Beginning NetBeans IDE

for Java Developers

■ ■ ■

Geertjan Wielenga

Apress®

Beginning NetBeans IDE

ISBN-13 (pbk): 978-1-4842-1258-5

ISBN-13 (electronic): 978-1-4842-1257-8

Managing Director: Welmoed Spahr
Lead Editor: Steve Anglin
Technical Reviewer: Josh Juneau
Editorial Board: Steve Anglin, Louise Corrigan, Jonathan Gennick, Robert Hutchinson,
    Michelle Lowman, James Markham, Susan McDermott, Matthew Moodie, Jeffrey Pepper,
    Douglas Pundick, Ben Renow-Clarke, Gwenan Spearing, Steve Weiss
Coordinating Editor: Mark Powers
Copy Editor: Kezia Endsley
Compositor: SPi Global
Indexer: SPi Global
Artist: SPi Global

Distributed to the book trade worldwide by Springer Science+Business Media New York, 233 Spring Street, 6th Floor, New York, NY 10013. Phone 1-800-SPRINGER, fax (201) 348-4505, e-mail orders-ny@springer-sbm.com, or visit www.springeronline.com. Apress Media, LLC is a California LLC and the sole member (owner) is Springer Science + Business Media Finance Inc (SSBM Finance Inc). SSBM Finance Inc is a Delaware corporation.

For information on translations, please e-mail rights@apress.com, or visit www.apress.com.

Apress and friends of ED books may be purchased in bulk for academic, corporate, or promotional use. eBook versions and licenses are also available for most titles. For more information, reference our Special Bulk Sales–eBook Licensing web page at www.apress.com/bulk-sales.

Any source code or other supplementary material referenced by the author in this text is available to readers at www.apress.com/9781484212585. For additional information about how to locate and download your book's source code, go to www.apress.com/source-code/. Readers can also access source code at SpringerLink in the Supplementary Material section for each chapter.

To the NetBeans community, all over the world!

Contents at a Glance

Contents

About the Author

Geertjan Wielenga (@geertjanw) is a product manager in the NetBeans team. He lives and works in Amsterdam. He is a Java technology enthusiast, evangelist, trainer, speaker, and writer.

His journey into software was long and winding. He spent most of his youth in South Africa, where he studied law at the University of Natal in Pietermaritzburg. On graduating, suspecting that the world of suits and ties was not for him, he decided to travel for a while and see where events would lead him. In early 1996, he found himself as a proofreader for a software organization in the Netherlands called SuperNova, which was a 4GL language that rose and fell while Java was just beginning its upward trajectory. After having worked at various other software organizations in the Netherlands, such as Seagull and Uniface, he moved to Vienna, Austria and joined Coca-Cola Computer Services, which at that time supplied most of the ERP needs of the Coca-Cola Company around the world. When he had an opportunity in 2004 to move to Prague, Czech Republic to work on the free and open source NetBeans IDE, he took the chance to continue his adventures elsewhere.

He discovered that NetBeans IDE was a unique product, project, and ecosystem. NetBeans is used all over the world at schools, universities, open source projects, and large organizations, and Geertjan became inspired and continually enthused by the open source ecosystem and the central role that the NetBeans community was playing in it. At the time at Sun Microsystems, the place of NetBeans IDE was unambiguously as the enabler of Java learning and Java productivity around the world, as well as the driver of a wonderful and diverse ecosystem that had spread to all the nooks and crannies of the software development universe. With the change to Oracle, the focus became even more specifically on Java and gradually on JavaScript. Since NetBeans IDE is pluggable and extensible, NetBeans has been able to take this change in stride.

Now, in the 20th year of Java's existence, Geertjan is happy and proud of the role NetBeans has played in it, as well as his own small personal contributions to the process. He's looking forward to the next 20 years of Java and many more books about NetBeans IDE!

About the Technical Reviewer

Josh Juneau (@javajuneau) has been developing software since the mid-1990s. PL/SQL development and database programming were the focus of his career in the beginning, but as his skills developed, he began to use Java and later shifted to it as a primary base for his application development.

Josh has worked with Java in the form of graphical user interfaces, web, and command-line programming for several years. During his tenure as a Java developer, he has worked with many frameworks, such as JSF, EJB, and JBoss Seam.

Josh began using NetBeans IDE in the early 2000's at version 3.x, and has been an avid user ever since. His favorite NetBeans features include the excellent Maven support, the life-saving NetBeans Debugger and NetBeans Profiler, the seamless support for JSF frameworks, and the ability to easily create entity classes from a database with a few clicks via the wizard.

About the Illustrator

Martien Bos (martienbos.com) lives and works in Amsterdam. He studied industrial design at the Technical University Delft and at the École Nationale Supérieure de Création Industrielle Les Ateliers in Paris and Dutch language and culture at the University of Amsterdam. He's a mostly self-taught illustrator.

While studying in Amsterdam, Martien was the editor of *Nymph* literary magazine, which was subsequently taken over by a publisher for whom he illustrated a number of books. Not long thereafter, he made a series of portraits of well-known authors for many newspapers in the Netherlands, including *NRC Handelsblad, PZC, De Stentor, Tubantia,* and *BN/De Stem.* He's also created illustrations for the Spanish *Barcelona Magazine* and the Belgian newspaper *De Standaard.*

As well as making portraits, he produces a range of illustrations for publishers, magazines, cultural e-zines, and educational institutions, and has on several occasions displayed his work in Amsterdam. His ambitions for the future are focused on narrative work, including an illustrated six-page story in the Belgian digital magazine *Stroke.*

Acknowledgments

I would like to thank the many people without whom this book would not have been possible. A team of highly skilled people—who I really have enjoyed working with—has greatly assisted me in creating this work.

First, I would like to thank the people at Apress involved in this project. Thanks to Steve Anglin for coming up with the idea for this book and for his assistance and insight in putting the initial table of content together. Thanks to project Manager Mark Powers for gently pushing me along and for keeping everything well scheduled and organized. Your experience and professionalism helped to make the book-writing process considerably easier than it otherwise might have been. Kezia Endsley, who copy edited the book, I would like to thank very much for your finely tuned eye and the precision and dedication you applied to the task. When I saw how many comments you had on each chapter I delivered, I knew this book would be even better than I had hoped. As a result, this book is not only full of new and interesting insights into NetBeans IDE, but also concisely written and consistently formulated.

Next, many, many thanks to Josh Juneau. Not sure exactly when I first met Josh, probably at JavaOne some years ago! He's an author in his own right and a very focused and technically savvy supporter of all things NetBeans. The second I was asked to provide a technical reviewer, I thought of Josh. Aside from many insights and shared wisdom, he's contributed a large part of the Chapter 9 on profiling and tuning, with thanks to Andrew Binstock from the *Oracle Java Magazine*, who let us reuse parts of an article that Josh published there.

Jaroslav Tulach and the original group of students in Prague, in the Czechoslovakia of 1995, need a very special thanks for their revolutionary insights and ideas, which they translated into what we now all know as NetBeans IDE. Without them, and of course without James Gosling and his team, who came up with Java in the first place, you, the reader of this book, would definitely not be holding this book in your hands! Many thanks to the NetBeans team, all the engineers over the many years, especially those still working on NetBeans today and who continue to make NetBeans a little bit better every day.

Furthermore, I'd like to thank the NetBeans community all over the world. In particular, the enthusiastic NetBeans Dream Team—that is, the community of volunteer evangelists that has helped over many years make NetBeans a fun and worthwhile environment for me and so many others to work in.

Special thanks to those who underwent the process of getting their portraits done for this book! That's certainly a unique aspect, for which Martien Bos did a fantastic job. Each chapter begins with a portrait of a well-known NetBeans user, together with a quote that relates to the chapter. Thanks to everyone involved in this, it certainly adds something special and meaningful, and helps visualize the diversity of the NetBeans community and highlights some of the many places around the world where it is used.

There's also a small army of volunteers who read this book at various stages of the writing process. In particular, I'd like to thank Constantin Drabo, Glenn Holmer, Pieter van den Hombergh, Benno Markiewicz, Hermien Pellissier, and Brett Ryan. Not all your comments made it into the book, though I am sure there will be many more editions of it where your insights will be used.

Throughout this text, reference and use has been made of earlier books written about NetBeans IDE, in particular, *NetBeans IDE Field Guide* (Prentice Hall, 2006) by Patrick Keegan and others and *Pro NetBeans IDE 5.5 Enterprise Edition* (Apress, 2007) by Adam Myatt.

Of course, I'd also like to thank my parents and Hermine, my wife! Thanks; your support, encouragement, and presence have helped in so many different and immeasurable ways.

Foreword

NetBeans started as a student project named Xelfi at the Faculty of Mathematics and Physics at Charles University, Prague, in the Czech Republic. We originally wanted to create Delphi for the XWindow system, though later we decided to switch to Java and create the first integrated development environment (IDE) for Java written in Java.

In 1995, I and 80 other students were supposed to select a final software project with which to complete our studies. There was a huge gathering where various professors presented their projects, hoping to attract the attention of the students. For example, there was a project to control a real robot; the previous year's group had managed to move it and even speed it up, until it hit a wall. The goal for the next team working on this project was to slow the robot down or even stop it, to avoid a crash. Nice—but a bit too hardware-oriented, and I was more of a software guy. There was also project to build a database system for a hospital—a nice and valuable goal to help poor patients, though I was not a huge fan of SQL and similar technologies. And so on, and so on. When the presentation by the professors was over, I still didn't know which project I should join.

However, I wasn't alone! Several other guys were also disappointed with the choices that had been presented. We chatted a bit and agreed on what we'd like to do—we came up with the idea to build an IDE, something like Delphi, but to run on Linux. That is, for the XWindow system. Luckily there was a visiting professor from the US named Adam Dingle. We contacted him and, though he didn't really know what it would be like to lead seven students in a software project, he agreed to do it. We officially announced the project and started holding weekly meetings. A usual meeting lasted around an hour. In that time, we chatted about our great design, our various plans, and then went to the pub! It was hard work, though we managed to keep it up for almost a year. Without producing a single line of code!

During that time, we did manage to participate in another project in which we used the new, cool language called Java. It didn't feel that bad, so at one of the Xelfi before-the-pub meetings, I suggested we use Java instead of C. The response was overwhelming: No, never! And so we continued our regular meetings for the next three months, still without writing a single line of code. When I later proposed to use Java again, the timing was better, and this time the suggestion got accepted. We all started to learn and code in Java. Our progress was good. Java really delivered on the promise to run everywhere—I was an OS/2 user, there were a few Linux users, and of course a bunch of students using Windows. We ended up providing a single GUI toolkit on all these platforms, which was something we had struggled to unify when working on the C version of Xelfi. In a few months, the IDE was working and even ready to help us pass our final exam!

We passed the exam with excellent marks. Some people say that it was because at that time none of the reviewers were able to actually execute a Java program. As a result, they couldn't really try Xelfi themselves and had to trust our demo and, as good demoers, we obviously knew which features to avoid showing. The only material they could study was our documentation and we had an enormous amount of that thanks to another Java invention: Javadoc! We impressed everyone by generating hundreds and hundreds of pages, describing—well, rather just listing—all the methods we had in our system. It was no surprise that everyone was impressed.

However, of course, the IDE was not fake at all. We actually liked what we did and so some of us tried to push Xelfi further. We started to offer Xelfi as a shareware, asking for $20 per copy. We didn't make much money in this way, but—and that is more important—we attracted a lot of attention. We were contacted by Roman Staněk, who was looking for investment opportunities and, in the autumn of 1997, the company which later turned into NetBeans was established. The rest, as they say, is history. James Gosling and Sun Microsystems came into the picture, which was later taken over by Oracle.

Speaking of James Gosling, he says this about NetBeans IDE, on the NetBeans Facebook page:

> *I live in NetBeans. I use it more than email. Everything works together smoothly; it doesn't feel like a bag of disconnected parts. All the tools are there. The refactoring tools are so good that they've replaced a huge amount of what I used to do with the editor - using them is not an occasional thing for me.*

NetBeans continues to innovate, to this day. And that is one thing that I continue to like about NetBeans IDE—its development team is continually striving for innovation. One of the best examples is, in my opinion, the NetBeans debugger, described in this book. Thanks to the excellent work of the NetBeans engineers and the close co-operation with the JDK team, the NetBeans debugger was the first to deliver mixed languages (e.g., Java/JavaScript) debugging for JDK8 and its Nashorn JavaScript engine. I am proud of that feature, because it later was copied to other IDEs, which, in my opinion, is a sign of extraordinary quality!

I wish you, the reader of this book, productivity and enjoyment as you learn about the key features of NetBeans IDE and apply the principles you learn here to your projects, at schools and universities, as well as in the enterprise.

—Jaroslav Tulach, Founder of NetBeans IDE

Preface

A constant search for fresh technology made my young Java life very exciting.

In the early 2000's, I started to write my first book *Enterprise Java Frameworks*, and bumped into NetBeans IDE. I liked the look and feel but hated the concepts behind it. Back then, NetBeans IDE was too complicated to use and I almost forgot about NetBeans altogether. . .

A few years later, NetBeans IDE 5 came out and was praised by Sun Microsystems engineers as "the only IDE you need" and was supposed to be especially powerful. Meanwhile, I had invested a lot in the Eclipse ecosystem. I was maintaining 35 client-specific workspaces with different and incompatible plugin-sets. But it worked well enough for me. However, I gave NetBeans IDE 5 a shot. My expectations were very low. I expected a configuration and plugin-installation party and an overly complicated IDE. The opposite was true. NetBeans IDE 5 was not only trivial to install; it was production-ready after a double-click.

The installation also contained the GlassFish application server, which I already used in my projects.

Nevertheless, I kept being skeptical about the integration and potential Sun-proprietary extensions. None of my prejudices turned out to be true, however. NetBeans output was IDE-agnostic, GlassFish integration was tight, though not proprietary. It was really hard to criticize anything.

At the same time, I was having similar positive experiences with the GlassFish application server and so I tried to explain the miracle to myself as "The New Sun Microsystems Wave of Quality." I have stuck with NetBeans IDE from version 5 and have never regretted the choice. Now I'm even frequently using NetBeans development builds in production and they are surprisingly stable.

What was also interesting was that there were no migration steps between the 35 Eclipse workspaces and NetBeans. I just opened the projects in NetBeans and seamlessly proceeded with my work. Back then, my projects were 50% Ant and 50% Maven, and both project types were immediately recognized by NetBeans without any additional configuration. Nowadays, I'm exclusively using Maven with NetBeans and I am still amazed by the nice integration.

However, NetBeans is mature, but not boring — the out-of-the-box Nashorn, JavaScript, and HTML 5 support in the recent NetBeans IDE 8 releases are very useful in my daily work. I use NetBeans daily as a capable editor for writing Nashorn automation scripts, for doing docker development, for exploring files, for editing HTML documents, for monitoring Jenkins, for debugging JavaScript, as well as for Java profiling and memory leak hunting.

Read this book, use NetBeans IDE, and save time!

—Adam Bien, Java EE enthusiast

Introduction

From this book you will gain structured insights into the key features that NetBeans IDE makes available, all for free. Starting from installation and your first "hello world" application in Java, you will travel through every key feature of the IDE, whether you are just beginning to learn Java or want to be productive in Java enterprise environments.

If there is one area on which this book particularly focuses, it is the Java Editor. More pages and screenshots are dedicated to this topic than to any other. The reason for this is quite simple. Writing Java code, quickly and efficiently, is what the IDE is all about. All the other features, while powerful, are secondary. Programming is all about your fingers being on the keyboard and your keyboard being a whirl of click-clacking while you input Java code into the editor. The editor is bursting with features to help you focus on your business logic. It has a host of functionality that has been developed with the single purpose of letting you write robust and useful applications that meet your business needs, including your users' many and diverging expectations. The better you become familiar with the treasures of the Java Editor in the IDE, the better equipped you will be to pass your exams at educational institutions and complete your sprints on time in the enterprise!

While the focus of the book is to equip you with everything you need to program Java applications effectively, you should be aware that the Java language itself is out of scope of this book. To learn about Java objects, methods, and the myriad of other Java syntax elements, many other books are available that will get you up and running quickly. In contrast to those books, this book is specifically focused on the IDE itself and aims to help you to get everything you can out of it. By the end of the book, you'll have a thorough overview of the IDE and its tools and you'll be a lot more productive than you might have hoped!

I wish you fun and productivity, whether you're at school in Java introductory courses, working for a startup, or at a large enterprise where you need to get your work done fast and efficiently. NetBeans is there to help you, and this book unlocks some of its deepest secrets.

NetBeans is the best IDE to start with when learning Java, because of its out-of-the-box experience. A simple click-through installation procedure provides all the tools you need, with a friendly and intuitive user interface to develop all kinds of Java applications.

—Zoran Sevarac,
assistant professor at the University of Belgrade, Serbia, and founder of Neuroph

CHAPTER 1

■ ■ ■

Installing and Setting Up

In this chapter, I introduce you to NetBeans IDE, after which I provide you with the information needed to get the IDE up and running. You'll see that the process is simple and soon you'll be able to work through a basic scenario, as described in Chapter 2, which guides you through the workflow of programming in Java with the IDE.

What Is NetBeans IDE?

The IDE is a 100% free and open source development environment that helps you create different kinds of software applications. In the context of this book, we will focus specifically on the IDE as an environment for developing Java applications. The IDE provides support for all types of Java applications, helping you develop projects that use all the Java technologies—Java SE, Java EE, Embedded, and Cloud.

The IDE is modular and can be extended via plugins. The features included in the download bundles that you will be introduced to in this chapter are extensive enough that you will not need to use any plugins, at least not initially.

Java is the language in which the IDE is written. It can run on operating systems on which the Java Development Kit (JDK) has been installed. Installers that guide you through the process of installing and setting up the IDE are available for Windows, Linux, and Mac OSX. The IDE can also be downloaded as a ZIP or TAR file, which can be useful if you want to use the IDE on an operating system for which no installer is provided.

For the purposes of this book, the IDE exists to simplify the development process of Java applications. Without the IDE, the edit-compile-debug cycle inherent in Java development is cumbersome and error prone. To overcome and help in the development process, the IDE integrates tools for these activities. Specifically, the IDE does the following:

- Notifies you of problems in your code and highlights them in the Java Editor.

- Assists you in coding quickly and efficiently using the editor's features such as code templates, code completion, and hints in the Java Editor.

- Shows documentation for classes and methods while you type in the Java Editor.

- Includes visual navigation assistance, including the Navigator and editor features such as code folding, together with many keyboard shortcuts to speed up coding.

- Provides hyperlinks in the Output window to let you jump from compilation errors to lines in the Java Editor where the related problematic code is found.

- Helps to manage changes across your application code by managing references to names of packages, classes, and methods throughout your code. When you move or rename code, the IDE finds related code affected by your changes and lets you control whether the related code should automatically be changed.

- Comes with a debugger and profiler that work together to help you identify problems in your code quickly and easily. As your code runs, you can step through it and set breakpoints, instead of needing to add print statements. The profiler lets you identify bottlenecks in your code, such as areas causing performance problems and deadlocks.

- Lets you integrate your development workflow into a single environment, including checking your code into and out of version control systems, such as Git, Mercurial, and Subversion.

Advantages of the IDE

Just like other development environments, the IDE consists of a set of editors and graphical tools for efficiently coding and quickly detecting problems. The IDE guides you from the point of project creation, through the editing process, to compilation, debugging, and the packaging of your applications.

While using the IDE, you can use its free and cutting-edge set of tools and features, without the disadvantages that you might associate with moving your code to a single integrated development environment. For example, the IDE is unique in that the project architectures and build structures it supports, based on Maven, Gradle, or Ant, are also based on open standards. Other IDEs enforce IDE-specific structures and processes on you, with proprietary metadata and other files, so that you need to change your application architecture when you want to run it outside the other IDEs. With NetBeans IDE, you can be sure that the work you do compiles and runs outside the IDE exactly as it does within it. This is especially convenient when you are using continuous build servers such as Hudson or Jenkins, as well as when you are using Maven as your build tool.

The IDE is consistently aligned with and even ahead of the curve in providing support for new and evolving software standards. When you are working with Java, you can be sure that the latest specifications and techniques are supported by the IDE and that all the assistance you get from it is based on the most recent standards. For example, the latest language features—in particular those that relate to lambdas and functional operations that have been introduced in Java SE 8—are supported in the IDE's Java Editor by means of refactoring tools, batch analyzers, Java hints, and syntax coloring.

New users of the IDE tend to be surprised by the array of features that are available "out of the box," that is, without requiring you to install any additional plugins. The IDE has a full-featured Java EE platform development environment built-in, again, out of the box. The editor, debugger, profiler, and project support available for Java SE applications are also available, without any setup or configuration, for Java EE development.

Downloading the IDE

You can download the IDE from the NetBeans.org web site:

```
http://www.netbeans.org/downloads/index.html
```

You can also download it, together with the JDK, from the Oracle.com web site:

```
http://www.oracle.com/technetwork/java/javase/downloads
```

It's best to use the latest available version of the JDK and IDE. At the time of this writing, the latest version of the IDE is NetBeans IDE 8.1. NetBeans IDE 8.1 is used throughout this book, and the assumption is that you are using NetBeans IDE 8.1 while working through this book.

Figure 1-1 shows the download bundles available on NetBeans.org.

NetBeans IDE 8.1	Download				8.0.2 | 8.1	Development | Archive

Email address (optional): _____   IDE Language: English ▼   Platform: Windows ▼

Subscribe to newsletters: ☑ Monthly ☐ Weekly   Note: Greyed out technologies are not supported for this platform.
☑ NetBeans can contact me at this address

NetBeans IDE Download Bundles

Supported technologies *	Java SE	Java EE	HTML5/JavaScript	PHP	C/C++	All
④ NetBeans Platform SDK	●	●				●
④ Java SE	●	●				●
④ Java FX	●	●				●
④ Java EE		●				●
④ Java ME						●
④ HTML5/JavaScript		●	●	●		●
④ PHP			●	●		●
④ C/C++					●	●
④ Groovy						●
④ Java Card™ 3 Connected						●
Bundled servers						
④ GlassFish Server Open Source Edition 4.1		●				●
④ Apache Tomcat 8.0.20		●				●

	Download	Download	Download ×86 / Download ×64	Download ×86 / Download ×64	Download ×86 / Download ×64	Download
	Free, 95 MB	Free, 190 MB	Free, 100 - 96 MB	Free, 100 - 96 MB	Free, 102 - 99 MB	Free, 213 MB

Figure 1-1. *NetBeans IDE download bundles*

The NetBeans IDE download bundles contain the features described in Table 1-1. For the instructions in this book, you need the Java EE download bundle. In general, when you are learning the Java language, the Java SE download bundle is all you need because it includes the Java Editor, debugger, and profiler. However when you are employed in an organization as a Java developer, you normally create applications that use the Java EE platform, since Java EE is an integrated solution for creating complex enterprise Java web applications. The Java EE download bundle provides tools that are helpful when working with the Java EE platform. In short, the Java EE download bundle encompasses the full set of Java features that the IDE provides and is the download bundle you should download and install when working through this book.

Table 1-1. *NetBeans IDE Download Bundles*

Download Bundle	Features
Java SE	Provides features for creating Java desktop applications, with tools for JavaFX and Swing for the user interface, including a Java Editor, Java debugger, and Java profiler.
Java EE	Provides the same features as the Java SE distribution, together with tools for working with the Java EE platform such as for Java servlets, Java Server Faces, Java Persistence API, Enterprise Java Beans, Java RESTful Web Services, and code generators for working with frameworks such as PrimeFaces. Includes tools for registering and deploying to GlassFish and Tomcat, as well as managing applications deployed to these servers.
C/C++	Provides features for developing C and C++ applications, including project templates, editors, code generators, debugger, and make file wizard for configuration management.
HTML5/JavaScript and PHP	Provides features for HTML5 web applications, with editors, templates, and code generators for HTML5, JavaScript, and CSS3, as well as for creating hybrid mobile applications with Cordova for deployment to iOS and Android. Includes a JavaScript debugger, tools for SASS and LESS, and JavaScript framework support, such as for Knockout.js and AngularJS. The PHP features include editors, code templates, code generators, and a debugger, as well as integration with MYSQL and other database servers.
All	Provides all the tools described above in one download bundle. It is unlikely you will need the "All" distribution and you are recommended to use one of the other download bundles, specifically, the download bundle that most closely matches your actual requirements.

■ **Note**   For Java development, that is, if you want to use the Java SE, Java EE, or All distributions, having the IDE and only the Java Runtime Environment (JRE) installed on your system is not sufficient for running the IDE. You need to have the JDK, that is, the Java Development Kit, which includes the JRE. The IDE relies on development tools provided by the JDK, such as the `javac` compiler, and takes advantage of other parts of that download, such as JDK sources that it includes. Go here to download the latest version of the JDK:

`http://www.oracle.com/technetwork/java/javase/downloads`

Installing the IDE

Once you have downloaded the IDE, installing it is simple. Start by making sure that you have a suitable version of the JDK installed on your system, which must be JDK 7 or higher. Open a command prompt and run the following:

```
java -version
```

You should see output comparable to the following:

```
java version "1.8.0_40-ea"
Java(TM) SE Runtime Environment (build 1.8.0_40-ea-b23)
Java HotSpot(TM) 64-Bit Server VM (build 25.40-b25, mixed mode)
```

You can see that JDK 8 Update 40 is installed. If the command is not recognized, go to http://www.oracle.com/technetwork/java/javase/downloads, download the latest version of the JDK and install it.

Once the JDK is installed, you can begin installing the IDE. On Windows, double-click the installer of the IDE, which you downloaded in the previous section. On Mac OSX or Linux, launch the installer from the command prompt. Step through the installer wizard, as described next.

1. Figure 1-2 shows the first screen in the wizard that you use to install the IDE. As you can see, together with the IDE, you can install the GlassFish server and the Apache Tomcat server. GlassFish is useful if you want to work with Java EE, while Apache Tomcat is focused on Java web applications, which do not make full use of the Java EE platform. For the purposes of this book, you should install the GlassFish server so that you can use the IDE tools that relate to the Java EE platform.

Figure 1-2. *Welcome to the NetBeans IDE installer*

Figure 1-3 shows the licensing terms that you need to agree to when using the IDE.

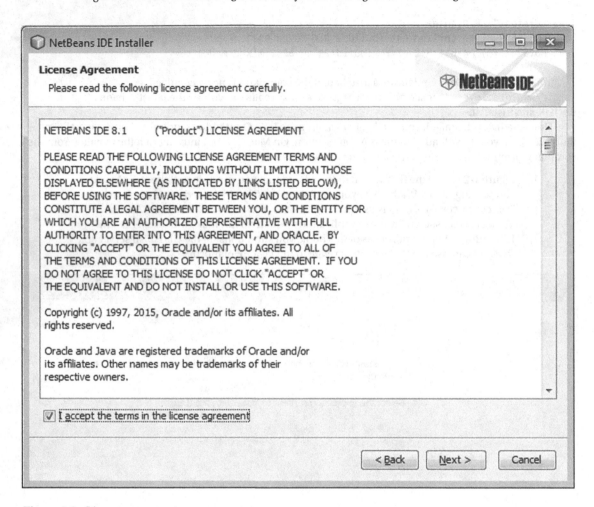

Figure 1-3. *License agreement*

2. In Figure 1-4 you can see that you need to specify the location where the IDE will be installed, together with the JDK that will be used to start it. If you need to change the JDK used to start the NetBeans IDE after you have installed it, you can use the netbeans.conf file, which is in the installation directory's etc folder, to point to a different JDK.

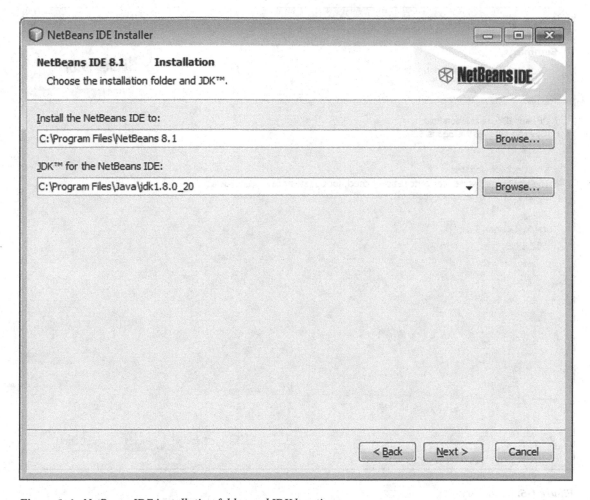

Figure 1-4. *NetBeans IDE installation folder and JDK location*

3. Once you have gone through Steps 1-3, the installer shows where the IDE will be installed. If you click the Check for Updates checkbox, the IDE will notify you when new versions of installed features are available and prompt you to let the IDE install them.

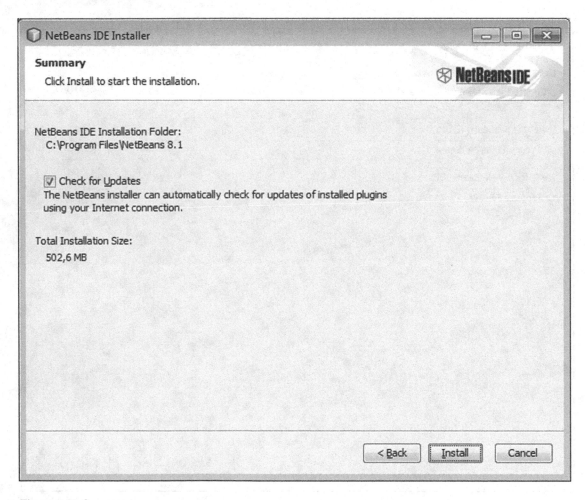

Figure 1-5. *Summary*

Once you have gone through these steps, the IDE begins the installation process, as shown in Figure 1-6.

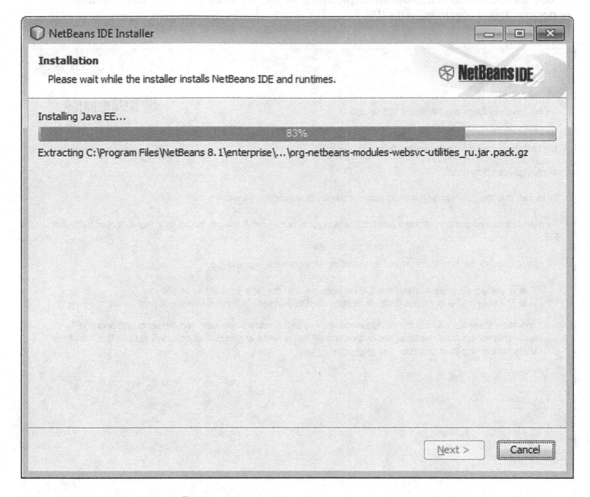

Figure 1-6. *NetBeans IDE installation*

As shown in Figure 1-7, the installer informs you when the installation process is complete. You can help the IDE engineers improve the IDE by letting the IDE periodically and automatically submit anonymous data of your usage of the IDE.

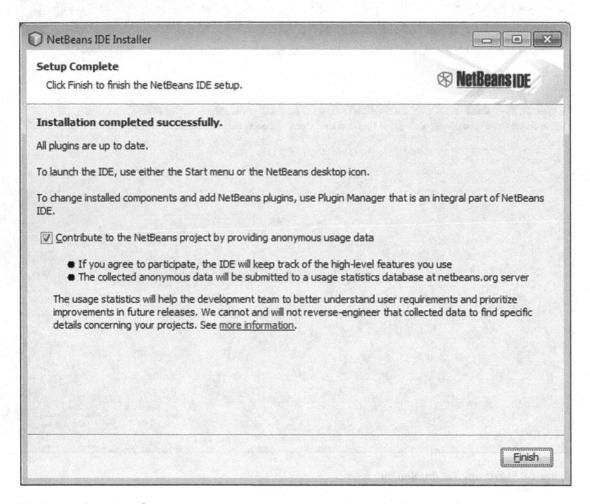

Figure 1-7. *Setup complete*

That's all you need to do, NetBeans IDE is now installed, as you can see in Figure 1-8. As you can see, the installer guides you through selecting a JDK on your system to run the IDE and, on Windows, can create desktop icons and Start menu items to launch the IDE from.

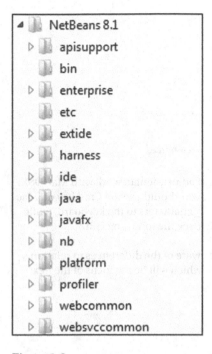

Figure 1-8.

Using Mac OSX

Although the IDE runs on Windows, Linux, and Mac OSX, it is important to be aware of the differences in terms of how you will work with the IDE. To be consistent, and to not clutter the book with operating system-specific differences, all images and descriptions assume that you are using Windows. On Linux distributions, the IDE behaves identically to Windows, although, of course, the IDE itself looks quite different. On Mac OSX the IDE not only looks different, it also behaves differently in certain specific ways. It's important to be aware of these differences, to avoid a lot of frustration, not only in this book, but when using the IDE itself.

Most importantly, whenever the book tells you to open the Options window by going to Tools ➤ Options in the menu bar in the IDE, if you are using Mac OSX, you should instead go to NetBeans ➤ Preferences, as shown in Figure 1-9.

Figure 1-9. *Accessing the Options window on Mac OSX via NetBeans ➤ Preferences*

The keyboard shortcuts used throughout the book also need a slight adjustment to work with Mac OSX. In general, whenever you see a keyboard shortcut that uses the Ctrl key, you should use the Cmd key on Mac OSX instead. For example, on Windows and Linux you use Ctrl+C to copy characters to the keyboard, while on Mac OSX you use Cmd+C instead. For full details and more examples, see the following URL: https://netbeans.org/kb/articles/mac.html.

Now that you have downloaded and installed the IDE and you are aware of the differences in relation to Mac OSX, you are ready to create your first "hello world" application, which will be the focus of the next chapter.

NetBeans is simply a complete and well organized toolbox. Everything is easy to find and on-hand when you need it. NetBeans works out of the box, no further assembly is required, and it's really intuitive to use. New users are productive right from the start.

—Anton Epple,
founder and owner of Eppleton IT Consulting

CHAPTER 2

■ ■ ■

Getting Started

In this chapter, you'll work through a simple "Hello World" example in Java using NetBeans IDE. After that, I'll show you the example projects that the IDE provides to help you get started with a variety of technologies. The chapter rounds off with an exploration of the IDE's main windows. It's a good idea to spend some time familiarizing yourself with the key components of the workspace that the IDE provides.

Hello World

When you have started the IDE, you are presented with a Welcome window, with links to interesting content, as shown in Figure 2-1.

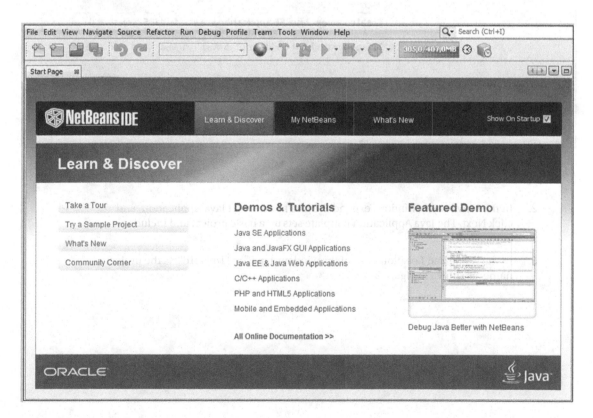

Figure 2-1. *Welcome screen*

To help you make the IDE come alive, this section provides a quick run-through of setting up, compiling, and running a "Hello World" project.

1. To set up the project, start by choosing File ➤ New Project. The New Project window opens, as shown in Figure 2-2.

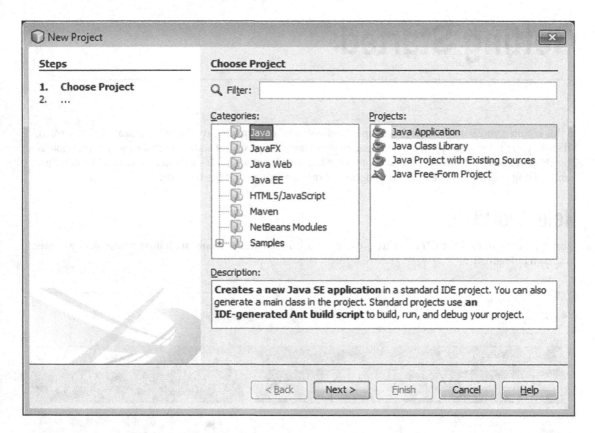

Figure 2-2. *The New Project window*

2. In the New Project window, expand the Java node, select Java Application, and click Next. The Java Application template sets up a basic project and includes a main class.

3. In the Name and Location page of the window, type "HelloWorld" as the project name, as shown in Figure 2-3.

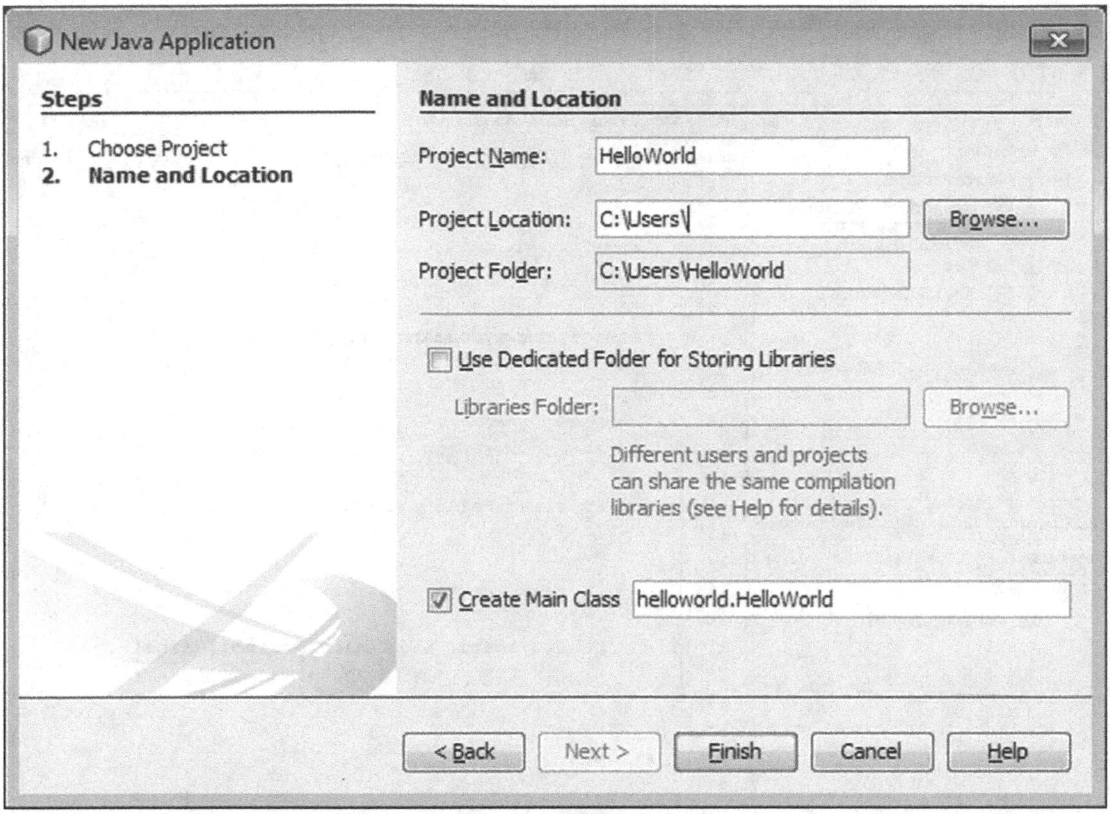

New Java Application

Steps

1. Choose Project
2. **Name and Location**

Name and Location

Project Name: HelloWorld

Project Location: C:\Users\   [Browse...]

Project Folder: C:\Users\HelloWorld

☐ Use Dedicated Folder for Storing Libraries

Libraries Folder: [   ]   [Browse...]

Different users and projects can share the same compilation libraries (see Help for details).

☑ Create Main Class   helloworld.HelloWorld

[< Back] [Next >] [Finish] [Cancel] [Help]

Figure 2-3. Setting the name and location in the New Project window

4. In the Create Main Class field, change `helloworld.HelloWorld` to
    `com.mydomain.myproject.HelloWorld`. When you enter a fully-qualified class
    name in this field, the IDE will generate directories for each level of the package
    structure when you complete this process. Click Finish.

The IDE creates a new Java project for you, as shown in Figure 2-4.

- HelloWorld
  - Source Packages
    - com.mydomain.myproject
      - HelloWorld.java
  - Libraries
    - JDK 1.8 (Default)

Figure 2-4. Newly created Java project

Once you have finished the window, the IDE runs a scan of the classpath that has been set for the
project to enable features such as code completion to work. Several windows are now populated, as shown
in Figure 2-5.

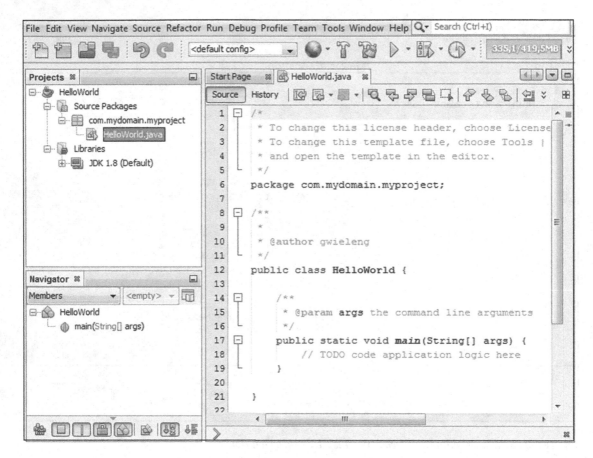

Figure 2-5. *Windows populated when Java project is created*

The windows that you see in Figure 2-5 are described next.

- The Projects window is in the top-left side of the workspace. It provides access to your sources, any tests you might have, and your classpath. You can display multiple projects in the Projects window.

- The Navigator is in the bottom-left portion of the workspace. It provides an easy way for you to view and access members of the currently selected class.

- The Source Editor covers the main area of the workspace. It provides tabs for multiple documents, such as Java files. A tab for the HellowWorld.java class automatically opens.

Let's now modify, build, and run the project.

1. In the Source Editor, click within the main method at the end of the line that reads // TODO code application logic here. Press the Enter key and then type the following statement.

    ```
    System.out.println("Hello World!");
    ```

    A different way to do this, one that is faster and makes use of code templates, is to type the characters sout and then press the Tab key. Also, instead of sout, you can type soutv and press the Tab key, and you will see the nearest variable referenced in the System.out.println statement.

2. Press Ctrl+S to save the file.

3. Press F11 (or choose Build ➤ Build Main Project) to compile and package the application. This command triggers a script that the IDE has generated and maintains for the project. The Output window opens and displays the output from the script as it runs through its targets, as shown in Figure 2-6.

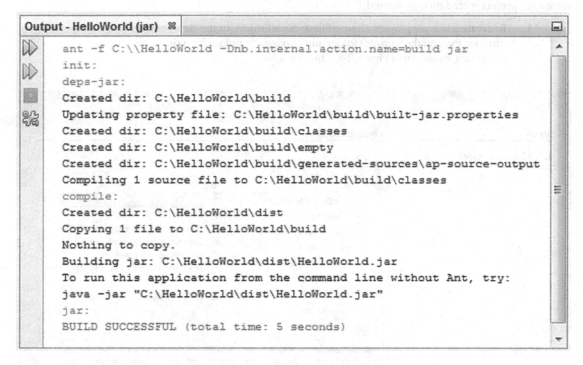

```
Output - HelloWorld (jar)  ✕                                              ▬
▷▷   ant -f C:\\HelloWorld -Dnb.internal.action.name=build jar          ▲
▷▷   init:
     deps-jar:
■    Created dir: C:\HelloWorld\build
🧩   Updating property file: C:\HelloWorld\build\built-jar.properties
     Created dir: C:\HelloWorld\build\classes
     Created dir: C:\HelloWorld\build\empty
     Created dir: C:\HelloWorld\build\generated-sources\ap-source-output
     Compiling 1 source file to C:\HelloWorld\build\classes
     compile:
     Created dir: C:\HelloWorld\dist
     Copying 1 file to C:\HelloWorld\build
     Nothing to copy.
     Building jar: C:\HelloWorld\dist\HelloWorld.jar
     To run this application from the command line without Ant, try:
     java -jar "C:\HelloWorld\dist\HelloWorld.jar"
     jar:
     BUILD SUCCESSFUL (total time: 5 seconds)                           ▼
```

Figure 2-6. Output window

4. Press F6 (or choose Run ➤ Run Main Project) to run the project. The Output window should display the "Hello World!" message from your application, as shown in Figure 2-7.

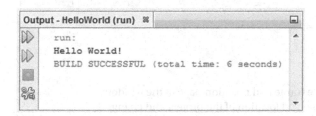

```
Output - HelloWorld (run)  ✕                               ▬
▷▷   run:                                               ▲
▷▷   Hello World!
     BUILD SUCCESSFUL (total time: 6 seconds)
■
🧩                                                      ▼
```

Figure 2-7. "Hello World!" message in Output window

Note that you do not need to build and run your applications separately. When you run the project, any files that have not been built into Java classes will automatically be built for you. With that, you have created and run your first application in the IDE!

Trying Out the IDE with Sample Code

If you want to check out the features of the IDE on working code without touching your existing files or you just want to see what a working project looks like in the IDE, you can open one or more of the IDE's sample projects.

When you create a sample project, the sample code is copied into a directory of your choosing and all necessary project metadata is generated.

1. To create a sample project, choose File ➤ New Project. In the New Project window, expand the Samples folder and choose a template from one of the categories, as shown in Figure 2-8. Then click Next.

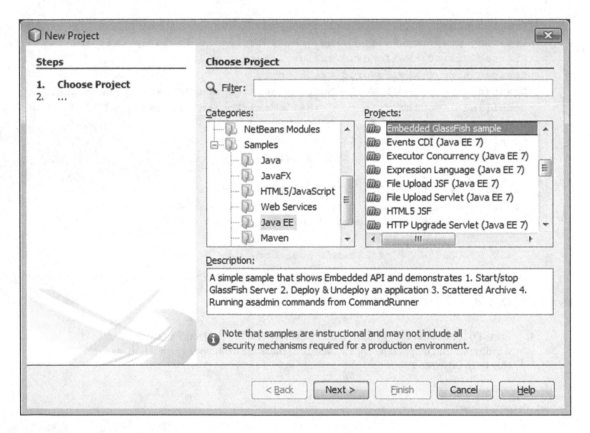

Figure 2-8. *Samples in the New Project window*

2. Choose a sample and click Next. On the Name and Location page of the window, check the generated values for the name and location of the project and change them, if you wish. Then click Finish.

Exploring the IDE

You'll now orientate yourself by taking a tour through all the windows that comprise the IDE. There are so many windows that it's not possible to capture them in a single image. Many of them are shown in Figure 2-9. In subsequent sections, I'll go through each of the windows in turn.

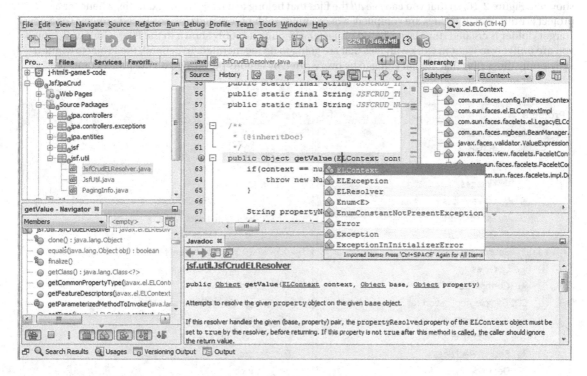

Figure 2-9. *Most windows open in the IDE*

The windows in the IDE can be grouped into five categories, depending on the view they provide.

- Project views

- File views

- Hierarchy views

- Service views

- Supporting views

Project Views

The Projects window (Ctrl+1) is the main entry point to your project sources. It shows a logical view of the important project content; that is, it shows you the files you are most likely to want to work with, organized in folders that you are likely to easily understand.

Together with the Projects window, the IDE provides the Files window (Ctrl+2), both of which are shown in Figure 2-10, so that you can see *all* the files that belong to a project. For example, whenever a project is built, that is, its files are compiled, a new "build" folder is created (for Ant-based projects) or a new "target" folder is created (for Maven-based projects), although it is only shown in the Files window, because you are unlikely to want to work with files that are going to be regenerated. In general, the Projects window shows only those files that are not going to be overwritten by actions performed on the project or its files.

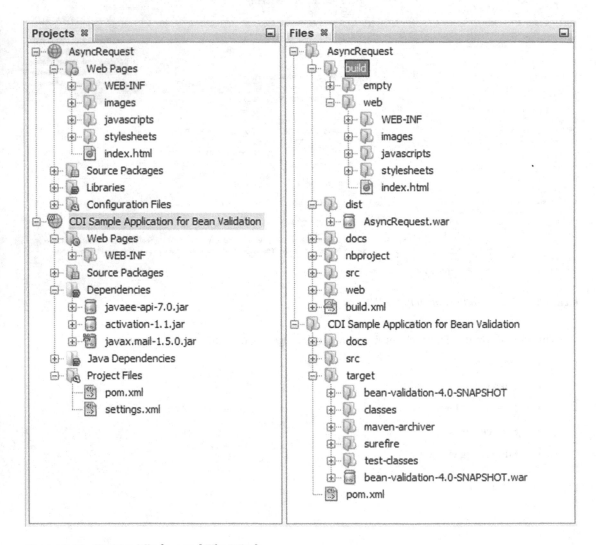

Figure 2-10. *Projects Window and Files Window*

A third project view is provided by the Favorites window (Ctrl+3). The Favorites window gives you access to all the folders and files on disk. It is equivalent to a file browser, built into the IDE. In the Favorites window, you can add arbitrary folders and files that you find on your disk so that you can easily access and browse folders and files within the IDE that are of particular interest to you. By default, the user directory is added to this window, although you can remove it, add other folders and files, or do combinations of these.

File Views

The Navigator window (Ctrl+7), shown in Figure 2-11, provides a compact view of the currently selected file and simplifies navigation between different parts of the file.

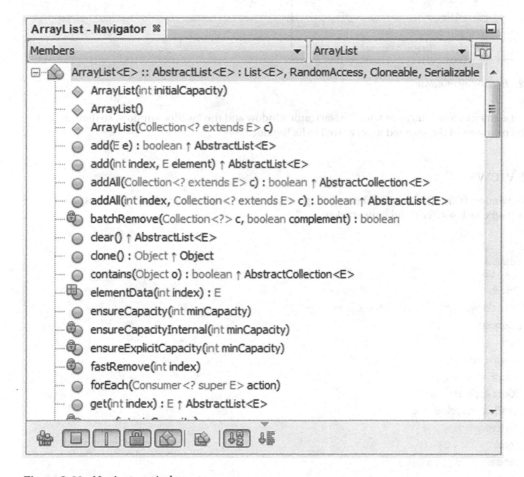

Figure 2-11. *Navigator window*

For example, for Java files, the Navigator window shows a list of constructors, methods, and fields, while for HTML and CSS files, it shows the logical structure of the selected document.

Hierarchy Views

The Hierarchy window (Alt+F12), shown in Figure 2-12, displays the supertypes and subtypes of the currently selected Java file or the currently selected Java type under the cursor in the editor.

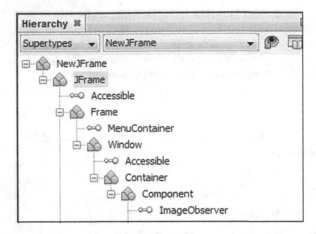

Figure 2-12. *Hierarchy window*

The Hierarchy window integrates with the Navigator window and the Javadoc window, so that you can easily see the elements of the selected item, as well as its Javadoc.

Service Views

The Services window (Ctrl+5), shown in Figure 2-13, gives you access to many ancillary resources, such as databases, servers, web services, and issue trackers.

Figure 2-13. *Services window*

You can start and stop databases and servers directly in the IDE. When working with databases, you can add, remove, and modify your data in the IDE. When you deploy an application to a server, you can manage your deployed resources because they are displayed in the Servers node. You can connect to a bug database, such as Issuezilla or Bugzilla, and list issue reports for your project right in the IDE.

Supporting Views

The windows available to support the project views, file views, and service views are the Output window, Properties window, Action Items window, Tasks window, and Notifications window.

Output Window

The Output window (Ctrl+4), shown in Figures 2-6 and 2-7, is a multi-tabbed window that displays processing messages from the IDE. It is displayed automatically when you encounter compilation errors, debug your program, and generate Javadoc documentation. You can configure the display options for the Output window in the Options window.

If the file that contains the error is open, the Source Editor jumps to the line containing each error as you move the insertion point into the error in the Source Editor. You can also use the F12 and Shift+F12 keyboard shortcuts to move to the next and previous error in the file.

When you run a program that requires user input, a new tab appears in the Output window. This tab includes a cursor. You can enter information in the Output window as you would on a command line.

Properties Window

The Properties window (Ctrl+Shift+7), shown in Figure 2-14, displays the properties of the currently selected item. For example, most items that can be represented in the Projects, Files, or Navigator windows have properties that can be viewed in the Properties window.

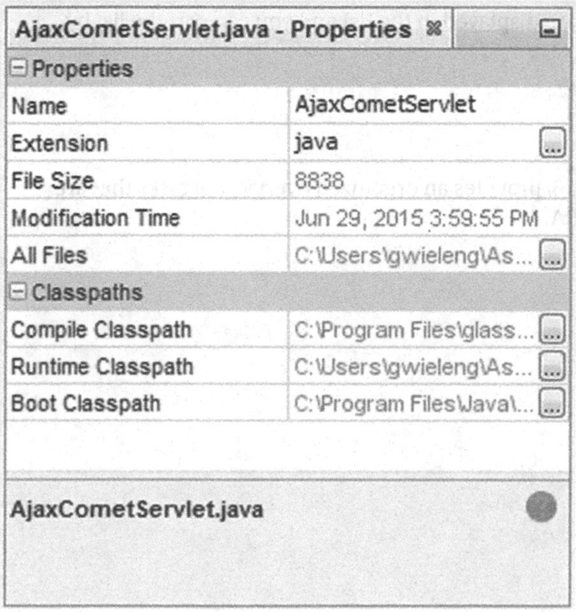

AjaxCometServlet.java - Properties ⌗	▬
⊟ Properties	
Name	AjaxCometServlet
Extension	java
File Size	8838
Modification Time	Jun 29, 2015 3:59:55 PM
All Files	C:\Users\gwieleng\As...
⊟ Classpaths	
Compile Classpath	C:\Program Files\glass...
Runtime Classpath	C:\Users\gwieleng\As...
Boot Classpath	C:\Program Files\Java\...
AjaxCometServlet.java	●

Figure 2-14. *Properties window*

Depending on the currently selected item, you can edit the values of some properties in the Properties window. To change a property value, click the property's value field. The appearance of the field changes depending on the type of value required.

Action Items Window

The Action Items window (Ctrl+6), shown in Figure 2-15, displays a unified list of problems that you need to resolve in your various files and projects.

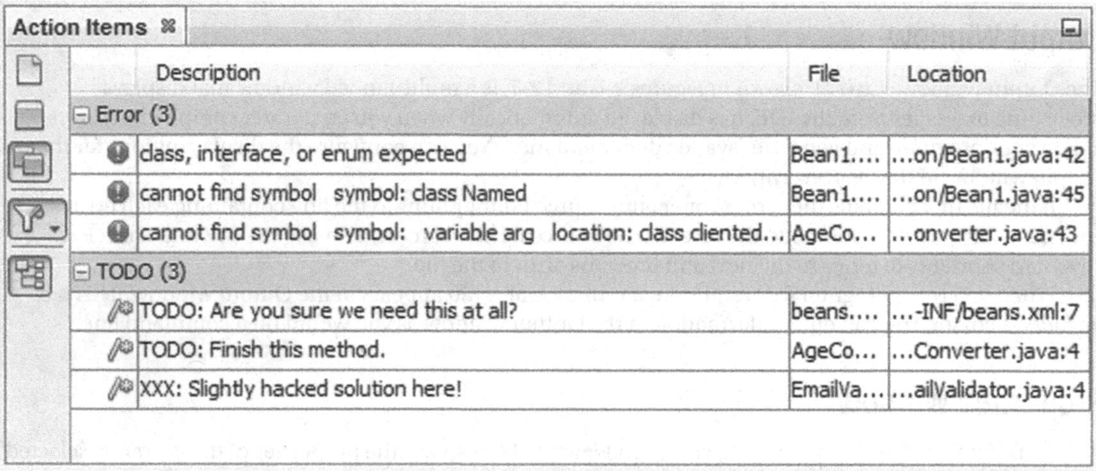

	Description	File	Location
	Error (3)		
	class, interface, or enum expected	Bean1....	...on/Bean1.java:42
	cannot find symbol symbol: class Named	Bean1....	...on/Bean1.java:45
	cannot find symbol symbol: variable arg location: class cliented...	AgeCo...	...onverter.java:43
	TODO (3)		
	TODO: Are you sure we need this at all?	beans....	...-INF/beans.xml:7
	TODO: Finish this method.	AgeCo...	...Converter.java:4
	XXX: Slightly hacked solution here!	EmailVa...	...ailValidator.java:4

Figure 2-15. *Action Items window*

You can use filters to determine the entries that are displayed in the list and you can sort the list by clicking a column heading.

Tasks Window

The Tasks window (Ctrl+Shift+6), shown in Figure 2-16, provides an organized overview of tasks that are recorded in a task repository, such as Bugzilla and JIRA.

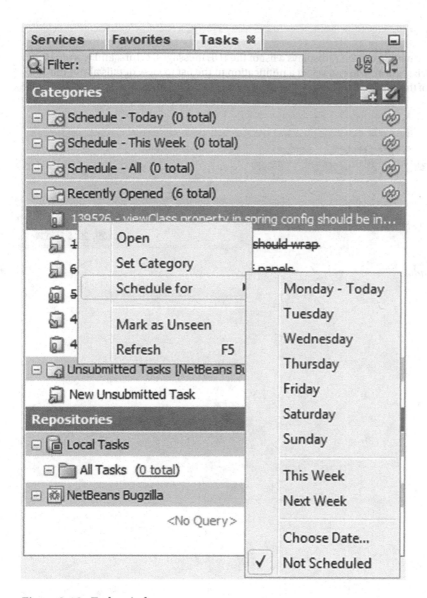

Figure 2-16. *Tasks window*

Notifications Window

The Notifications window, shown in Figure 2-17, displays a list of the IDE messages, errors, and warnings that occurred in the current IDE session. You can select a notification in the list to view details about the notification in the right pane of the window.

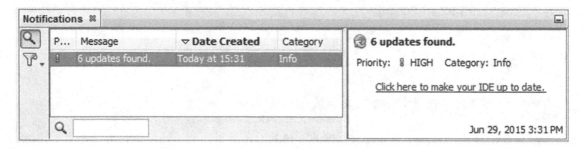

Figure 2-17. *Notifications window*

I don't have time to learn every little Event, Action or Handler type available and NetBeans provides suggestions and syntax auto-completion with a key press automagically. This feature is so smooth it has replaced Internet searching for me.

—Sean Phillips,
Ground Systems Engineer, NASA MMS and JWST Missions

CHAPTER 3

■ ■ ■

Java Editor

NetBeans IDE provides a collection of interrelated tools to support Java application development. However, it is the Source Editor, in particular, where you will spend most of your time. Given that fact, a lot of attention has been focused on providing features and subtle touches in, and around, the Source Editor to help developers code faster and more efficiently. This chapter examines in detail the ways you can use the Source Editor to simplify and speed up common coding tasks, specifically for Java files.

Overview

While you are writing, editing, and refactoring Java code, many editor features are available to you. For example, one of these is code completion, sometimes also known as "intellisense," shown in Figure 3-1. Use it to learn about the context in which your cursor is located and to generate code or provide information applicable to that context.

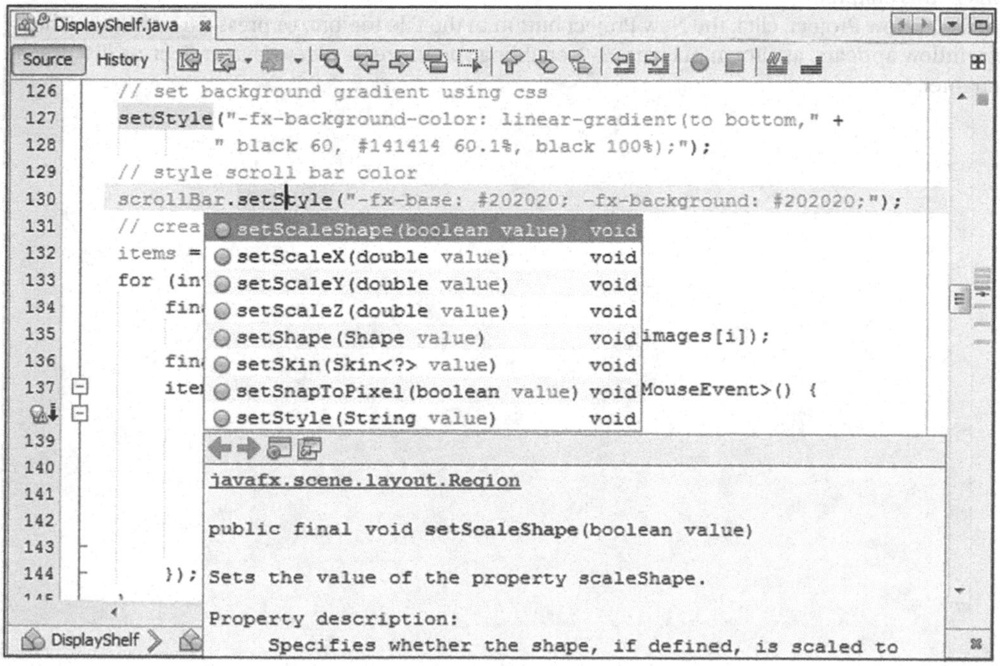

Figure 3-1. *Code completion*

Keyboard shortcuts for code generation features and for navigation through files in your application ensure that your hands rarely need to leave the keyboard.

Be aware that the Source Editor is a collection of different types of editors, each of which contains features specific to certain files. For example, when you open a Java file, which is the focus of this chapter, there is a syntax-highlighting scheme specifically for Java files, along with code completion, refactoring, and other features relevant to Java files. Likewise, when you open JSP, HTML, XML, and other types of files, you are exposed to a set of features applicable to those types of files.

Perhaps most importantly, the Source Editor is tightly integrated with other parts of the IDE, which greatly streamlines your workflow. For example, you can define breakpoints directly in the Source Editor and trace Java code as it executes. Similarly, when compilation errors are reported in the Output window, you can jump to the source of those errors by clicking the error or pressing F12.

Getting Started

This section helps you get comfortable with the layout and structure of the Source Editor. The most immediate tasks relating to getting started with the Source Editor are described here. Subsequent sections will go into details on specific features. Here, you learn about the most basic initial concerns users have, based on user questions on mailing lists and elsewhere, when they are new to the Source Editor.

Opening a File

Before starting to work with the Source Editor, you will typically want to have a NetBeans project set up. You can then open an existing Java file in the project or create a new Java file from a template. The next chapter goes through these tasks in detail, so they aren't covered in detail here. Instead, you'll go through the basic processes quickly, to get you to a point where you have a Java file in the Source Editor in preparation for the other sections in this chapter.

Choose File ➤ New Project, click the New Project button in the File toolbar, or press Ctrl+Shift+N. The New Project window appears, as shown in Figure 3-2, enabling you to create a new Java project, as discussed in the next chapter.

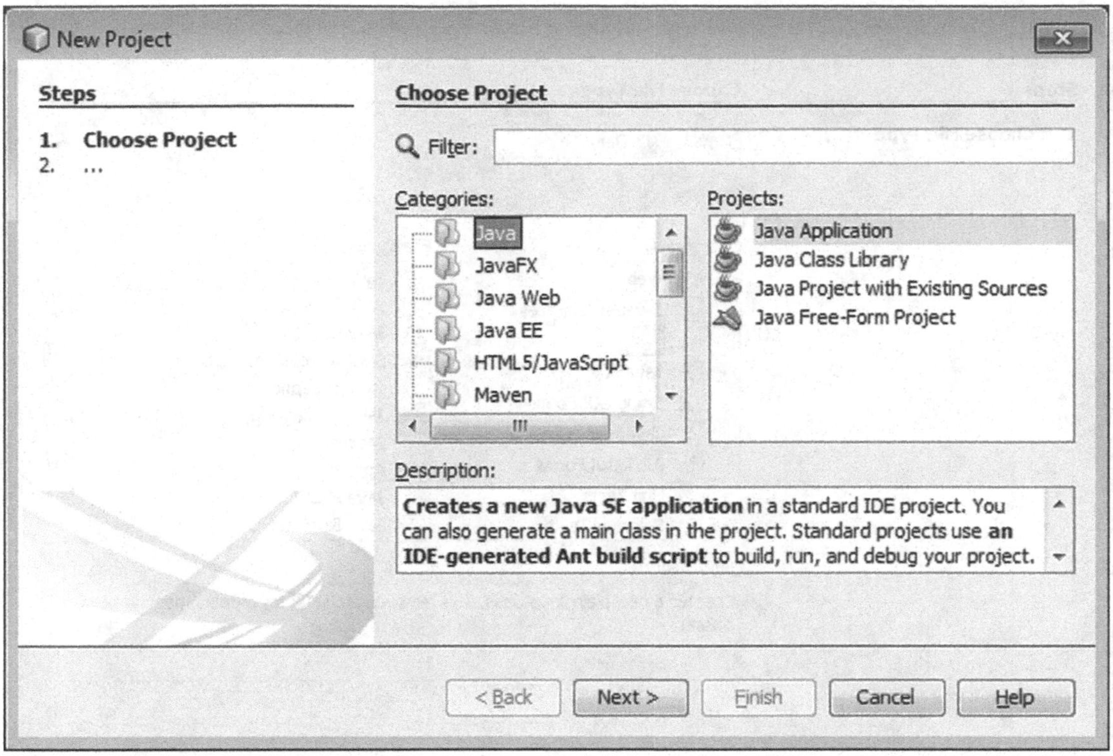

Figure 3-2. *New Project window*

Once you have a project, you'll want to create new files in it. To create a new Java file in a project, choose File ➤ New File, click the New File button in the File toolbar, or press Ctrl+N. The New File window appears, as shown in Figure 3-3, enabling you to create a new Java file.

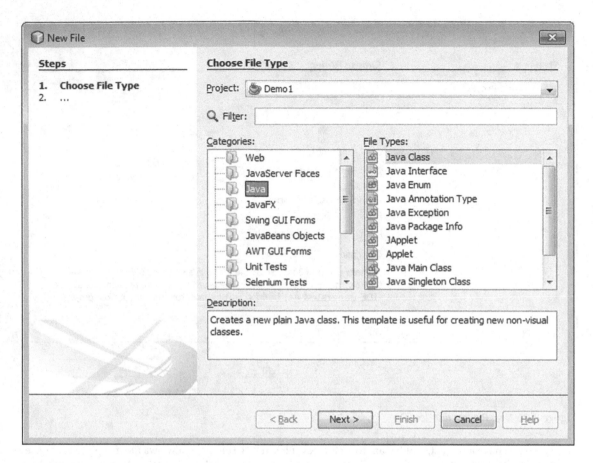

Figure 3-3. *New File window*

Opening a File Without a Project

If you would like to code in Java without setting up a project, you can use File ➤ Open File to open a specific Java file on disk. Use File ➤ Open Recent File (Ctrl+Shift+T) to open the file that you have most recently closed since opening the IDE.

Alternatively, you can use the Favorites window (Ctrl+3), shown in Figure 3-4. The Favorites window enables you to make arbitrary folders and files on your system accessible to the IDE.

However, note that although the Favorites window can be useful if you just want to open and edit a few files quickly, it is not designed for full-scale Java application development, such as usage of the refactoring tools, for example.

To use the Favorites window to give you access to the Source Editor without needing to create a project, choose Favorites from the Window menu, or press Ctrl+3. This will open the Favorites window. Add the folder where you want the file to live (or where it already lives) by right-clicking in the Favorites window, choosing Add to Favorites, and choosing the folder from the file chooser. In the Favorites window, navigate to the file that you want to edit and double-click it to open it in the Source Editor. If you want to create a new file, right-click a folder node, choose New, and then create a new folder or file in the folder.

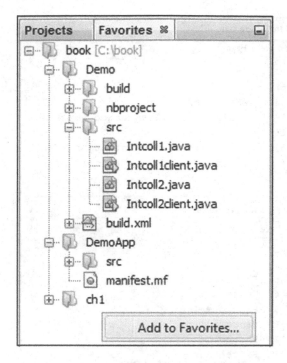

Figure 3-4. *The Favorites window*

Reconfiguring the Source Editor

Now that you have one or more Java files open, it's time to get comfortable! The first step is to set up the Source Editor the way you'd like it to be.

To begin with, you'll be happy to know you can split the Source Editor to view multiple files simultaneously or to view different parts of the same file, as shown in Figure 3-5. To split the Source Editor window to view multiple files, make sure at least two files are already open. Click a tab on one file, hold down the mouse button, and drag the tab to the far left, far right, or bottom of the Source Editor. Release the mouse button when the red outline that appeared around the tab when you started dragging changes to a rectangle. This indicates the placement of the split window.

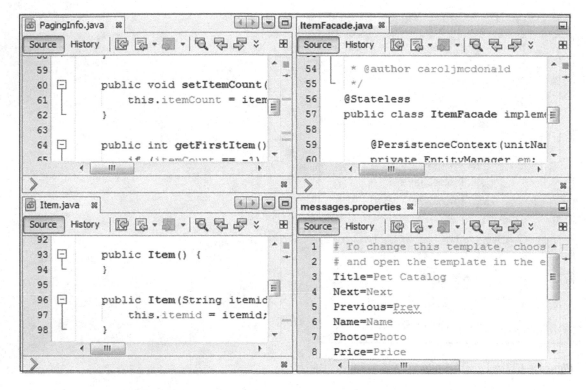

Figure 3-5. *Viewing multiple files simultaneously*

You can view different parts of the same file simultaneously, as shown in Figure 3-6, using a variety of different tools in the IDE.

- Clone Document. Right-click the file's tab in the Source Editor and choose Clone Document to create a second tab for the same document. If needed, drag and drop one of the tabs to create a split Source Editor area. See the previous procedure on dragging and dropping Source Editor tabs.

- Split Document. Right-click the file's tab in the Source Editor and choose Split Document. Then choose Vertically or Horizontally, depending on how you want to split the document.

- Split Document Button. Drag the Split Document button, from the top right of each editor document, vertically or horizontally to split the editor according to your needs.

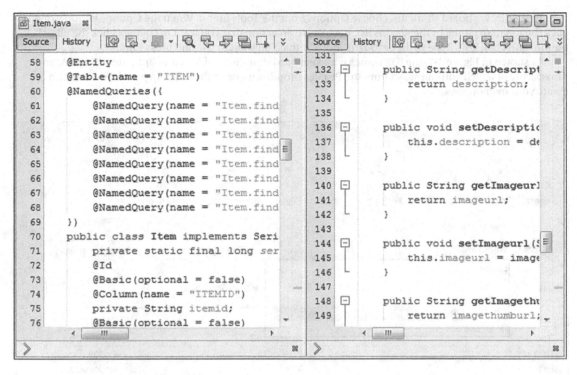

Figure 3-6. *Splitting a single file*

Next, let's explore the actions you can take to make more space for your code.

- Double-click the file's tab. When you do this, the file takes the entire space of the IDE except for the main menu and row of toolbars. You can make the other windows reappear as they were by double-clicking the tab again.

- Make other windows "sliding" windows. Make other windows sliding windows by right-clicking their tabs and choosing Minimize, which minimizes them. They will appear only when you click or mouse over a button representing that window on one of the edges of the IDE. You can return the window to its normal display by clicking the button in the sliding window.

- Hide the IDE's toolbars. You can toggle the display of the main toolbars in the View menu, where you can choose Toolbars. Then, individually, you can choose the toolbars that you want to hide or display. You can toggle the display of the Source Editor's toolbar in the View menu by choosing Show Editor Toolbar.

Changing Keyboard Shortcuts, Fonts, and Colors

You can change default keyboard shortcuts or map other available commands to shortcuts. If you are familiar with keyboard shortcuts defined in other IDEs, you can choose to use those instead of the defaults provided by NetBeans IDE.

Moreover, if you are comfortable with fonts and colors in other IDEs or editors, or for some reason you don't like the default colors used in the editor or in the IDE as a whole, you can relatively easily switch to your preferred font and color combinations.

To modify keyboard shortcuts, choose Options from the Tools menu. When the Options window opens, click the Keymap panel. In the Actions list, navigate to an action that you want to change, click the ellipsis button, and click Edit. Type in the keyboard shortcut that you want to use and press Enter.

As shown in Figure 3-7, the IDE comes with keyboard shortcut profiles for Eclipse, IntelliJ IDEA, and Emacs, any of which you can select from the Profiles dropdown box in the Keymap panel. You can also create your own profiles.

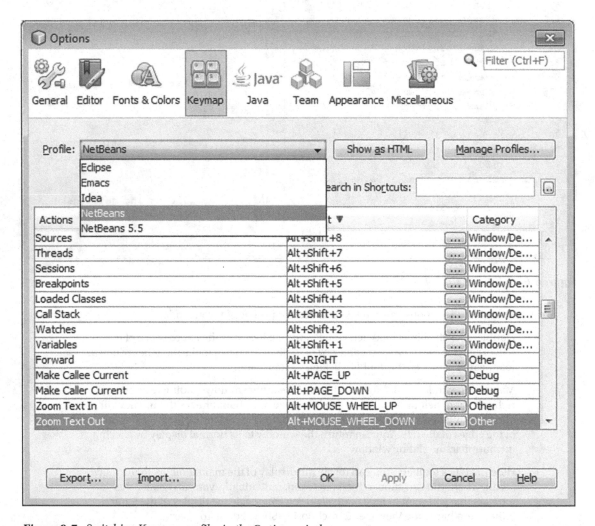

Figure 3-7. *Switching Keymap profiles in the Options window*

To modify the fonts and colors of the Source Editor, choose Options from the Tools menu. When the Options window opens, click the Fonts & Colors panel, as shown in Figure 3-8. Choose a profile from the Profile dropdown box. If you want to fine-tune a profile, use the Category list to navigate to a class member that you want to modify, and then use the Font, Foreground, Background, Effects, and Effect Color components as needed. Use the Preview area to make sure you have customized according to your requirements. Then press Enter.

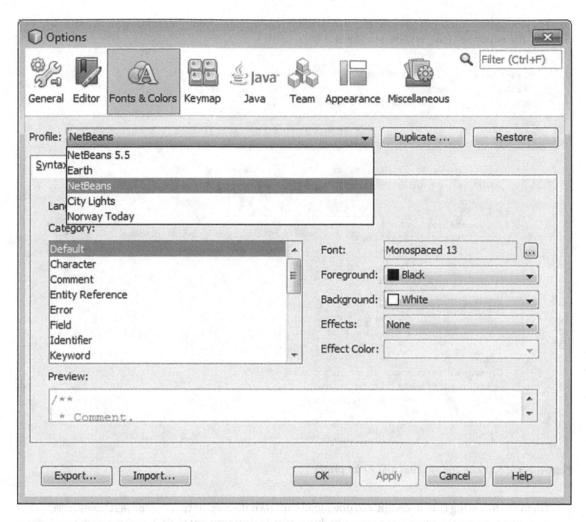

Figure 3-8. *Switching Fonts & Colors profiles in the Options window*

For example, if you select Norway Today from the Profile dropdown without making any further changes, the editor will look as shown in Figure 3-9.

```
62    @Stateless
63    @Path("/greeting")
64    public class HelloWorldResource {
65
66        @EJB
67        private NameStorageBean nameStorage;
68        /**
69         * Retrieves representation of a HelloWorldResource
70         * @return an instance of String
71         */
72        @GET
73        @Produces("text/html")
74        public String getGreeting() {
75            return "<html><body><h1>Hello "+nameStorage.getName()+"!</h1></body></html>";
76        }
77
78        /**
79         * PUT method for updating an instance of HelloWorldResource
80         * @param content representation for the resource
81         * return an HTTP response with content of the updated or created resource.
82         */
83        @PUT
84        @Consumes("text/plain")
85        public void setName(String content) {
86            nameStorage.setName(content);
87        }
88
89    }
```

Figure 3-9. *"Norway Today" Font and Color profile*

Go to the following URL to design and download your own themes: `http://netbeansthemes.com`.

Nowadays, dark backgrounds are increasingly popular in development tools. You can switch to a dark background throughout the IDE by installing the Dark Look & Feel Themes plugin.

To do so, choose Plugins from the Tools menu. When the Plugin Manager opens, click the Available Plugins panel. Select and install the Dark Look and Feel Themes plugin, as shown in Figure 3-10.

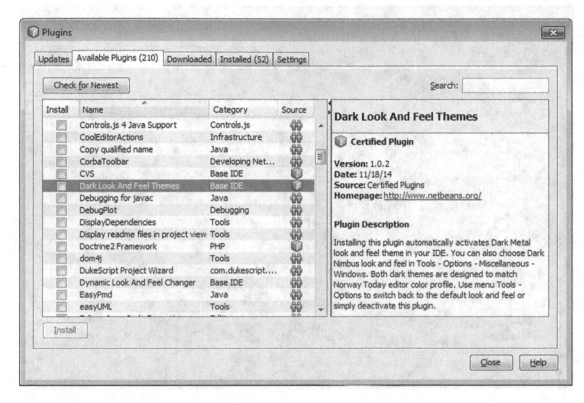

Figure 3-10. *Dark Look and Feel Themes plugin*

After installing the plugin and restarting the IDE, the IDE looks as shown in Figure 3-11.

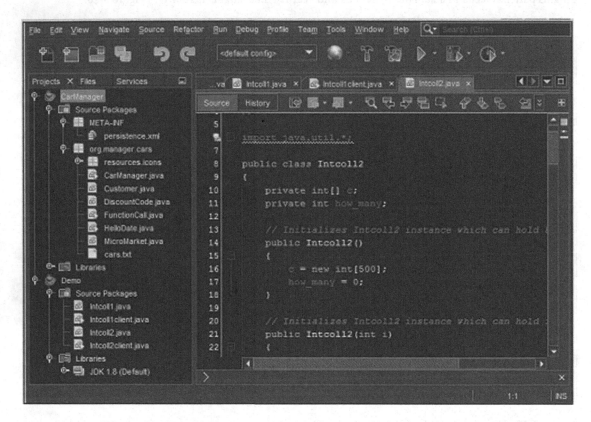

Figure 3-11. *Dark Metal look and feel*

However, the plugin provides two different dark themes. Moreover, various other themes are provided by default, defined by Swing "Look & Feel" implementations.

To switch between themes, choose Options from the Tools menu. When the Options window opens, click the Appearance panel, as shown in Figure 3-12. Use the Preferred Look and Feel dropdown to switch themes.

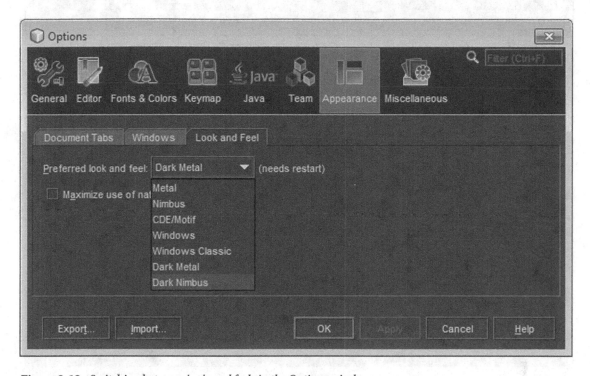

Figure 3-12. Switching between look and feels in the Options window

After switching themes to Dark Nimbus and restarting the IDE, it looks as shown in Figure 3-13.

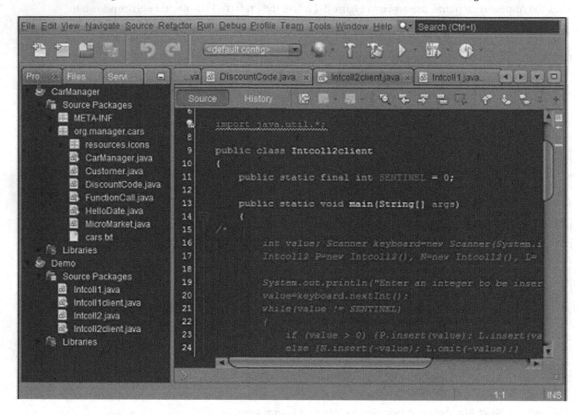

Figure 3-13. *The Dark Nimbus look and feel*

Comparing Differences Between Two Files

You can generate a side-by-side comparison of two files with the differing lines highlighted.

To compare two files, right-click on the two files you want to compare. Choose Tools and then choose Diff, as shown in Figure 3-14.

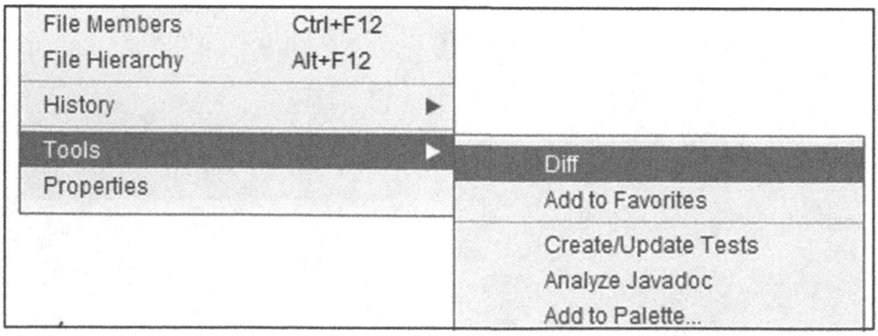

File Members	Ctrl+F12	
File Hierarchy	Alt+F12	
History	►	
Tools	►	Diff
Properties		Add to Favorites
		Create/Update Tests
		Analyze Javadoc
		Add to Palette...

Figure 3-14. *Diff menu item in the Tools menu*

The Diff window appears in the Source Editor, as shown in Figure 3-15.

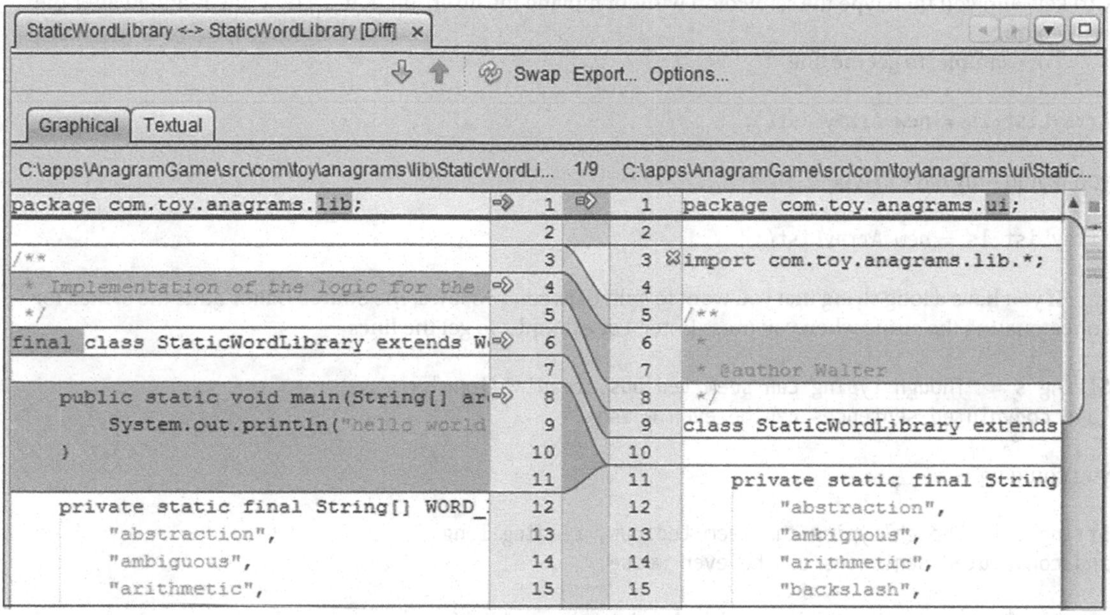

Figure 3-15. *Diff window*

In comparing the document, the colors in the Diff window show deleted lines (red), changed lines (blue), and added lines (green).

Note that the Diff item appears in the Tools menu only when two (and no more than two) files are selected in the Projects, Files, or Favorites window.

Typing

When you're typing in the Source Editor, one of the first things that you will notice is that the closing characters are automatically inserted when you type the opening character. For example, if you type a quote mark, the closing quote mark is inserted at the end of the line. Likewise, parentheses(()), brackets ([]), and curly braces ({}) are completed for you.

While this might seem surprising at first, the feature was designed to not get in your way. If you type the closing character yourself, the automatically inserted character is overwritten. Also, you can end a line by typing a semicolon (;) to finish a statement. The semicolon is inserted at the end of the line after the automatically generated character or characters.

See the following subtopics for information on how to use the insertion of matching closing characters.

Finishing and Concatenating

When the Source Editor inserts matching characters at the end of the line, this would appear to force you to move the insertion point manually past the closing character before you can type the semicolon.

In fact, you can hold down the Ctrl key and type the semicolon without moving the insertion point, and it will be placed at the end of the line automatically. When you hold down the Shift key together with the Ctrl key, and you then type the semicolon without moving the insertion point, a new line is added after the semicolon.

For example, to get the line

```
ArrayList ls = new ArrayList();
```

you would only have to type

```
ArrayList ls = new ArrayList(;
```

If you have a long string that you want to split between two lines, the Source Editor adds the syntax for concatenating the string when you press Enter. For example, to get the lines

```
String s = "Though typing can seem tedious, reading long" +
"and convoluted sentences can be even worse."
```

you could type

```
String s = "Though typing can seem tedious, reading long
and convoluted sentences can be even worse.
```

The final three quote marks and the plus sign (+) are added for you.

If you want to break the line without creating the concatenation, press Shift+Enter.

Matching Other Words in a File

If you are typing a word that appears elsewhere in your file, you can use a keyboard shortcut to complete that word according to the first word found in the Source Editor that matches the characters you have typed. This word-match feature works for any text in the file. It also searches through files that you have been recently working in (in the order that you have last accessed the files). Press Ctrl+K to search backward from the cursor for a match. Press Ctrl+L to search forward from the cursor for a match.

For example, if you have defined the method refreshCustomerInfo on line 100 and now want to call that method from line 50, you can type ref and then press Ctrl+L. If there are no other words that start with ref between lines 50 and 100, the rest of the word refreshCustomerInfo will be filled in. If a different match is found, keep pressing Ctrl+L until the match that you want is filled in.

For typing variable names, you might find that the word match feature is preferable to code completion, since the IDE only has to search a few files for a text string, compared to the code completion feature, where the IDE searches the whole classpath.

Text Selection Shortcuts

To enable you to keep both hands on the keyboard, a number of shortcuts allow you to select text, deselect text, and change the text that is selected. See Table 3-1 for a selection of these shortcuts.

Table 3-1. *Text Selection Shortcuts*

Shortcut	Description
Alt+Shift+J	Selects the current identifier or other word that the insertion point is on.
Ctrl+Shift+[	Selects all the text between a set of parentheses, brackets, or curly braces. The insertion point must be resting immediately after either the opening or closing parenthesis/bracket/brace.
Alt+Shift+Period (Alt+Shift+Comma)	Selects the current code element. Upon subsequent pressings, incrementally increases (Alt+Shift+Period) or decreases (Alt+Shift+Comma) the size of the selection to include surrounding code elements. For example, if you press Alt+Shift+Period once, the current word is selected. If you press it again, the rest of the expression might be selected. Pressing a third time might select the whole statement. Pressing a fourth time might select the whole method.
Shift+Right (Shift+Left)	Selects the next (previous) character or extends the selection one character.
Ctrl+Shift+Right (Ctrl+Shift+Left)	Selects the next (previous) word or extends the selection one word.
Shift+Down (Shift+Up)	Creates or extends the text selection one line down (up).
Shift+End (Shift+Home)	Creates or extends the text selection to the end (beginning) of the line.
Ctrl+Shift+End (Ctrl+Shift+Home)	Creates or extends the text selection to the end (beginning) of the document.
Shift+Page Down (Shift+Page Up)	Creates or extends the text selection one page down (up).

Macros

You can record macros in the IDE to reduce what would normally involve a long set of keystrokes to one keyboard shortcut. In macros, you can combine the typing of characters in the Source Editor and the typing of other keyboard shortcuts.

To record a macro:

1. Put the insertion point in the part of a file in the Source Editor where you want to record the macro.

2. Click the Start Macro Recording button in the Source Editor's toolbar to begin recording.

3. Record the macro using any sequence of keystrokes, whether it is typing characters or using keyboard shortcuts. Mouse movements and clicks (such as menu selections) are not recorded.

4. Click in the Source Editor's toolbar to finish recording.

5. In the Macro field of the Recorded Macro window that appears, fine-tune the macro, if necessary.

6. Click Add to assign a keyboard shortcut to the macro. In the Add Keybinding window, press the keys that you want to use for the keyboard shortcut. (For example, if you want the shortcut Alt+Shift+Z, press the Alt, Shift, and Z keys.) If you press a wrong key, click the Clear button to start over.

Be careful not to use a shortcut that is already assigned. If the shortcut you enter is an editor shortcut, a warning appears in the dialog box. However, if the key combination is a shortcut that applies outside of the Source Editor, you will not be warned.

You can assign a new shortcut in the Options window. Choose Tools ➤ Options, click the Editor panel, select the Macros tab, and then click the Set Shortcut button.

Code Snippets

The Source Editor has several features for reducing the keystrokes needed for typing code. And you can access many of these features without using the mouse, having to use menus, or remembering scores of keyboard shortcuts.

Arguably the most important mechanisms for generating code are the following:

- Ctrl+spacebar. This shortcut opens the code completion box, as shown in Figure 3-16. The code completion box contains a context-sensitive list of ways you can complete the statement you are currently typing and of other code snippets you might want to insert in your code.

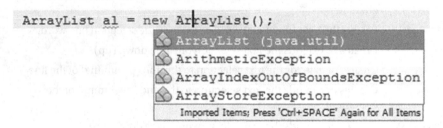

Figure 3-16. *Code completion*

- Multi-keystroke. Abbreviations for longer snippets of code called code templates. These abbreviations are expanded into the full code snippet after you press the spacebar, as shown in Figure 3-17.

Figure 3-17. *Code templates*

- Alt+Insert. This shortcut opens a small popup, shown in Figure 3-18, from which code snippets can quickly be generated.

Figure 3-18. *Code generators*

- Alt+Enter. You can use this shortcut to display suggestions the IDE has regarding missing code and then have the IDE insert that code. The IDE notifies you that it has a suggestion by displaying a light bulb icon in the left margin of the line you are typing, as shown in Figure 3-19.

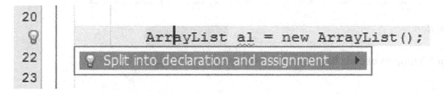

Figure 3-19. *Java hints*

In addition to saving keystrokes and use of the mouse, these features assist in preventing typos and also help you find the right class and method names.

The following sections illustrate how to get the most out of these features when coding in Java.

Code Completion

When you are typing Java identifiers in the Source Editor, you can use the code completion feature to help you finish expressions. In addition, Javadoc documentation appears and displays documentation for the currently selected item in code completion.

A variety of types of code generation tools have been added to the code completion feature. Using code completion, you can do the following:

- Fill in names of classes and class members while reading the related Javadoc documentation, as shown in Figure 3-20.

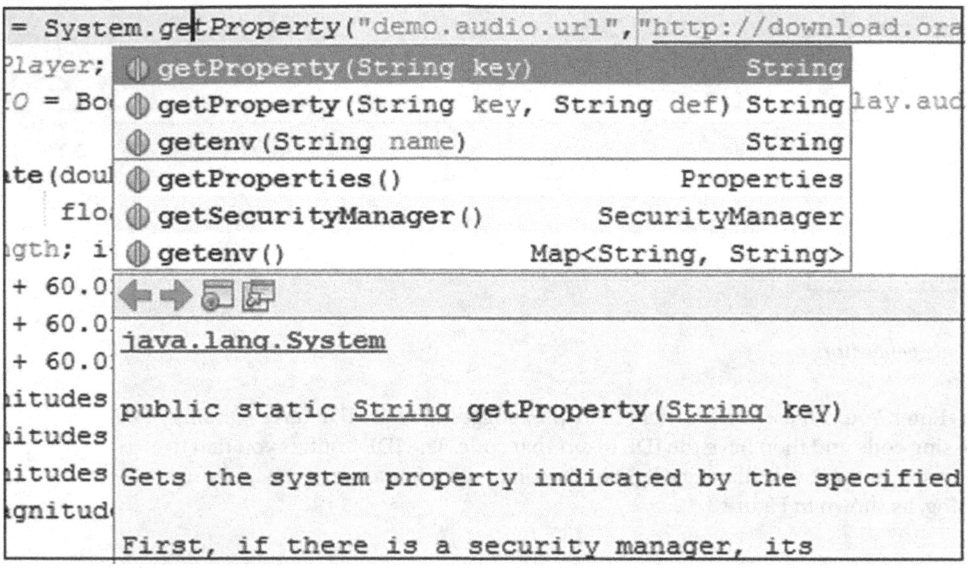

```
= System.getProperty("demo.audio.url", "http://download.ora
Player;       getProperty(String key)                String
O = Bo        getProperty(String key, String def) String lay.aud
              getenv(String name)                    String
te(dou        getProperties()                    Properties
   flo        getSecurityManager()          SecurityManager
gth; i        getenv()                 Map<String, String>

+ 60.0
+ 60.0        java.lang.System
+ 60.0
itudes        public static String getProperty(String key)
itudes
itudes        Gets the system property indicated by the specified
gnitud
              First, if there is a security manager, its
```

Figure 3-20. Code completion

- Generate whole snippets of code from dynamic code templates, as shown in Figure 3-21.

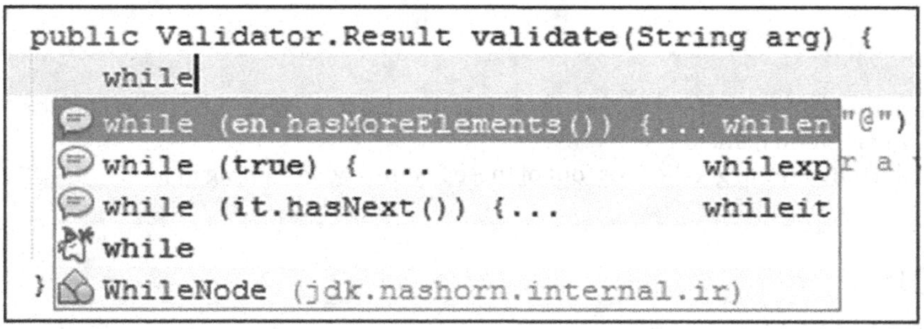

```
public Validator.Result validate(String arg) {
    while
       while (en.hasMoreElements()) {... whilen "@")
       while (true) { ...                   whilexp r a
       while (it.hasNext()) {...            whileit
       while
}      WhileNode (jdk.nashorn.internal.ir)
```

Figure 3-21. Dynamic code templates

- Generate getter and setter methods, as shown in Figure 3-22.

```
41    public class Person {
42
43        String name;
44        int age;
45
46        |
47        🔷 Person() - generate
48        🔷 Person(String name, int age) - generate
49        🔵 clone() - override                    Object
50        🔵 equals(Object obj) - override        boolean
51        🔵 finalize() - override                    void
52        🔵 getAge() - generate                        int
53        🔵 getName() - generate                    String
54        🔵 hashCode() - override                      int
```

Figure 3-22. *Generate getters and setters*

- Generate skeletons for abstract methods of classes extended by and interfaces implemented by the current class and override inherited methods, as shown in Figure 3-23.

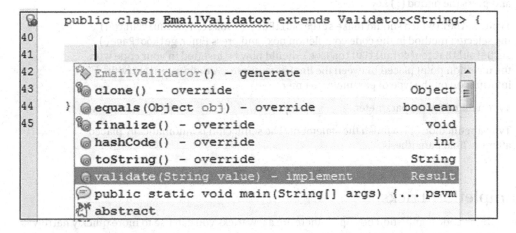

```
      public class EmailValidator extends Validator<String> {
40
41        |
42        🔷 EmailValidator() - generate
43        🔵 clone() - override                    Object
44    }   🔵 equals(Object obj) - override        boolean
45        🔵 finalize() - override                    void
          🔵 hashCode() - override                      int
          🔵 toString() - override                  String
          🔵 validate(String value) - implement   Result
          🔵 public static void main(String[] args) {... psvm
          🔷 abstract
```

Figure 3-23. *Override inherited methods*

- Generate skeletons of anonymous inner classes, as shown in Figure 3-24.

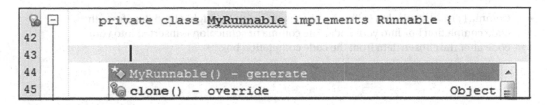

```
      🔒 ⊟  private class MyRunnable implements Runnable {
42
43            |
44            🔷 MyRunnable() - generate
45            🔵 clone() - override                    Object
```

Figure 3-24. *Generate anonymous inner classes*

A variety of mechanisms are provided to open the code completion box:

- Ctrl+spacebar. Type the first few characters of an expression and then press Ctrl+spacebar (or Ctrl+\).

- Pause. Pause after typing a period (.) in an expression.

- Space. Type a space, and then pause for a moment.

The code completion box opens with a selection of possible matches for what you have typed so far. To narrow the selection in the code completion box, continue typing the expression. To complete the expression and close the code completion box, do one of the following:

- Type. Continue typing until there is only one option left and then press Enter.

- Scroll. Scroll through the list using the arrow keys or your mouse to select a value, and then press Enter.

To close the code completion box without entering any selection, press Esc.

To complete the expression and leave the code completion box open, select a completion and press the period (.) key. This is useful if you are chaining methods. For example, if you want to type

```
getRootPane().setDefaultButton(defaultButtonName)
```

you might do the following:

- Type getRo (which would leave only getRootPane() in the code completion box) and press the period (.) key.

- Type .setDef (which should make setDefaultButton(JButton defaultButton) the selected method in the code completion box) and press Enter. getRootPane(). setDefaultButton(defaultButtonName) should now be inserted in your code with the insertion point placed between the final parentheses. A tooltip appears with information on the type of parameter to enter.

- Type a name for the parameter.

- Type a semicolon (;) to finish the statement. The semicolon is automatically placed after the final parenthesis.

Code Completion Tricks

When typing with the code completion box open, there are a few tricks you can use to more quickly narrow the selection and generate the code you are looking for. For example:

- Camel Case. If you want to create an instance of HashSet, you can type private HS and press Ctrl+spacebar to display HashSet (and other classes that have a capital H and a capital S in their names).

- Comma (,) and semicolon (;) keys. Use these to insert the highlighted item from the code completion box into your code. The comma or semicolon is inserted into your code after the chosen item from the code completion box.

- Tab. You can fill in text that is common to all of the remaining choices in the list by pressing Tab. This can save you several keystrokes (or use of the arrow keys or mouse) when the selection in the code completion box is narrowed to choices with the same prefix. For example, if you are working with a Hashtable object ht and you have typed ht.n, there will be two methods beginning with notify (notify() and notifyAll()). To more quickly narrow the selection to just notifyAll(), press Tab to expand ht.n to ht.notify and then type A. You can then press Enter to complete the statement with notifyAll().

Customizing Settings for Code Completion

If you prefer to use different shortcuts for code completion, you can change those shortcuts in NetBeans IDE. From the Options menu, choose Tools. The Options window opens. In the Options window, click Editor and select Keymap, as shown in Figure 3-25. In the Search filter, type code completion. The related shortcuts will be shown so that you can fine-tune them to your taste.

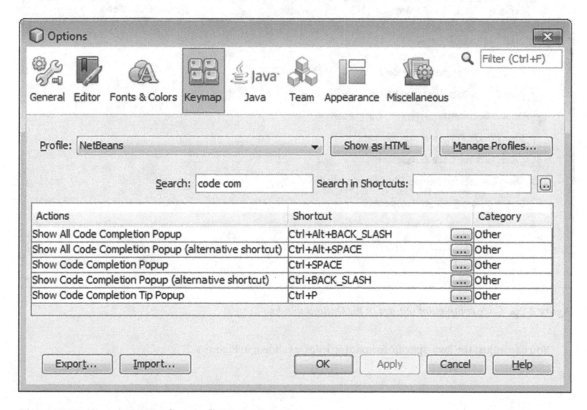

***Figure 3-25.** Customizing code completion actions*

To adjust general formatting rules, choose Tools from the Options menu. The Options window opens. In the Options window, click Editor and select Code Completion, as shown in Figure 3-26. In the Language dropdown, when All Languages is selected, fine-tune the general settings to your taste.

As you can see in Figure 3-26, if you find the code completion box to be more of a nuisance than a help, you can disable automatic appearance of the code completion popup. Code completion will still work if you manually activate it by pressing Ctrl+spacebar or Ctrl+\.

Another typical setting you might find useful is that you can leave automatic appearance of the code completion popup enabled but disable the bulkier Javadoc code completion dialog box. The Javadoc popup can be manually invoked with Ctrl+Shift+spacebar.

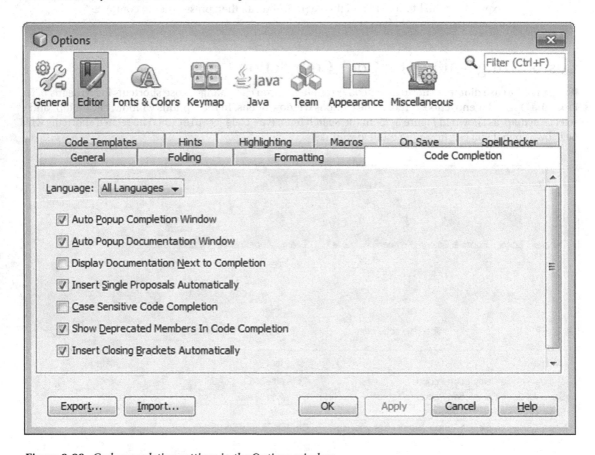

Figure 3-26. *Code completion settings in the Options window*

You can adjust the Java-specific formatting rules, as shown in Figure 3-27.

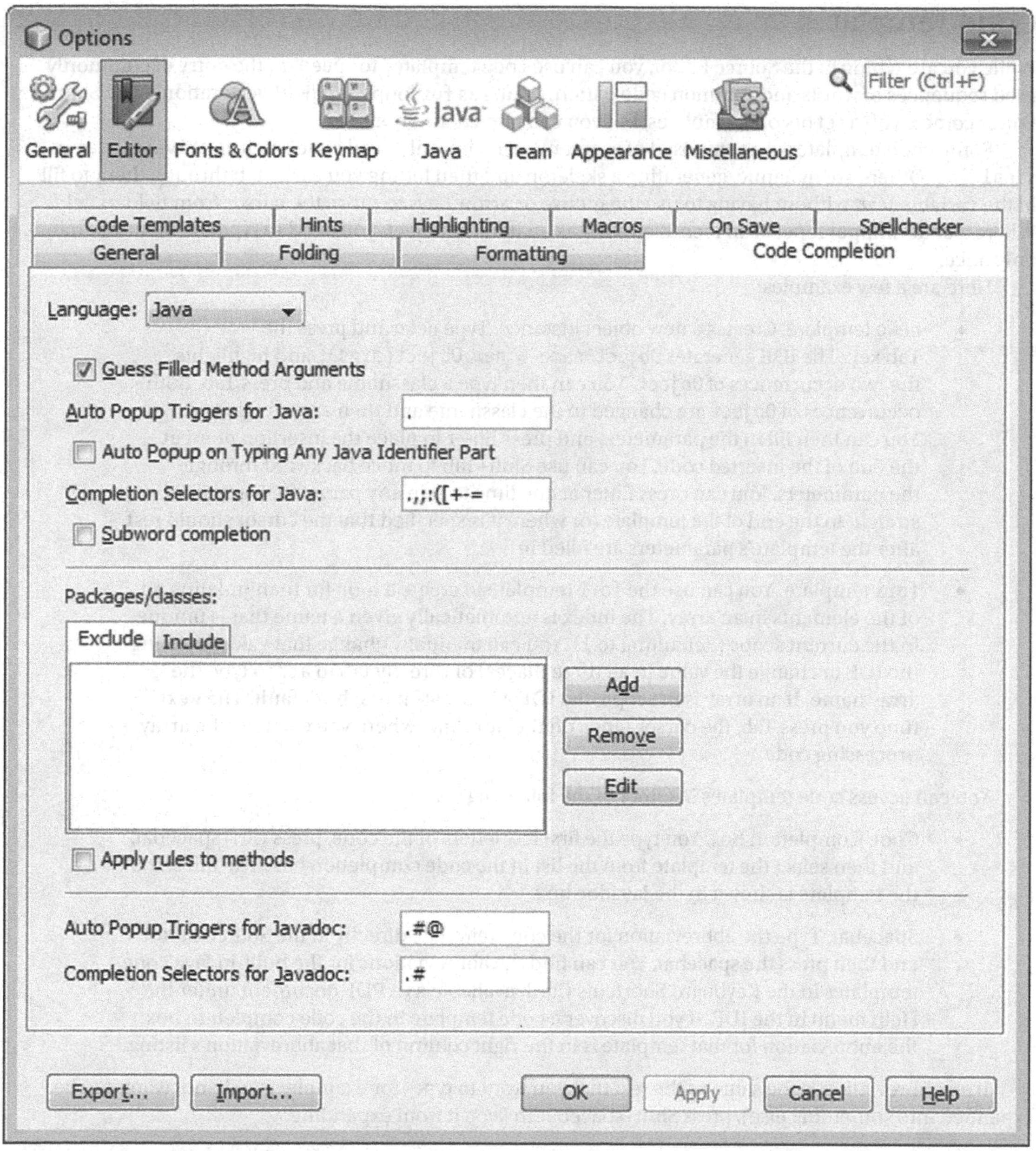

Figure 3-27. Java-specific code completion in the Options window

Templates

As you get more comfortable with the IDE, you should try to make the most of the many facilities it provides. For example, you can significantly cut down on the amount of typing you need to do if you spend some time learning about the IDE's many different kinds of templates. This section introduces the IDE's code templates and file templates. By the end of this section, you should be typing a lot less than before!

Code Templates

While you are typing in the Source Editor, you can use code templates to speed up the entry of commonly used sequences of words and common code patterns, such as for loops and field declarations. The Source Editor comes with a set of code templates, but you can also create your own.

Some code templates are composed of segments of commonly used code, such as `private static final int`. Others are dynamic, generating a skeleton and then letting you easily tab through them to fill in the variable text, without having to use the mouse or arrow keys to move the cursor from field to field. Where a code snippet repeats an identifier, such as an iterator object, you need to type the identifier name only once.

Here are a few examples:

- `newo` template. Creates a new object instance. Type `newo` and press the Tab key. The IDE generates `Object name = new Object(args);` and highlights the two occurrences of `Object`. You can then type a classname and press Tab. Both occurrences of `Object` are changed to the classname and then `args` is selected. You can then fill in the parameters and press Enter to place the insertion point at the end of the inserted code. You can use Shift+Tab to move backward through the parameters. You can press Enter at any time to skip any parameters and jump straight to the end of the template (or where it is specified that the cursor should rest after the template's parameters are filled in).

- `fori` template. You can use the `fori` template to create a loop for manipulating all of the elements in an array. The index is automatically given a name that is unique in the current scope (defaulting to `i`). You can manually change that value (causing the IDE to change the value in all three places) or directly tab to `arr` to type the array name. If an array is in scope, the IDE will use its name by default. The next time you press Tab, the cursor lands on the next line, where you can type the array processing code.

You can access code templates in either of the following ways:

- Code Completion Box. You type the first few letters of the code, press Ctrl+spacebar, and then select the template from the list in the code completion box. The full text of the template is shown in the Javadoc box.

- Spacebar. Type the abbreviation for the code template directly in the Source Editor and then press the spacebar. You can find the abbreviations for the built-in Java code templates in the Keyboard Shortcuts Card, available as a PDF document under the Help menu in the IDE. If you discover a code template in the code completion box, the abbreviation for that template is in the right column of that abbreviation's listing.

If an abbreviation is the same as the text that you want to type (for example, you do not want it to be expanded into something else), press Shift+spacebar to keep it from expanding.

Adding, Changing, and Removing Code Templates

The code templates that come with the IDE are representative of the kind of things you can do with code templates, but they represent only a tiny fraction of the number of potentially useful templates.

You can modify existing code templates and create entirely new ones to suit the patterns that you use frequently in your code.

To create a new code template:

1. Choose Tools ➤ Options, click Editor in the left panel, and select the Code Templates tab.

2. Click New.

3. In the New Code Template window, type an abbreviation for the template and click OK.

4. In the Expanded Text field, insert the text for the template. See the "Code Template Syntax" section later in this chapter for information on how to customize the behavior of your templates.

5. Click OK to save the template and exit the Options window.

    To modify a code template:

1. Choose Tools ➤ Options, click Editor in the left panel, and select the Code Templates tab.

2. Select a template from the Templates table and edit its text in the Expanded Text field.

3. Click OK to save the changes and exit the Options window.

You cannot directly change the abbreviation for a code template. If you want to assign a different shortcut to an existing template, select that shortcut, copy its expanded text, create a new code template with that text and a different abbreviation, and then remove the template with the undesired abbreviation.

To remove a code template:

1. Choose Tools ➤ Options, click Editor in the left panel, and select the Code Templates tab.

2. Select a template from the Templates table and click Remove.

3. Click OK to save the changes and exit the Options window.

Code Template Syntax

In code templates, you can set up the variable text to provide the following benefits for the template user:

-   Display a descriptive hint for the remaining text that needs to be typed.

-   Enable typing of an identifier once and have it generated in multiple places.

-   Make sure that an import statement is added for a class.

-   Specify a type of which a parameter of the code template is an instance. The IDE will automatically generate an appropriate value for that parameter when the template is used to insert code.

-   Automatically set up a variable name for an iterator, making sure that that variable name is not already used in the current scope.

-   Set a location for the cursor to appear in the generated snippet once the static text has been generated and the variable text has been filled in.

For example, you might want to easily generate something like the following code for a class that you instantiate often:

```
FileWriter filewriter = new FileWriter(outputFile);
```

In the definition for such a code template, you could use something like the following:

```
${fw type = "java.io.FileWriter"
    editable="false"} ${filewriter} = new ${fw}(${outputFile});
```

When the template is inserted into the code, the following things happen:

- `${fw type = "java.io.FileWriter" editable="false"}` is converted to `FileWriter` in the inserted code.

- `${fw}` is also converted to `Filewriter` (as it is essentially shorthand for the previously defined `${fw type = "java.io.FileWriter" editable="false"}`).

- `${filewriter}` and `${outputFile}` generate text (`filewriter` and `outputFile`, respectively).

- `filewriter` is selected. You can type a new name for the field and then press Tab to select `outputFile` and type a name for that parameter. Then you can press Tab or Enter to place the cursor after the whole generated snippet.

You could further refine the code template by defining an `instanceof` attribute for `${outputFile}` (such as `OutputFile instanceof = "java.io.File"`). This would enable the IDE to detect an instance of that class and dynamically insert the name of the instance variable in the generated snippet instead of merely `outputFile`.

Changing the Expander Shortcut for Code Templates

If you find that the code templates get in your way because they inadvertently get invoked when you type certain strings, you can configure the IDE to activate the templates with a different key or key combination. This enables you to continue using the code template feature without having to individually change any templates that get in your way.

To change the code template expander key, choose Tools ➤ Options, click Editor in the left panel, and select the Code Templates tab. Select the preferred key or key combination from the Expand Template On dropdown list. Click OK to save the change and exit the Options window.

File Templates

You can customize the templates from which you create files. You can also create your own templates and make them available in the New File wizard. This might be useful if you need to add standard elements in all of your files, such as copyright notices, or you want to change the way other elements are generated, as shown in Figure 3-28.

Figure 3-28. *File templates*

There are several macros you can use in templates to generate text dynamically in the created files. These macros are identifiable by the double underscores that appear both before and after their names.

To edit a template:

1. In the Tools menu, choose Templates. The Template Manager opens.

2. Expand the appropriate category node and select the template that you want to edit.

3. Where possible, click Open in Editor, edit the template, and then save it.

Not all of the templates listed in the Template Manager can be modified at the user level. In some cases, the templates are available in the New File wizard but do not represent file constructs, such as those in the Enterprise and Sun Resources categories.

To create a new file template based on another template:

1. In the Tools menu, choose Templates. The Template Manager opens.

2. Expand the appropriate category node and select the template that you want to use as a starting point.

3. Click Duplicate.

4. A new node appears for the copied template. _1 is appended to the template's name.

5. Click Open in Editor.

6. Edit the file, incorporating any of the template macros that you want to use, and save it. If the template is for a Java class, you can use the filename for the classname and constructor name. These are automatically adjusted in the files you create from the template.

To import a file template:

1. In the Tools menu, choose Templates. The Template Manager opens.

2. Select the category folder for the template.

3. Click Add to open the Add Template window.

4. Navigate to and select the file that you want to import as a template. Then click Add.

Java Hints

When the IDE detects an error for which it has identified a possible fix, or a suggestion for a different way to express your code, a light bulb icon appears in the left margin of that line, as shown in Figure 3-29.

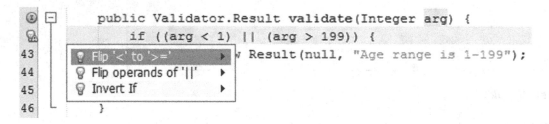

Figure 3-29. Java hints

You can click the light bulb or press Alt+Enter to display a list of possible fixes. If one of those fixes suits you, you can select it and press Enter to have the fix generated in your code.

Often, the "error" is not a coding mistake but is related to the fact that you have not filled in the missing code. In those cases, the editor hints simply automate the entry of certain types of code. Other times, the code is not "wrong," but could be expressed in a different way, so the editor hint suggests the alternative ways of expressing your code.

For example, assume you have just typed the following code, but x is not defined anywhere in the class.

```
int newIntegerTransformer () {
  return x;
}
```

If your cursor is still resting on the line of the return statement, the icon will appear. If you click the icon or press Alt+Enter, you will be offered three possible solutions. You can select one of those hints to generate the code.

For example, the IDE can provide hints for and generate the following solutions to common coding errors.

- Add a missing import statement.

- Insert abstract methods that are declared in a class' implemented interfaces and abstract superclasses.

- Insert a method parameter.

- Create a missing method.

- Create a missing field.

- Create a missing local variable.

- Initialize a variable.

- Insert a cast.

- Add a throws clause with the appropriate exception.

- Surround the code with a try-catch block including the appropriate exception.

- To modify Java hints, choose Options from the Tools menu. In the Options window, click Editor and select Hints, as shown in Figure 3-30. In the Hints list, specify the hints you want to enable. In the Show As dropdown, specify the priority of the hint.

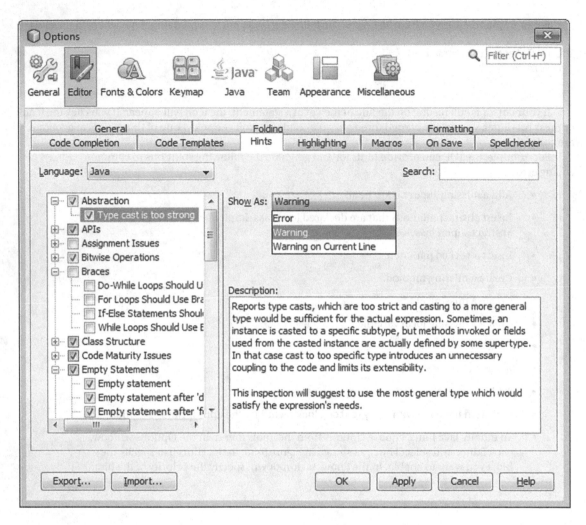

Figure 3-30. *Customizing Java hints*

Java Members

The Java Editor has tools especially created for specific kinds of Java members.

Implements and Overrides

When you extend a class or implement an interface, you have abstract methods that you need to implement and possibly non-abstract methods that you can override. The IDE has several tools that help you generate these methods in your class:

- Editor hints. When you add the `implements` or `extends` clause, a light bulb icon appears in the left margin. You can click this icon or press Alt+Enter to view a hint to implement abstract methods. If you select the hint and press Enter, the IDE generates the methods for you. This hint is available only when your cursor is in the line of the class declaration.

- Code completion. You can generate methods to implement and override
  individually by pressing Ctrl+spacebar and choosing the methods from the code
  completion box.

JavaBeans

The IDE has a few levels of support for creating JavaBeans components. You can use the following features:

- Code completion. When you have a field in your class without a corresponding
  get or set method, you can generate that method by pressing Ctrl+spacebar and
  choosing the method from the code completion box.

- Refactor/Encapsulate Fields. You can use the Encapsulate Fields command to
  generate get and set methods, change the field's access modifier, and update code
  that directly accesses the field to use the getters and setters instead.

- BeanInfo Generator. In the Projects window, you can right-click a JavaBeans
  component and choose BeanInfo Editor. If a BeanInfo class does not exist, it will be
  generated for you.

Imports

When you use the IDE's code completion and editor hints features, import statements are generated for you automatically.

For example, if you have the code completion box open and you start typing a simple classname instead of its fully-qualified classname (for example, you type Con and then select ConcurrentHashMap from the code completion box), the following import statement will be added to the beginning of the file:

```
import java.util.concurrent.ConcurrentHashMap;
```

For cases where these mechanisms are not sufficient for the management of import statements, you can use the following commands:

- Fix Imports (Alt+Shift+F). Automatically inserts any missing import statements for
  the whole file. import statements are generated by class (rather than by package).
  For rapid management of your imports, use this command.

- Fast Import (Alt+Shift+I). Enables you to add an import statement or generate the
  fully qualified classname for the currently selected identifier. This command is useful
  if you want to generate an import statement for a whole package or if you want to use
  a fully qualified classname inline instead of an import statement.

Javadoc

The IDE gives you a few ways to access documentation for JDK and library classes.

- To glance at documentation for the currently selected class in the Source Editor, press Ctrl+Shift+spacebar. A popup window appears with the Javadoc documentation for the class. This popup also appears when you use code completion. You can dismiss the popup by clicking outside of the popup.

- To open a web browser on documentation for the selected class, right-click the class and choose Show Javadoc (or press Alt+F1).

- To open the index page for a library's documentation in a web browser, choose View ➤ Documentation Indices and choose the index from the submenu.

Documentation for some libraries is bundled with the IDE. However, you might need to register the documentation for other libraries in the IDE for the Javadoc features to work.

Paradoxically, JDK documentation is available through a popup in the Source Editor but not through a browser by default. This is because the Javadoc popup in the Source Editor picks up the documentation from the sources that are included with the JDK. However, the browser view of the documentation requires compiled Javadoc documentation, which you have to download separately from the JDK.

Formatting

When you type or have code generated in the Source Editor, your Java code is automatically formatted in the following ways by default:

- Class members are indented four spaces.

- Continued statements are indented eight spaces.

- Tabs are converted to spaces.

- Opening curly braces are placed on the same line as the declaration of the class or method.

- The opening parenthesis has no space before it.

If your file loses correct formatting, you can reformat the whole file by selecting Source ➤ Format (Alt+Shift+F). If you have one or more lines selected, the reformatting applies only to those lines. If you have a node selected in the Projects window, such as a project or a package, or combinations of multiple projects, packages, and files, the reformatting applies only to the content of those nodes.

When you have copied code, you can have it inserted with correct formatting by pasting with the Ctrl+Shift+V shortcut. When you want to copy from the clipboard, press Ctrl+Shift+D to show a popup of the content of the clipboard (the history of your copied text) and select the item you want to paste.

If you want to see spaces and line endings, choose View ➤ Show Non-printable Characters. The editor then looks as shown in Figure 3-31.

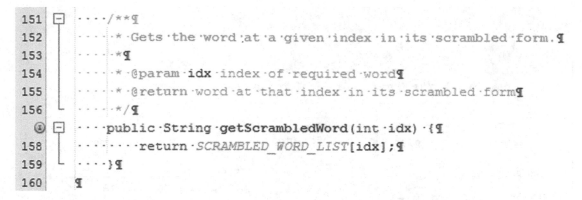

```
151    ····/**¶
152    ·····* ·Gets ·the ·word ·at ·a ·given ·index ·in ·its ·scrambled ·form.¶
153    ·····*¶
154    ·····* ·@param ·idx ·index ·of ·required ·word¶
155    ·····* ·@return ·word ·at ·that ·index ·in ·its ·scrambled ·form¶
156    ·····*/¶
       ····public ·String ·getScrambledWord(int ·idx) ·{¶
158    ·········· ·return ·SCRAMBLED_WORD_LIST[idx];¶
159    ····}¶
160    ¶
```

Figure 3-31. *Show non-printable characters*

Indenting Blocks of Code Manually

You can select multiple lines of code and then indent all those lines by pressing Tab or Alt+Shift+Right.

You can reverse indentation of lines by selecting those lines and then pressing Shift+Tab or Alt+Shift+Left.

The editor toolbar has two buttons that you can use for indenting and unindenting the selected lines of code, as shown in Figure 3-32.

Figure 3-32. *Indenting blocks of code manually*

Changing Formatting Rules

For various file types, you can adjust formatting settings, such as for number of spaces per tab, placement of curly braces, and so on.

To adjust formatting rules for Java files, choose Tools from the Options menu. The Options window opens. In the Options window, click Editor and select Formatting, as shown in Figure 3-33. In the Formatting tab, you can fine-tune the settings to your taste.

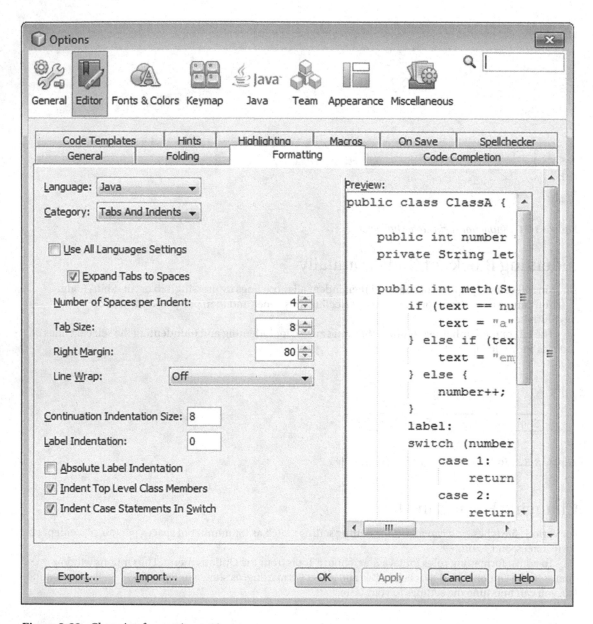

Figure 3-33. *Changing formatting settings*

Navigation

It can be pretty frustrating knowing you have a piece of code somewhere, but not knowing where it is exactly. This section shows you ways of quickly moving around your file and your project to quickly and efficiently manage your Java code.

Navigating Within the Current Java File

- The IDE provides several tools to make it easier to view and navigate a given Java file:Navigator. Appears below the Projects window and provides a list of members (for example, constructors, fields, and methods) in the currently selected Java file.

- Bookmarks window. Enables you to jump back to specific places in the file.

- Jump List. Enables you to jump between areas where you have been working.

- Keyboard shortcuts. Enable you to scroll around the editor.

- Code folding. Enables you to collapse sections of code (such as method bodies, Javadoc comments, and blocks of import statements), thus making a broader section of your class visible in the window at a given time.

Viewing and Navigating Members of a Class

The Navigator provides a list of all members (constructors, methods, and fields) of your class, as shown in Figure 3-34.

Figure 3-34. Navigator

Double-click a member in this list to jump to its source code in the Source Editor. Alternatively, instead of using the mouse, press Ctrl+7 to give focus to the Navigator window. Then begin typing the identifier until the Navigator locates it and press Enter to select that identifier in the Source Editor.

You can use the filter buttons at the bottom of the Navigator to hide non-public members, static members, fields, and/or inherited members.

Moving the Insertion Point and Scrolling the Window

There is a wide range of keyboard shortcuts that you can use to move the insertion point, that is, the cursor, quickly around the editor, instead of simply pressing the left and right arrow keys to move one character left and right or the up and down arrow keys to move it one character up and down, as shown in Table 3-2.

Table 3-2. *Cursor Movement Shortcuts*

Shortcut	Description
Ctrl+Right (Ctrl+Left)	Moves the insertion point to the next word (previous word).
Ctrl+Home (Ctrl+End)	Moves the insertion point to the top (bottom) of the file.
Home (End)	Moves the insertion point to the start (end) of the statement.
Ctrl+Up (Ctrl+Down)	Scrolls up (down) without moving the insertion point.
Alt+Shift+Home/End/Insert	Scrolls the window so that the current line moves to the top, bottom, or middle of the window, without moving the insertion point.
Ctrl+[	Moves the insertion point to the parenthesis, bracket, or curly brace that matches the one directly before your insertion point.

Customizing Code Folds

You can set bookmarks in files to make it easy to find areas of your projects that you are working with frequently. You can then cycle through all your bookmarks by pressing Ctrl+Shift+Period (next bookmark) or Ctrl+Shift+Comma (previous bookmark).

To bookmark a line in a file, click in the line and press Ctrl+Shift+M. To remove a bookmark, also use Ctrl+Shift+M.

You can open the Bookmarks window by choosing Window ➤ IDE Tools ➤ Bookmarks. Alternatively, choose the final item in the popup that appears when you cycle through the bookmarks via Ctrl+Shift+Period and Ctrl+Shift+Comma. The Bookmarks window displays all bookmarks throughout all applications, enabling you to create an easy path through the relevant parts of the applications you're working on, as shown in Figure 3-35.

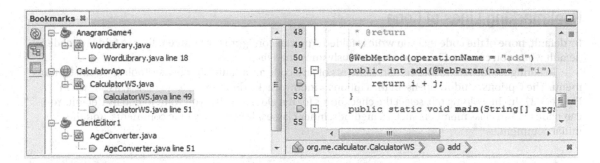

Figure 3-35. *Bookmarks window*

Hiding Sections of Code

You can collapse (or "fold") low-level details of code so that only one line of that block is visible in the Source Editor, leaving more room to view other lines. Methods, inner classes, import blocks, and Javadoc comments are all foldable.

Collapsible blocks of code are marked with a minus icon in the left margin next to the first line of the block. The rest of the block is marked with a vertical line that extends down from the icon. Collapsed blocks are marked with a plus icon. You can click one of these icons to fold or expand the particular block it represents, as shown in Figure 3-36.

```
40      @WebService()
41      public class CalculatorWS {
42
43  ⊞      /** Web service operation ...6 lines */
49         @WebMethod(operationName = "add")
50  ⊟      public int add(@WebParam(name = "i") int i, @WebParam(name = "j") int j) {
51             return i + j;
52         }
53
54      }
```

Figure 3-36. *Hiding sections of code*

You can also collapse and expand single or multiple blocks of code with keyboard shortcuts and menu items in the View ➤ Code Folds menu and the Code Folds submenu in the Source Editor. Table 3-3 lists the related commands and shortcuts.

Table 3-3. *Code Folding Shortcuts*

Shortcut	Description
Ctrl+NumPad-Minus	Collapse Fold
Ctrl+NumPad-Plus	Expand Fold
Ctrl+Shift+NumPad-Minus	Collapse All
Ctrl+Shift+NumPad-Plus	Expand All

Bookmarking Lines of Code

By default, none of the code that you write is folded. You can configure the Source Editor to fold Java code by default when you create a file or open a previously unopened file.

To configure the IDE to fold certain elements of Java code automatically, choose Tools from the Options menu. The Options window opens. In the Options window, click Editor and select Folding, as shown in Figure 3-37. In the Folding tab, select the checkboxes for the elements that you want folded by default. You can choose from class members such as methods, inner classes, imports, Javadoc comments, and the initial comment.

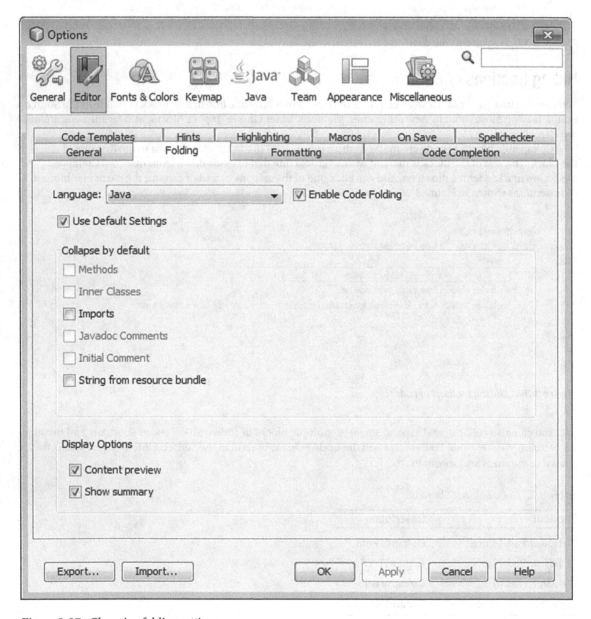

Figure 3-37. *Changing folding settings*

Navigating from the Source Editor

The IDE includes handy shortcuts for navigating among files, different bits of code, and different windows. The more of these shortcuts you can incorporate into your workflow, the less your fingers will have to stray from your keyboard to your mouse.

Switching Between Open Files

Besides using the Source Editor's tabs and dropdown list, you can switch between open files using keyboard shortcuts.

- Ctrl+Tab. Opens a popup showing all open files, as shown in Figure 3-38. Hold down the Ctrl key and press the Tab key multiple times until the file that you want to view is selected. Then release both keys to close the box and display the file.

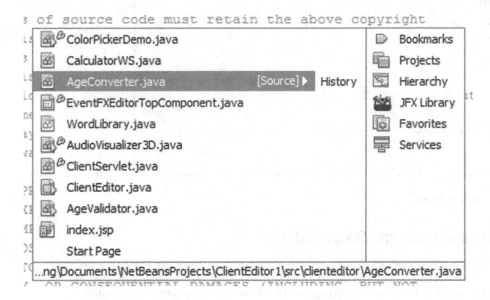

Figure 3-38. *Popup switcher*

- Shift+F4. Opens a dialog box that lists all open files, as shown in Figure 3-39. You can use the mouse or the arrow keys to select the file that you want to view and press Enter to close the dialog box and display the file.

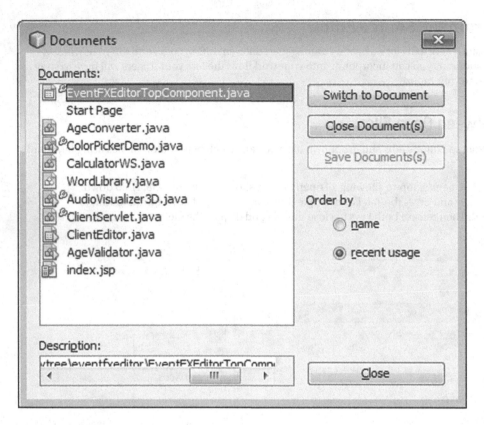

Figure 3-39. *Document switcher*

Jumping to Related Code and Documentation

The shortcuts in the list below enable you to jump to parts of the current file or other files that are relevant to the selected identifier. The first six of these shortcuts are available from the Navigate menu and the Go To submenu of the Source Editor's contextual (right-click) menu. The Show Javadoc command is available straight from the Source Editor's contextual menu.

- Alt+O (or Ctrl-click). Go to Source jumps to the source code for the currently selected class, method, or field, if the source is available. You can achieve this either by pressing Alt+O with the identifier selected or by holding down the Ctrl key, hovering the mouse over the identifier until it is underlined in blue, and then clicking it.

- Alt+G. Go to Declaration jumps to the declaration of the currently selected class, method, or field.

- Ctrl+B. Go to Super Implementation jumps to the super implementation of the currently selected method (if the selected method overrides a method from another class or is an implementation of a method defined in an interface).

- Ctrl+G. Go to Line jumps to a specific line number in the current file.

- Alt+Shift+O. Go to Class enables you to type a classname and then jumps to the source code for that class if it is available to the IDE.

- Alt+Shift+E. Go to Test jumps to the unit test for the selected class.

- Alt+F1. Show Javadoc displays documentation for the selected class in a web browser. For this command to work, Javadoc for the class must be made available to the IDE through the Java Platform Manager (for JDK documentation) or the Library Manager (for documentation for other libraries).

Jumping Between Areas Where You Have Been Working

When you are working on multiple files at once or in different areas of the same file, you can use the Jump List buttons in the Editor toolbar, as shown in Figure 3-40, to navigate directly to areas where you have been working instead of scrolling and/or switching windows.

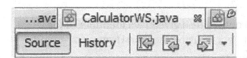

Figure 3-40. *Jump List buttons*

The Jump List is essentially a history of lines where you have done work in the Source Editor, as shown in Figure 3-41.

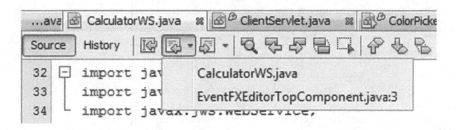

Figure 3-41. *Expanded Jump List*

Jumping from the Source Editor to a File's Node

When you are typing in the Source Editor, you can jump to the node that represents the current file in other windows. This can be useful, for example, if you want to navigate quickly to another file in the same package or you want to browse versioning information for the current file.

- Ctrl+Shift+1. Select the node for the current file in the Projects window.

- Ctrl+Shift+2. Select the node for the current file in the Files window.

- Ctrl+Shift+3. Select the node for the current file in the Favorites window.

Search and Replace

There are different types of searches available for different types of needs. Depending on the type of activity you want to perform, you can use different aspects of the search/replace tool, each of which is described here.

- Find Usages command. Find occurrences of an identifier for a class, method, or field in your project.

- Rename command. Rename a class, method, or field throughout your project.

- Ctrl+F in a file. Find and replace specific character combinations in an open file.

- Ctrl+F on a project. Find files that match search criteria based on characters in the file, characters in the filename, file type, and/or date.

Finding Usages

When you are working in the Source Editor, you can quickly find out where a given Java identifier of the currently selected class, method, or field name is used in your project by using the Find Usages command, which displays the Find Usages window, as shown in Figure 3-42.

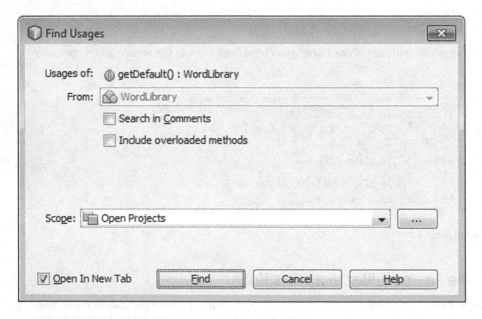

Figure 3-42. *Find Usages window*

To display the Find Usages window to find occurrences of a specific identifier in your code, start in the Source Editor. Then move the insertion point/cursor to the class, method, or field name that you want to find occurrences of. Then press Alt+F7. Alternatively, you can right-click in the editor and choose Find Usages. Another way to start finding usages is to, in the Edit menu, choose Find Usages. In the Find Usages window, specify settings such as whether the search should be performed in the comments, and click Find.

Find Usages improves upon a Find command in a text editor by being sensitive to the relevance of text in the Java language context.

Depending on the kind of identifier you have selected and which options you have selected in the Find Usages window, the Usages window appears at the bottom of the IDE and displays your results, as shown in Figure 3-43.

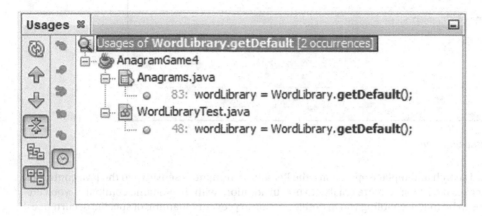

Figure 3-43. *Usages results*

The Usages window displays statements that contain a combination of the following items, depending on the identifier:

- Classes and interfaces. A declaration of a method or variable of the class or interface, a usage of the type, such as at the creation of a new instance, importing a class, extending a class, implementing an interface, casting a type, or throwing an exception, a usage of the type's methods or fields, and subtypes.

- Methods. The calling of the method and any overriding methods.

- Fields. The getting or setting of the field's value.

- Comments. Any comments that reference the identifier.

You can navigate to a given occurrence of a class, method, or field name by double-clicking the occurrences line in the Usages window.

Renaming

If you want to rename a class, method, or field, you can use the Refactor ➤ Rename command to update all occurrences of the identifier in the project to the new name, as shown in Figure 3-44.

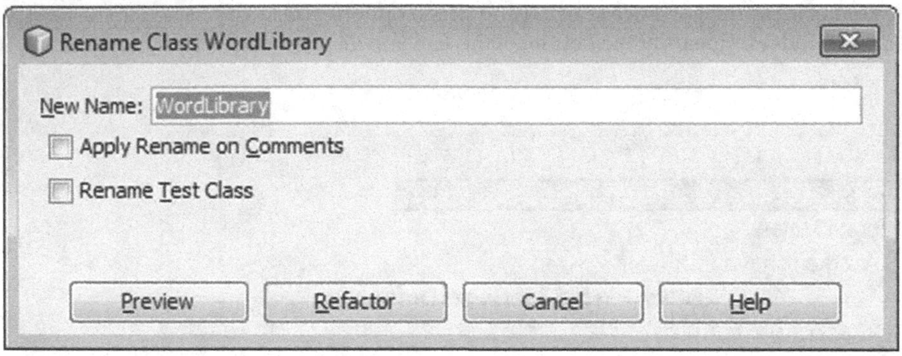

Figure 3-44. Rename window

Unlike standard search and replace operations, the Rename command is sensitive to the Java context of your code, which makes it easier and more reliable to use. In addition, with the Rename command, you can preview the changes to be made, enabling you to deselect items to prevent renaming of specific occurrences, as shown in Figure 3-45.

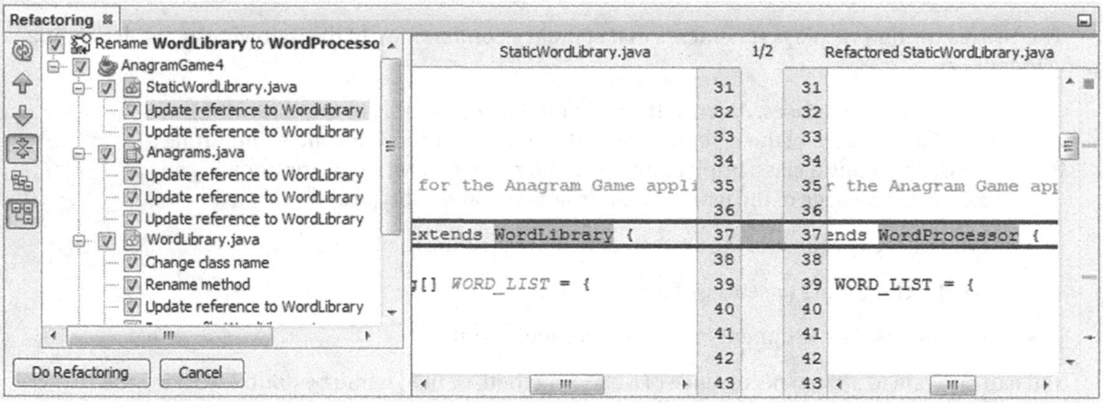

Figure 3-45. Refactoring preview

To rename a class, method, or field name, start in the Source Editor. Move the insertion point to an occurrence in the code of the class, method, or field name that you want to rename. Press Ctrl+R or right-click and, in the Refactor menu, choose Rename. In the Rename dialog box, type the new name for the element. If you want occurrences of the name in comments to also be changed, check the Apply Name on Comments checkbox. In the Rename window, click Next. If you have deselected the Preview All Changes checkbox, the changes are applied immediately. If you leave the Preview All Changes checkbox selected, the Refactoring window appears with a preview of the changes.

In the Refactoring window, which appears at the bottom of the IDE, verify the occurrences that are set to change. If there is an occurrence that you do not want to change, deselect that line's checkbox. Click Do Refactoring to apply the changes. If you later find that the refactoring has had some consequences that you would like to reverse, you can press Ctrl+Z or choose Undo from the Edit menu.

You can initiate the process of renaming a class or interface by renaming it inline in the Projects window. You do this by typing Ctrl+R on the node to be renamed.

Finding

If you quickly want to find a combination of characters in your file, click in the file that you want to search, choose Edit ➤ Find (Ctrl+F), and type the text that you want to find in the Find window, which is integrated in the bottom of the editor, as shown in Figure 3-46.

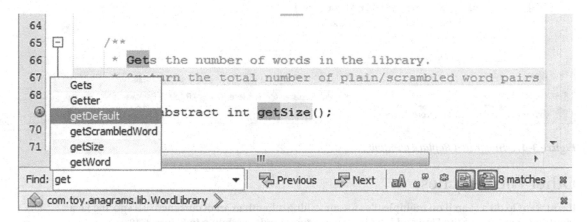

Figure 3-46. *Integrated Find window*

Some tips on using the Find dialog box:

- In the Find dialog box, you can use a regular expression as your search criterion by pressing Alt+G or by clicking the Regular Expression button.

- Unlike the Find Usages command, the Find command allows you to search for parts of words, do case-sensitive searches (press Alt+C or click the Match Case button), and highlight matches in the current file (press Alt+H or click the Highlight Matches button).

- You can jump between occurrences of the search string by pressing F3 (next occurrence) and Shift+F3 (previous occurrence).

- To select the word in which the cursor is resting and start searching for other occurrences of that word, press Ctrl+F3.

Replacing

Finding what you're looking for is often only the start of a task. More often than not, you need to replace the code that you have found. This section helps you with that task.

To search and replace text, click in the appropriate file, press Ctrl+H, and fill in the Find What and Replace With fields, as shown in Figure 3-47.

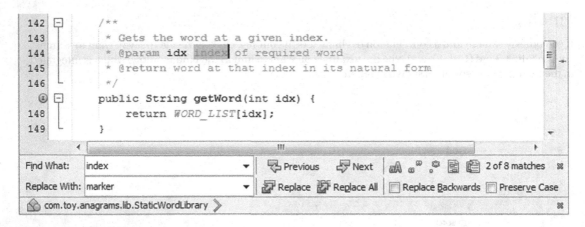

```
142    /**
143     * Gets the word at a given index.
144     * @param idx index of required word
145     * @return word at that index in its natural form
146     */
    public String getWord(int idx) {
148        return WORD_LIST[idx];
149    }
```

Find What: index — Previous — Next — 2 of 8 matches

Replace With: marker — Replace — Replace All — Replace Backwards — Preserve Case

com.toy.anagrams.lib.StaticWordLibrary

Figure 3-47. *Integrated Replace window*

Other File Searches

If you want to do a search on multiple files for something other than an occurrence of a specific Java identifier, you can use the Find and Find in Projects commands, as shown in Figure 3-48.

Find in Projects

Containing Text:

(The text will be used literally)   (test)

Match Case   Whole Words   Match: Literal

Scope: Selection (AnagramGame4)

Search in Archives   Search in Generated Sources

File Name Patterns: (all files)

(Example: *.java, FZP??.jsp)

Use Ignore List (edit)   File Path Regular Expression (test)

Please specify text to find or file name pattern.

Open In New Tab   Find   Close   Help

Figure 3-48. *Find in Projects window*

These commands enable you to search files in a folder, in a project, or in all projects. You can base these commands on any combination of the following types of criteria:

- Matches to a substring or regular expression on text in the file

- Matches to a substring or regular expression on the filename

- Dates the files were modified

- File type

To initiate such a file search, in the Edit menu, choose Find in Projects to search all files in all open projects. Alternatively, in the Projects window, right-click the node for the folder or project that you want to search in and choose Find (or press Ctrl+F). Yet another approach is to right-click a folder in the Files window and choose Find (or press Ctrl+F).

After you initiate the search, fill as many search criteria as you want. After you enter the criteria in the Find or Find in Projects window and click Search, the results are displayed in the Search Results window, with nodes for each matched file. For full-text searches, these nodes can be expanded to reveal the individual lines where matched text occurs. You can double-click a match to open that file in the Source Editor (and, in the case of full-text matches, jump to the line of the match).

The dialog box that appears when you press Ctrl+F or choose Edit ➤ Find (or Edit ➤ Find in Projects) depends on which IDE window has focus. If you have the Source Editor selected, the Find dialog box integrated into the bottom of an individual file appears. If you have a node selected in the Projects window (or one of the other tree-view windows), the dialog box for searching in multiple files is opened.

Tracking Notes

The IDE has an Action Items window that provides a way for you to write notes in your code and then view all of these notes in a centralized location. To write a note, also known as an "action item," to yourself, you use patterns such as XXX or TODO anywhere in your code.

You can use the Action Items window as the center of operations when cleaning up loose ends in your code, as shown in Figure 3-49, which lists all the action items for you.

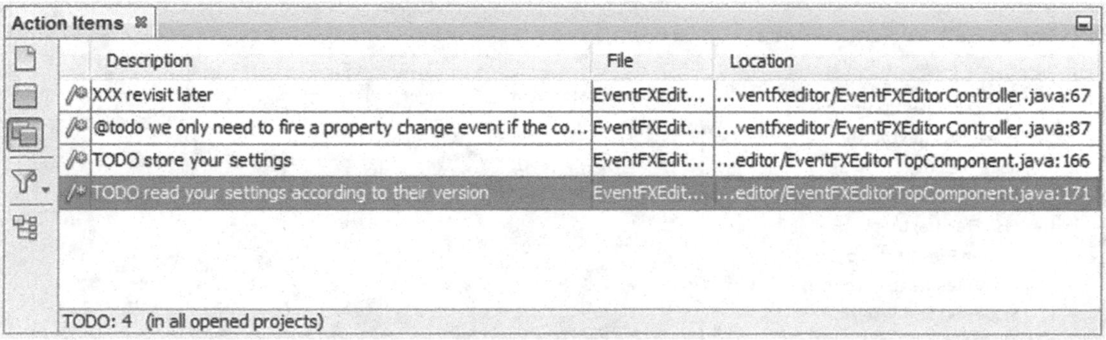

Action Items ✕			
	Description	File	Location
	XXX revisit later	EventFXEdit...	...ventfxeditor/EventFXEditorController.java:67
	@todo we only need to fire a property change event if the co...	EventFXEdit...	...ventfxeditor/EventFXEditorController.java:87
	TODO store your settings	EventFXEdit...	...editor/EventFXEditorTopComponent.java:166
	TODO read your settings according to their version	EventFXEdit...	...editor/EventFXEditorTopComponent.java:171
	TODO: 4 (in all opened projects)		

Figure 3-49. *Action Items window*

A line is displayed in the task list if it is "tagged with" (contains) any of the following text.

When you type one of these tags in your code, it must be typed as a whole word for the IDE to recognize it. For example, if you do not put a space between the tag and the note, the note will not appear in the Action Items window.

To view the Action Items window, choose Window ➤ Action Items (or press Ctrl+6).

Once you have displayed the Action Items window, you can view tasks for the current file, for all open files, or for a specific folder by clicking the corresponding button on the left of the Action Items window.

You can sort task-list items by task, location, or priority by clicking the corresponding column titles. See "Displaying Tasks by Priority" later in this chapter for information on displaying the Priority column.

You can jump from an entry in the task list straight to the line in the code where you wrote the note by double-clicking the entry.

Adding, Removing, and Changing Action Item Tags

To change the tags that are used for the Action Items window, choose Tools from the Options menu. The Options window opens. Click Team and select Action Items, as shown in Figure 3-50. In the Action Items tab, use the Add, Edit, and Remove buttons to modify the content of the Action Items list.

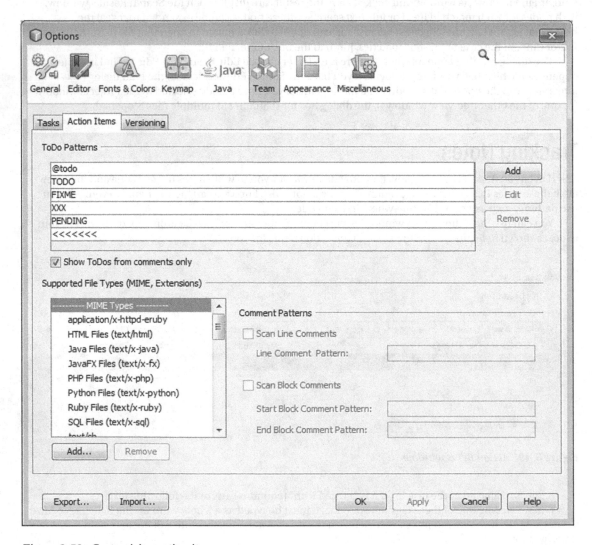

Figure 3-50. Customizing action items

Filtering Action Items

You can further limit the entries displayed in the Action Items window by creating and using filters. When you use a filter, only entries that match criteria specified by the filter are displayed. Criteria include text that needs to appear in the note, the priority of the task, and/or the filename.

To create a filter, click Edit from the Filter dropdown to the left of the Action Items window, as shown in Figure 3-51. In the Edit Filters dialog box, click the New button and then type a name for the filter in the Name field. Fill in the details. Optionally, add additional criteria in the Keywords tab and then fill in the details for the filters. You can select to have the filter match all or any of the criteria using the radio buttons at the top of the dialog box.

An entry for the newly defined filter appears in a Filter dropdown in the left of the Action Items window in the To Do Window toolbar.

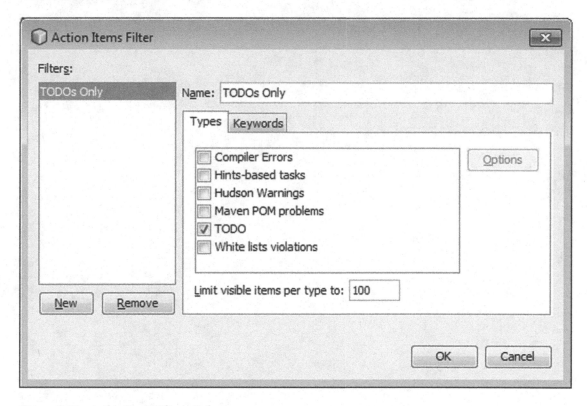

Figure 3-51. *Action Items Filter window*

Download, double click, and start coding. I use NetBeans for Java EE, Java SE, JavaFX, HTML5, and JavaScript coding, debugging, and profiling... out-of-the-box. NetBeans is a huge time-saver for me and my airhacks.com students.

—Adam Bien,
independent developer and pilot at airhacks.com

CHAPTER 4

■ ■ ■

Using Wizards and Plugins

In this chapter, I provide a general overview of both the workflow in the IDE and the tools it makes available for the key Java technologies that it enables you to use. Many wizards are included in the IDE, helping you to set up projects for each of the Java technologies—Java SE, Java EE, Embedded, and Cloud. The structure of this chapter is based on the Java Technologies outline on Oracle.com, as described at this URL:

https://www.oracle.com/java/technologies/index.html

When combined with many of the plugins that the NetBeans community makes available, the wizards described in this chapter give you absolutely everything you need to create any kind of Java application. For this reason, you will be introduced to the most useful plugins in the Plugin Manager, as well as the most useful wizards.

Once you complete this chapter, you should have a solid understanding of the IDE's application structuring principles and be able to quickly and effectively set up your development work in the IDE by using its wizards and their related plugins.

Overview

Rather than plowing through the remainder of this chapter, you may be interested in a quick overview of how to get started developing the kinds of Java applications that you're interested in. Table 4-1 provides an overview of the entry points in NetBeans for each of Java's technologies.

Table 4-1. *Getting Started with Java Technologies in the IDE*

Technology	Description	Getting Started
Java SE	Java platform, Standard Edition (Java SE) enables you to develop secure, portable, high-performance applications for the widest range of computing platforms possible. Java SE applications run on the computer desktop, as opposed to on a browser or a mobile device. Nowadays, these applications are sometimes referred to as "on-premise" applications.	In the IDE, open the New Project wizard (Ctrl+Shift+N). When you're getting started learning Java, you will probably want to use the simple Ant-based Java SE project template, available at Java ➤ Java Application in the New Project wizard. When you're more familiar with Java and you're interested in using the widely used Maven build system, go to Maven ➤ Java Application in the New Project wizard to get started creating your Java SE applications.
Java EE	Java platform, Enterprise Edition (Java EE) is the industry standard for enterprise Java computing. Java EE enables developers to write less boilerplate code, have better support for the latest web applications and frameworks, and access enhanced scalability and richer functionality.	In the IDE, open the New Project wizard (Ctrl+Shift+N). When you're getting started learning Java, you will probably want to use the simple Ant-based Java EE project template, available at Java Web ➤ Web Application in the New Project wizard. When you're more familiar with Java EE and you're interested in using the widely used Maven build system, go to Maven ➤ Web Application in the New Project wizard to get started creating your Java EE applications.
Embedded	Java Embedded products are designed and optimized to meet the unique requirements of embedded devices, such as microcontrollers, sensors (such as the Raspberry Pi), and gateways. They enable intelligent systems for M2M communications and the "Internet of Things" so you can do more with your devices.	In the IDE, go to Tools ➤ Java Platforms. Click Add Platform and select Remote Java Standard Edition. Click Next and you will be able to connect to the JDK installed on your embedded device. Once the embedded JDK is registered, you can deploy your Java applications to it, by setting the embedded JDK in the Project Properties window of the project you want to deploy to the embedded device.
Cloud	Java Cloud Services provide enterprise-grade platforms to develop and deploy business applications in the cloud. They enable you to maximize productivity with instant access to cloud environments that support any standard Java EE application, complete with integrated security and database access.	In the IDE, go to the Services window (Ctrl+5) and take a look at the Cloud node, where you can manage applications deployed to Java Cloud Services. Amazon Beanstalk is supported out of the box. Plugins are available for Oracle Cloud, Oracle Developer Cloud Service, Red Hat OpenShift, and Jelastic.

For adventurous readers, Table 4-1 should be enough to get you started with each of these technologies. For those wanting more detail, and for the adventurous readers who run into problems, the remainder of this chapter explores in detail each of the Java technologies and the tools the IDE provides to support them.

General

In this section, you are introduced to generic principles common to the IDE tooling structure and the application structure of all kinds of Java projects in the IDE. The IDE is opinionated on how your application structures should be visualized in the IDE. Mostly, once you understand the perspective from which the IDE approaches your applications, you will be more than satisfied with the approach the IDE takes.

For example, you will learn that the IDE only shows artifacts you are most likely to work with in the Projects window, while the Files window includes generated code, too. Without understanding these kinds of considerations, you will often be asking yourself questions like, "where is my build folder?" and "where is the JAR of the application I just built?"

Once you have examined the generic application structuring principles that the IDE follows, you will look in more detail at each of the Java technologies and the tools that the IDE provides for them.

Application Structure

When you create a new project in the IDE, it will open in the Projects window (Ctrl+1). The Projects window shows you the *logical structure* of your application. The logical structure consists of the folders and files that you are likely to want to work with directly and that will not change as a result of an automated process, such as a build process.

A variety of artifacts may be created when you cause an automated process to be performed on a project, such as a build process or a JUnit test process. These artifacts will not be shown in the Projects window. If you are looking for an artifact that was generated or automatically created in some way, open the Files window (Ctrl+2). The Files window has a dist folder that contains archive files, such as JAR, WAR, and EAR, that have been created for you in some way. In Ant-based projects, the Files window shows a build folder after a build process has been completed, while Maven-based projects show a target folder in the Files window after a build process is complete.

Figure 4-1 illustrates these points for an Ant-based project named AsyncRequest and for a Maven-based project named CDI Sample Application for Bean Validation. Both of these projects can be found in the Samples category of the New Project wizard.

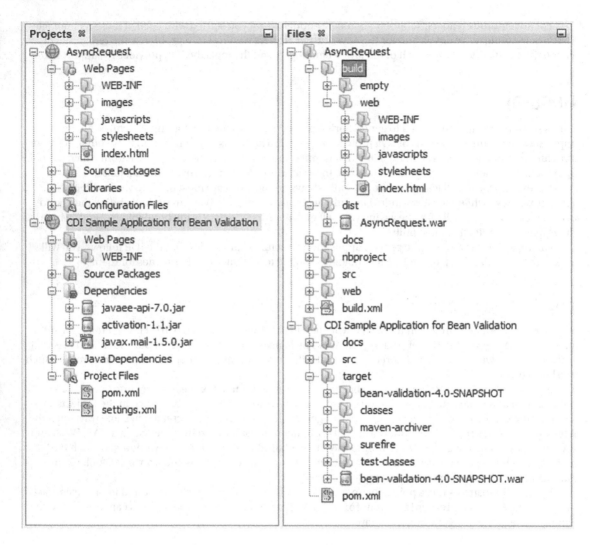

Figure 4-1. *Projects and Files windows*

Project Groups

A NetBeans project is a group of source files and the settings with which you build, run, and debug those source files. In the IDE, all development has to take place within a project. For applications that involve large codebases, it is often advantageous to split your application source code into several projects.

You can create groupings of projects so that you can open and close several projects at once. In addition, each group can have a different main project. After you create a project group, that project group is available in the Project Group menu. When you select a project group from that menu, all open projects outside of the project group are closed. If you want to close all open projects, choose File ➤ Project Group ➤ (none).

Viewing Java Packages

By default, as shown in the left-most image in Figure 4-2, each package is shown as a separate node in the application structure.

Figure 4-2. Java packages as list, tree, and reduced tree

However, a somewhat hidden feature in the IDE enables you to change how packages are displayed. Packages can be displayed as a list (left image), a tree (middle image), or a reduced tree (right image). You can switch between package layouts by right-clicking in the empty space in the Projects window and choosing the View Java Packages As submenu to select a different view layout for your packages. You don't have to do anything more; the package layout updates itself immediately.

Comprehensive Service Integration

Whenever you're wondering where the tools are for connecting to a database, server, or cloud service, the first place you should look is the Services window (Ctrl+5), shown in Figure 4-3.

Figure 4-3. Services window

91

The Services window is useful in the sense that it gives you a single access point to any imaginable external resource. Included in the Services window are access points to your databases, web services, servers, Maven repositories, Hudson continuous build servers, and issue trackers.

The services provide a uniform, standardized mechanism for working with them. In each case, right-click on the service to initialize, register, or start up an instance of the service. For example, right-click on the Servers node to register a locally installed GlassFish server so that you can manage it from the Service window, instead of from the command prompt or from the management console, which typically runs externally in the browser.

Plugin Manager

The IDE is unique in that, in principle, you should not require any additional plugins for basic Java development. However, because the IDE is relatively easy to extend, and has existed for over a decade, many people around the world have created plugins for it.

Use the Plugin Manager, shown in Figure 4-4, accessible under the Tools menu, to dynamically update the IDE from the registered update centers and to manage IDE plugins. Use the Available Plugins tab of the Plugins Manager to view and install new plugins available from the registered update centers.

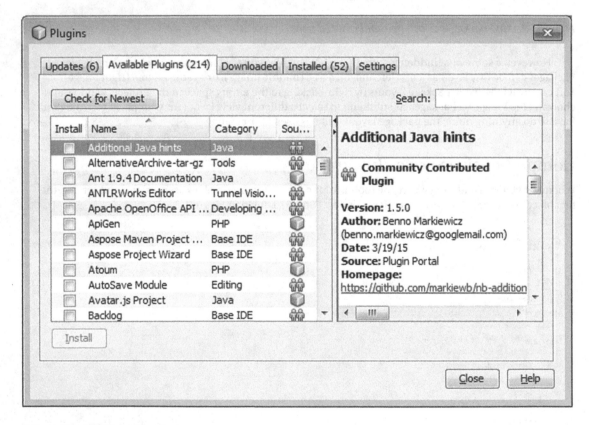

Figure 4-4. *Plugin Manager*

As you work through this chapter, you will occasionally be advised to use the Plugin Manager to install additional features into the IDE.

Though there are many plugins in the Plugin Manager, those listed in Table 4-2 are the ones that you may want to consider installing right away. These plugins are ambitious in terms of their feature set, they integrate with popular or "cool" external technologies, and they are comprehensive in relation to the subset of features currently made available by the plugin.

Table 4-2. *Plugins to Consider Installing Right Away*

Category	Description
DukeScript Project Wizard	Use this wizard to create a new DukeScript project using NetBeans. The wizard is based on Maven and takes care of the correct and simple configuration of the project. Use DukeScript and this wizard to develop applications that run on iOS, Android, Desktop, in the Browser or even as a NetBeans plugin.
EasyPmd	Performs code analysis by using PMD and shows the results both in the editor and in the Action Items window.
easyUML	Provides UML drawing features, code generation and creation of UML class diagrams from Java code. It is being developed at Open Source Software Development Center at Faculty of Organisational Sciences, University of Belgrade.
Eclipse Java Code Formatter	Helps you to conform to a common code style in a team of Eclipse JDT and NetBeans IDE users. The original formatting engine of Eclipse is embedded and allows you to format the source code the same way as your Eclipse co-workers do. You only have to provide an Eclipse formatter configuration file.
Gluon Plugin	Allows developers to create JavaFX applications that target the Android and iOS mobile platforms as well as the desktop platform using the same codebase.
Gradle Support	Allows opening directories containing a `build.gradle` file as a project in NetBeans. The opened project then can be used as a usual Java project.
jBatch Suite	Allows developers to design Java batch application models and automates Java code generation, using the Java Batch 1.0 specification. Batch processing is typified by bulk-oriented, non-interactive, background execution. Frequently long-running, it may be data or computationally intensive, execute sequentially or in parallel, and may be initiated through various invocation models, including ad hoc, scheduled, and on-demand.
JBoss Forge	Allows developers to quickly get started with various kinds of Maven-based Java EE applications.
Jindent	A powerful source code formatter for Java and C/C++. Jindent empowers you to transform any foreign Java/C/C++ source code to meet your preferred coding style or any common Java code convention.
JMeter	Provides a tight integration of Apache JMeter (2.4) into NB infrastructure. This plugin will install additional plugins, including Load Generator and Profiler/Load Generator Bridge.
JPA Modeler	Assists software developers in creating, designing, and editing Java persistence application business model visually as graphical diagrams. It automates Java code generation, using JPA 2.0 from JPA class diagrams.

(continued)

Table 4-2. (*continued*)

Category	Description
JRebel	A productivity tool that allows you to see changes you make to your code without the need to redeploy. It maps your project workspace directly to a running application so that the changes to classes and resources are immediately reflected in the application. It skips the build and redeploy phases. The IDE plugin bundles JRebel agent, automates server and project configuration, and provides debugger support.
Monet	This enables the same workflow for JavaFX rapid GUI design as is available today for Swing via the Matisse GUI Builder. Provides a design view on FXML files. A new multiview is provided by this plugin using the JavaFX Scene Builder.
Vaadin	Provides help with developing Vaadin projects, including wizards for project generation, a preferences page for updating Vaadin versions, setting widget set compilation parameters, as well as providing helper methods for frequently used commands.

Separate from the plugins made available in the Plugin Manager, there are many more at the NetBeans Plugin Portal (`http://plugins.netbeans.org`). Plugins in the Plugin Manager are those made available by the NetBeans team, as well as those created and verified by the NetBeans community. Plugins in the Plugin Portal are contributed by the NetBeans community. If they have not been verified, that is, tried out and approved by the NetBeans community, they will not be in the Plugin Manager. Before assuming that there is no support for a technology in the IDE, make sure to check both the Plugin Manager and the Plugin Portal. More often than not, someone in the NetBeans community will have created a NetBeans plugin to support your favorite technology.

Java SE

Java platform, Standard Edition (Java SE) enables you to develop secure, portable, high-performance applications for the widest range of computing platforms possible. By making applications available across heterogeneous environments, businesses can boost end-user productivity, communication, and collaboration—and dramatically reduce the cost of ownership of both enterprise and consumer applications.

Java SE applications run on the computer desktop, as opposed to the browser or a mobile device. These applications are sometimes referred to as "on-premise" applications. A complete end-to-end description of creating a Java SE application is provided in Chapter 2 of this book. The starting point for all these kinds of applications is to go to File ➤ New Project (Ctrl+Shift+N), which opens the New Project wizard. Choose the Java category, as shown in Figure 4-5.

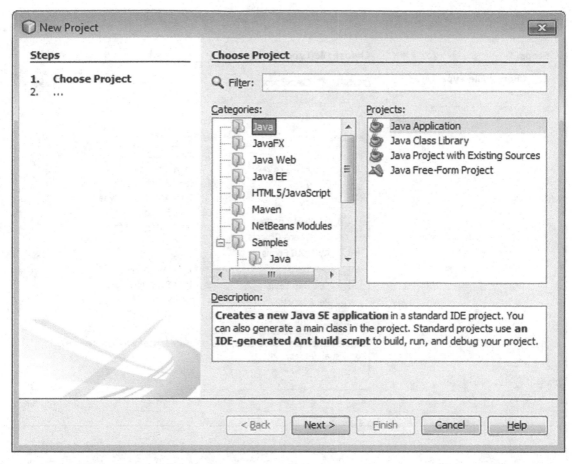

Figure 4-5. *Getting started with Java SE projects*

As you can see in Figure 4-4, different entry points are provided for getting started creating and working with Java SE applications in the IDE. Normally, you will use the Java Application project template to start your work in the IDE. Especially when you are first learning the Java language, this is the ideal entry point for the kind of work you are likely doing.

Three more specialized project templates are provided. The Java Class Library project template will create a new Java application without a main class. The idea is that you will use the project structure provided by this template for creating Java libraries, that is, bundles of Java code that provide a piece of generic functionality for a Java application. Use the Java Project with Existing Sources project template when you want to create a NetBeans project out of a set of folders on disk that contain Java source files, without there being a build.xml file. Ant drives these applications and the IDE will set up the Ant build script for you. Oftentimes, such an Ant build script already exists, in which case you would use the Java free-form project template, which lets you import an Ant build.xml file together with your Java sources. If you are using Maven instead of Ant as your build system, use the Maven category instead of the Java category in the New Project wizard. If your Maven project already exists on disk, simply open it via File ➤ Open Project, because the IDE automatically knows how to interpret your POM file. To create a new Maven project for Java SE applications, choose Maven ➤ Java Application or Maven ➤ JavaFX Application in the New Project wizard.

Once the application has been set up, you will want to create new files, typically new Java source files, in it. To do so, go to File ➤ New File (Ctrl+N), shown in Figure 4-6. In particular, the Java, JavaFX, Swing GUI Forms, JavaBeans Objects, and AWT GUI Forms categories relate directly to Java SE development.

95

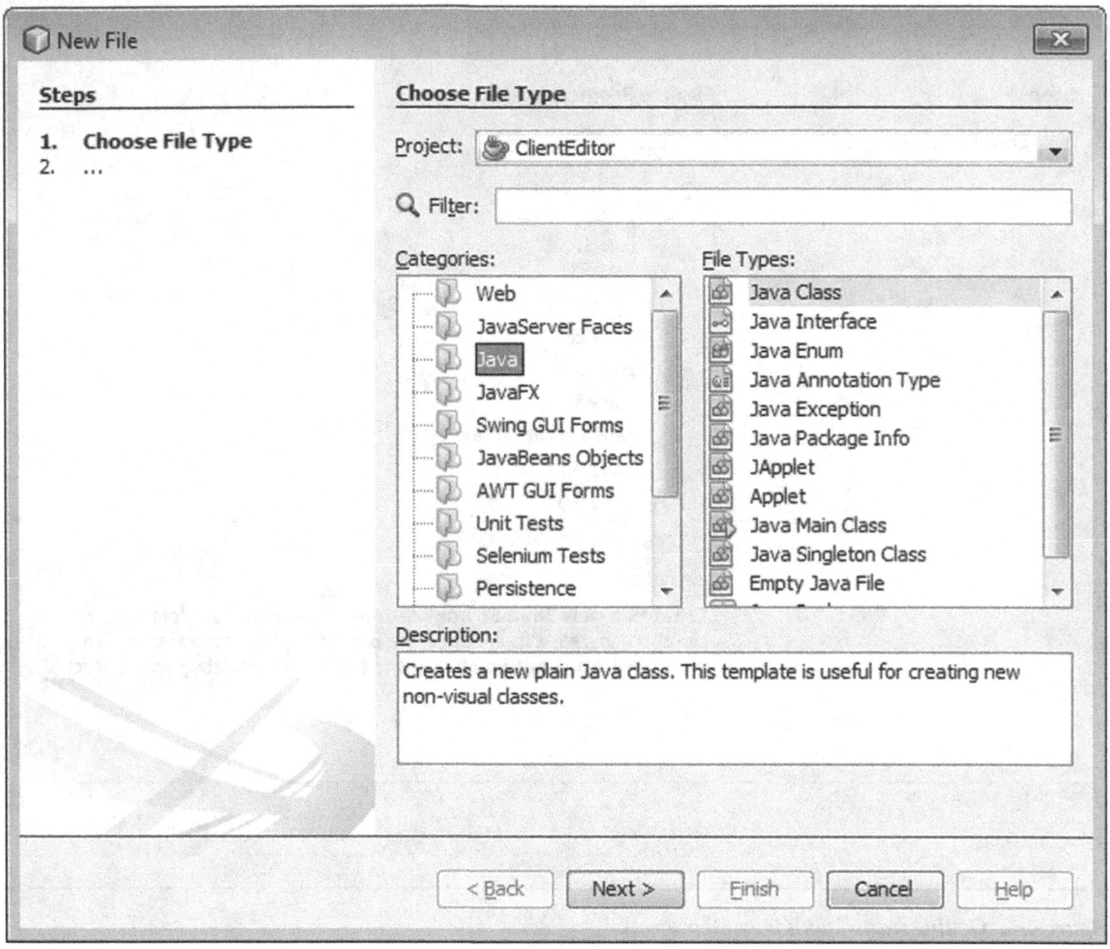

Figure 4-6. *Getting started with files in Java projects*

Depending on the kind of file you create, the IDE provides a variety of supporting features. In Chapter 3 of this book, the Java Editor is described in detail. In addition, the IDE provides the Matisse GUI Builder for the layout and design of Java Swing components and integration with the JavaFX Scene Builder for the layout and design of JavaFX components. Details on these GUI designers are found on the Java GUI Applications Learning Trail, on NetBeans.org, at the following URL: https://netbeans.org/kb/trails/matisse.html.

Be aware that you can configure each project you work with in the Project Properties window. Right-click a project and choose Properties. The Project Properties window, shown in Figure 4-7, opens. A range of configurations can be defined for each project you work on, from the JAR files on its classpath to compilation settings and runtime commands. For example, when you are working with Maven-based applications, you can map commands in your POM file to project commands so that when you press F6, which runs your project, you can execute goals that you have defined in your POM. Quite a range of features in the IDE can be configured, all in a unified location that the IDE makes available in the Project Properties window.

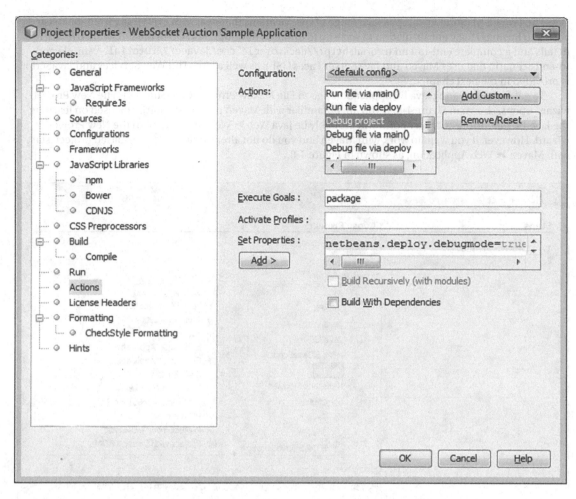

Figure 4-7. *Properties of Maven-based Java EE projects*

As you become more familiar with the IDE, you will probably increasingly want to use keyboard shortcuts rather than menu items and toolbar buttons. Hover with your mouse over the toolbar buttons to see their related keyboard shortcuts, such as F6 for Run and F11 for Build. In the Keymap section of the Options window, you can tweak and fine-tune all keyboard shortcuts that relate to working with your projects. For a list of keyboard shortcuts, go to Help | Keyboard Shortcuts Card.

Java EE

Java platform, Enterprise Edition (Java EE) is the industry standard for enterprise Java computing. With new features that enhance HTML5 support, increase developer productivity, and further improve how enterprise demands can be met, the Java EE platform enables developers to write less boilerplate code, have better support for the latest web applications and frameworks, and access enhanced scalability and richer functionality.

The Java EE platform encompasses a range of specifications that deal with everything from database access to business logic encapsulation to security to frontend development. Go to the following URL for full details and a complete end-to-end tutorial: http://docs.oracle.com/javaee/7/tutorial. A simple end-to-end scenario that uses Maven and Java Server Faces (JSF), as well as RESTful Web Services and JavaScript, is provided in the next chapter.

To get started creating Java EE applications, go to File ➤ New Project (Ctrl+Shift+N). The New Project wizard opens, shown in Figure 4-8. If you are unfamiliar with Maven and are primarily focused on learning the Java EE platform, your entry point will probably be Java Web ➤ Web Application in the New Project wizard. However, if you want to work with Maven and you do not already have a Maven-based project, start with Maven ➤ Web Application, as shown in Figure 4-8.

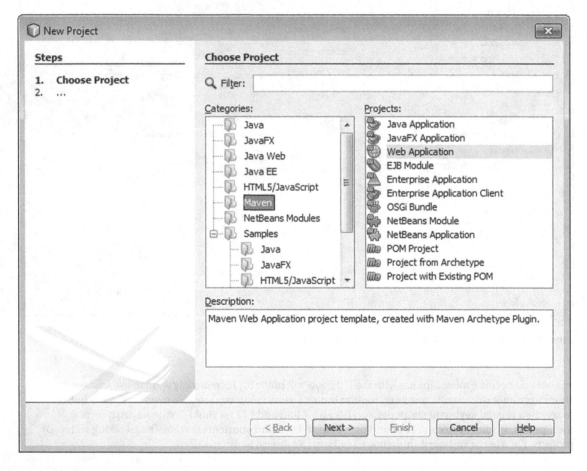

Figure 4-8. *Getting started with Java EE projects*

If you already have a Maven-based application on disk, that is, an application that includes a POM file, simply go to File ➤ Open Project. The IDE understands the POM file automatically and lays out your application in the IDE in a logical manner. The POM is further supported in a variety of ways. Open the POM by double-clicking on it and notice that the IDE shows you the effective POM, the source of the POM, as well as a graph view that shows the dependencies between the JARs registered in the POM.

Next, you are likely to want to create new files soon after you have set up your project. To do so, go to File ➤ New File in the IDE and, in particular, explore the Persistence and Web Services categories, shown in Figure 4-9.

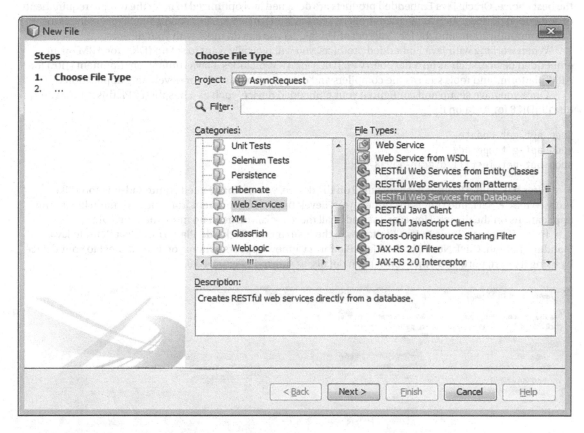

Figure 4-9. *Getting started with files in Java EE projects*

You will quickly see that in addition to helping you create simple Java source files, the IDE provides advanced code generators. Starting from a database or from one or more entity classes that conform to the JPA specification, the IDE can generate many artifacts for you. The code generators, such as the ones shown in Figure 4-9, are made possible by the fact that the artifacts are based on the specifications that are part of the Java EE platform. Specifications enable tool providers, such as the IDE, to know upfront the structure and content of files and other artifacts that need to be created. For example, if you want to expose the data in your database via RESTful Web Services, which are based on the JAX-RS specification, you simply need to step through the RESTful Web Services from Database wizard, shown in Figure 4-9. Explore the other code generators, read the descriptions, and notice how they relate directly to the specifications that the Java EE platform makes available.

Embedded

When you want more—more selection, more protection, and more power for embedded applications—Java is the best choice. Oracle Java Embedded products are designed and optimized to meet the unique requirements of embedded devices, such as microcontrollers, sensors, and gateways. They enable intelligent systems for M2M communications and the for "Internet of Things," so you can do more with your devices.

When working with Java Embedded products, you will typically want to set up JDK 8 for ARM on an embedded device, such as on a Raspberry Pi. JDK 8 for ARM includes a Java runtime environment (JRE) for ARM platforms and tools such as the compilers and debuggers necessary for developing applications.

Once you have set up and configured your embedded device, such as a Raspberry Pi, this is how you install JDK 8 for ARM on it:

```
sudo apt-get update
sudo apt-get upgrade
sudo apt-get install oracle-java8-jdk
```

After JDK 8 for ARM has been installed on the device, you normally need command-line tools like Putty, WinSCP, SSH, and others to connect your development environment from the command line to run applications on the device. However, instead of all those tools, you need no more than the IDE.

In the IDE, go to Tools ➤ Java Platforms in the main menu. Click Add Platform. Select Remote Java Standard Edition. Click Next. The Add Java Platform window appears, where you can connect to your device by using its host, port, and other connection details, as shown in Figure 4-10.

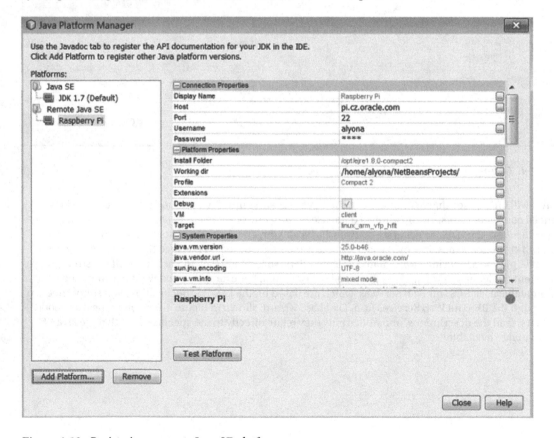

Figure 4-10. *Registering a remote Java SE platform*

Now that you have set up a remote Java SE platform in the IDE, you can create a standard Java SE project. In the Run tab of the Project Properties window of the project, specify that the project use the remote Java SE platform. You will be able to create, compile, run, debug, and profile the application on the device, just as if it were a local application.

Cloud

Java Cloud Services provide enterprise-grade platforms to develop and deploy business applications in the cloud. They enable you to maximize productivity with instant access to cloud environments that support any standard Java EE application, complete with integrated security and database access.

The list of cloud service providers available for use in the IDE is provided in Table 4-3.

Table 4-3. *Java Cloud Service Providers*

Company	Technology	Getting Started
Oracle	Oracle Cloud and Oracle Developer Cloud Service	In the IDE, go to Tools ➤ Plugins and search for Oracle Cloud. Install the plugin and look in the Cloud node in the Services window to get started.
Red Hat	OpenShift	In a browser, go to plugins.netbeans.org and search for OpenShift. Install the plugin and look in the Cloud node in the Services window to get started.
Jelastic	Jelastic	In a browser, go to plugins.netbeans.org and search for Jelastic. Install the plugin and look in the Cloud node in the Services window to get started.
Amazon	Amazon Beanstalk	In the IDE, go to the Services window. Expand the Cloud node and start using the Amazon Beanstalk provider.

Once you have set up a cloud service provider, you can specify that a Java EE application be deployed to it. In the same way as you would for any other server, in the Project Properties window of a project, you can specify the server to be used. In this case, the server will be the remote cloud service provider that you have registered.

For example, if you have registered the Oracle Cloud, you will see a new node in the Cloud node, as shown in Figure 4-11. In addition, you will see a new node in the Servers node and, when you deploy applications to the Oracle Cloud, you will be able to expand the Oracle Cloud node in the Servers node and manage the deployed artifacts.

Figure 4-11. Java EE applications deployed to the Oracle Cloud

Certain cloud service providers provide more than a remote location for deploying applications. For example, the Oracle Developer Cloud Service simplifies development with an automatically provisioned development platform that supports the complete development lifecycle. The focus of the Oracle Developer Cloud Services is to let you develop, deploy, and collaborate remotely. The Plugin Manager provides a plugin that integrates the Oracle Developer Cloud Service into the IDE, so that you can remotely use provisioned services made available by the Oracle Developer Cloud Service, such as GitHub and Hudson. Go to the following URL for further details: `https://cloud.oracle.com/developer_service`.

NetBeans provides comprehensive and complete end-to-end support for the Java EE platform. Develop, deploy, debug, and profile your Java EE applications on multiple application servers, with pleasure!

—Arun Gupta,
Director Technical Marketing and Developer Advocacy at Red Hat

CHAPTER 5

■ ■ ■

Putting the Pieces Together

In this chapter, you are going to do some work! While the previous chapters introduced you to everything you need to know to get started with Java development in NetBeans IDE, this chapter provides a sequential set of steps that you can take to put the pieces together and create a real application with the IDE.

You start this chapter by setting up tools and technologies such as a server and database, which you will need to serve up the application you will create and provide its data. Subsequently, you will create JPA entity classes, which represent tables in your database. The JPA entity classes will be generated from your database, in other words, you'll see that the tools in the IDE help you avoid the complexity of putting your code together. A lot can be automated, in fact, as far as possible anything that can be automated is automated by the IDE. Once you have your JPA entity classes, you'll learn how to expose them as RESTful Web Services, as well as how to consume them in a JSF-based frontend and in a JavaScript frontend.

By the end of this chapter, you will have all the skills and understanding needed when creating any kind of real application, specifically when you need to do so for applications that need to be deployed to a browser.

Setting Up

In this section, you learn how to connect to your database and start your application server.

Start in the Services window (Ctrl+3), where you can register your database server, connect to your databases, and modify data as needed. In this case, for the scenario you're working on, connect to the Sample database, which is a Derby database that is included with the Java EE distribution of NetBeans IDE. In the Services window, expand the Databases node, right-click the jdbc:derby node, and click Connect. The IDE connects to the Sample database.

Figure 5-1 shows the Services window with the Databases node expanded. The IDE has connected to the Sample database, so its tables are visible in the IDE.

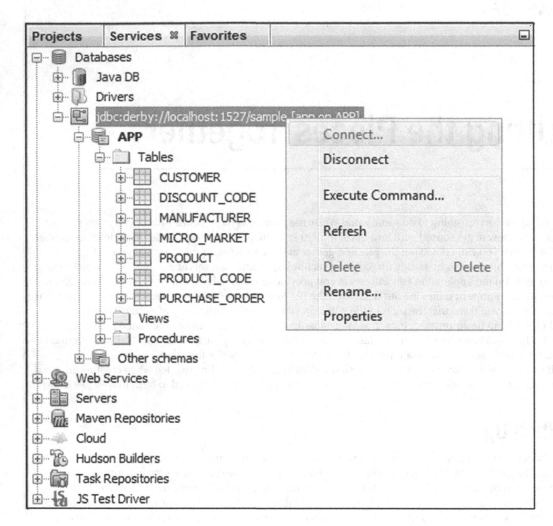

Figure 5-1. *Sample database started from the IDE*

Next, let's set up the application server.

Again in the Services window (Ctrl+3), expand the Services node to see the available application servers. Always make sure that the application server you're going to use supports the technology, and the version of the technology, that you want to use. In this chapter, you're going to deploy a Java EE application to GlassFish. The current version of GlassFish at the time of this writing is 4.1, while the current version of Java EE is Java EE 7. GlassFish 4.1 supports Java EE 7 and, therefore, this combination is a solid basis for a Java EE application.

GlassFish is bundled with the IDE. Therefore, when you installed the IDE, you should have installed GlassFish with it.

Right-click the GlassFish node and choose Start. The Output window (Ctrl+4) shows the output of the startup process. When the server is running, you should see a green arrow icon and you should be able to expand the node and see the Applications and Resources subnodes. When an application is deployed to GlassFish, you should see a new node added to the Applications node. This new node visualizes the deployed application and enables you to undeploy it after right-clicking on the node and choosing Undeploy.

Figure 5-2 shows the Services window with the Servers node expanded and the GlassFish server running.

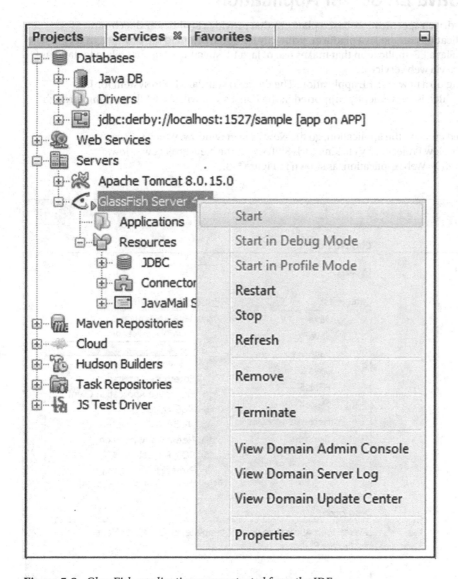

Figure 5-2. *GlassFish application server started from the IDE*

Now that the database and the application server are available and started, let's create and deploy the Java EE backend.

Creating the Java EE Server Application

Java EE is a community-driven specification-based platform that provides facilities and techniques for creating enterprise applications on the Java platform, primarily for deployment to the browser. In this section, you will create a Java EE application that makes use of Java EE specifications that relate to database access and data exposure via web services.

Let's begin by setting up a new Java EE application. The de-facto standard build system for Java applications is Maven , which is conveniently supported in the IDE, as you will see while working through the following steps.

1. To get started creating the application, go the New Project window, which you can do via File ➤ New Project or by clicking Ctrl+Shift+N. In the New Project window, choose Maven ➤ Web Application, as shown in Figure 5-3.

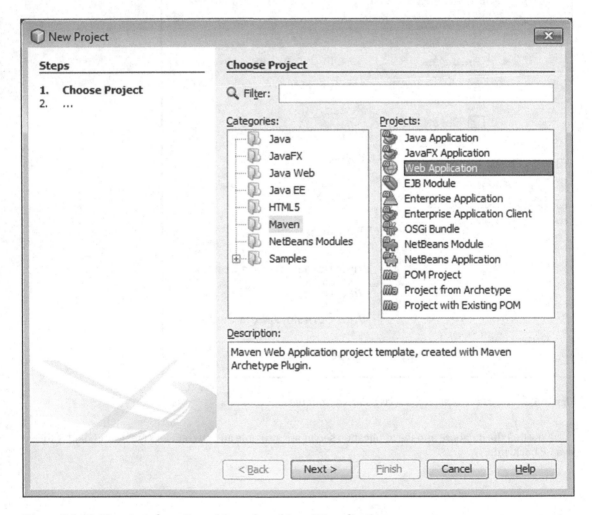

Figure 5-3. *Getting started creating a Maven-based Java EE application*

2. When you click Next, the "Name and Location" step of the wizard, shown in Figure 5-4, enables you to fill in Maven-specific settings. Aside from the name of the project and its location, you're prompted to specify the group ID, version, and optionally a package name, which will be treated as the main package of the application that will be created.

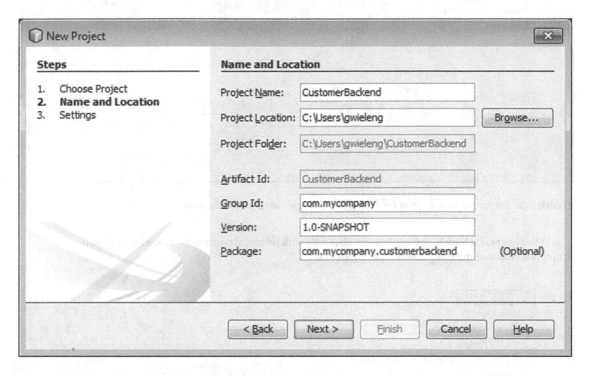

Figure 5-4. Maven settings for Maven-based Java EE application

■ **Note** The Maven group ID is an organizational setting; typically you would take the URL of your website and reverse it, so that if your site is mycompany.com, the group ID, as well as the package setting, would start off with com.mycompany. This creates a unique identifier or namespace for your application's base structure.

3. After clicking Next, select the application server to which the application will be deployed, as well as the Java EE version to which its artifacts and structure will comply; see Figure 5-5. Wizards and templates in the IDE will generate code conforming to the selected Java EE version. Here, choose GlassFish and Java EE.

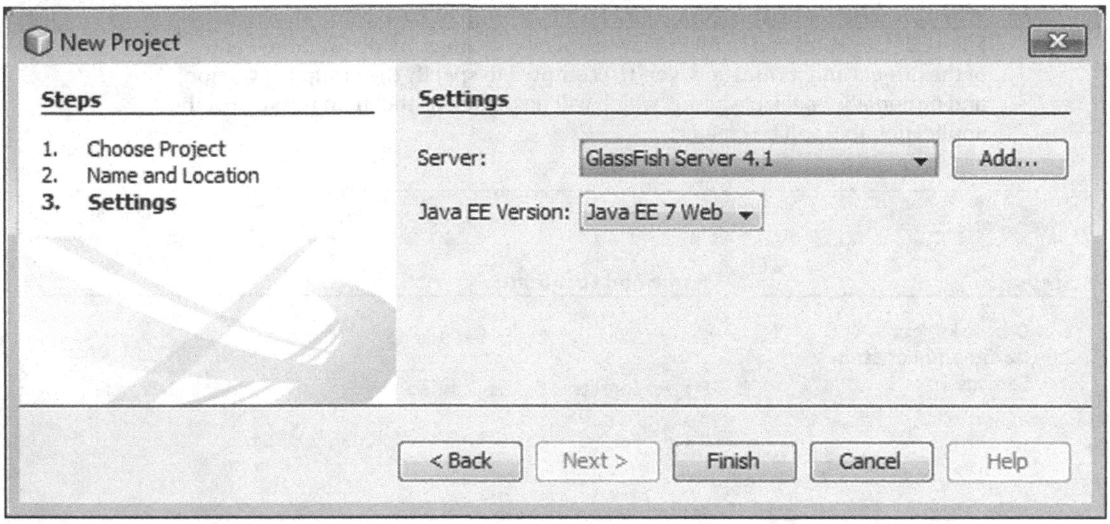

New Project

Steps

1. Choose Project
2. Name and Location
3. **Settings**

Settings

Server: GlassFish Server 4.1 ▼ Add...

Java EE Version: Java EE 7 Web ▼

< Back   Next >   Finish   Cancel   Help

Figure 5-5. *Server name and Java EE settings for Maven-based Java EE application*

When you click Finish, the application structure with its initial content is created and shown in the Projects window of the IDE, as shown in Figure 5-6.

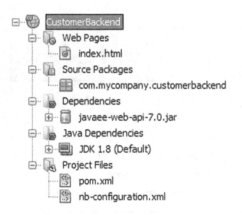

Figure 5-6. *Newly created Maven-based Java EE application*

Take a moment to explore the Maven-related facilities that the IDE makes available. For example, when you open the POM (`pom.xml`) file, you will notice multiple tabs, including a graph view. When you open the Navigator (Ctrl+7), you will notice a list of Maven goals, defined in the POM, which you can right-click to execute. When you go to the Action tab in the Project Properties window of the project, you can bind Maven goals to project commands, such as Build and Run, which you can invoke via keyboard shortcuts.

Now that you have created the structure and initial content of your Java EE backend, you're ready to generate into it your JPA entity classes from the Sample database, which you set up earlier in this chapter.

Generating JPA Entity Classes

The Java Persistence API (JPA) specification is focused on simplifying and standardizing data access. This is done by means of facilities such as Java annotations and a coherent XML file known as a "persistence unit," by defining the connection between the application and the databases it needs to access. The IDE further simplifies the JPA specification by letting you generate your JPA entity classes from tables in your database, as you will discover in this section.

In the New File window, which you can access via File ➤ New File or Ctrl+N, choose Persistence ➤ Entity Classes from Database, as shown in Figure 5-7.

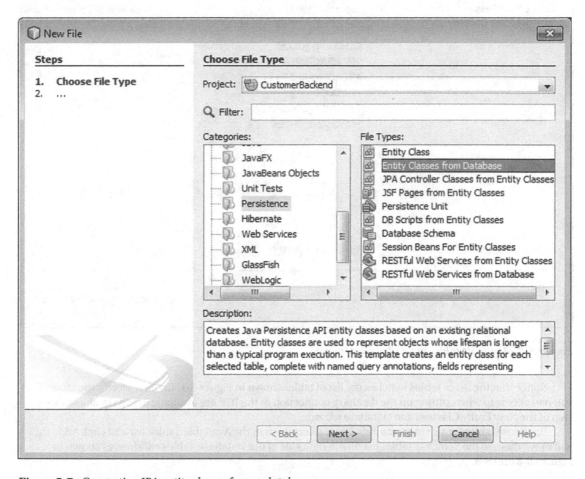

Figure 5-7. *Generating JPA entity classes from a database*

Also notice that the Persistence category in the New File window provides a number of other file generators. For example, if you want to expose your data as RESTful Web Services, choose RESTful Web Services from Database in the window shown in Figure 5-7, because this will generate your JPA entity classes together with your RESTful Web Services, all at the same time in a single process. Simultaneously, a persistent unit will be created. Notice that a persistence unit can also be created separately, by means of the Persistence Unit template, also shown in Figure 5-7.

When you click Next and select a data source, which in the case of this scenario is `jdbc/sample`, the available tables in the data source are listed in the Available Tables list, as shown in Figure 5-8.

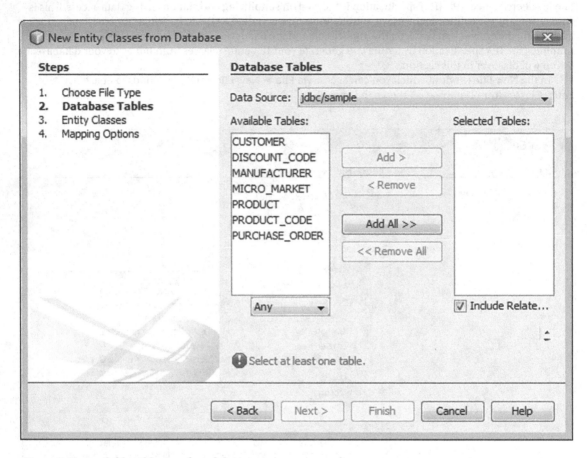

Figure 5-8. *Available tables in selected data source*

Notice that the list of tables matches the list of tables shown in Figure 5-1. In other words, the tables that you had access to when setting up the database connection in the IDE are available in the Database Tables step of the New Entity Classes from Database wizard.

To choose tables for use in your application, select them in the Available Tables list and click Add. This will move them to the Selected Tables list on the right side of the Database Tables window, as shown in Figures 5-8 and 5-9.

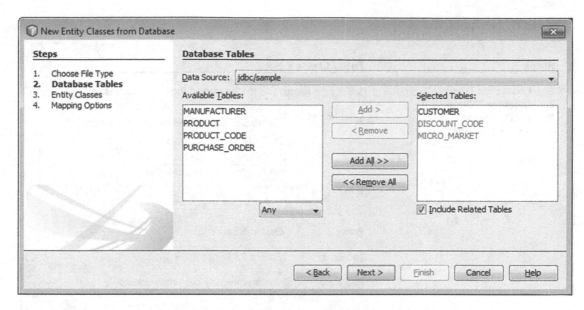

Figure 5-9. *Tables with foreign key relationships automatically included*

For purposes of this scenario, select CUSTOMER and click Add. This will move the CUSTOMER table to the Selected Tables list of the Database Tables window.

As you can see in Figure 5-9, tables with foreign key relationships are selected automatically.

When you click Next, you move to the Entity Classes step, as shown in Figure 5-10. The New Entity Classes step displays the Class Names list at the top, showing you the tables you selected, as well as the class names that will be used when the IDE automatically generates a JPA entity class to access the data from the related table.

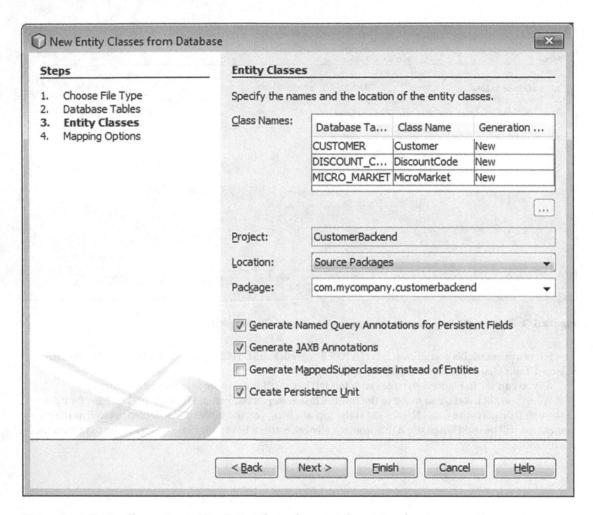

Figure 5-10. *Entity Classes step in New Entity Classes from Database wizard*

Also, if the class already exists, the Generation column, shown in Figure 5-10, displays "Update", instead of "New," to inform you that the IDE will override the existing JPA entity class with a new JPA entity class at the end of the New Entity Classes from Database wizard.

Notice that several checkboxes are selected by default, so the IDE will automatically generate named queries for persistent fields, JAXB annotations, and a persistence unit.

Although you can click Finish here, as shown in Figure 5-10, you can also click Next to fine-tune the settings so that the generated code will match your requirements exactly, as shown in Figure 5-11.

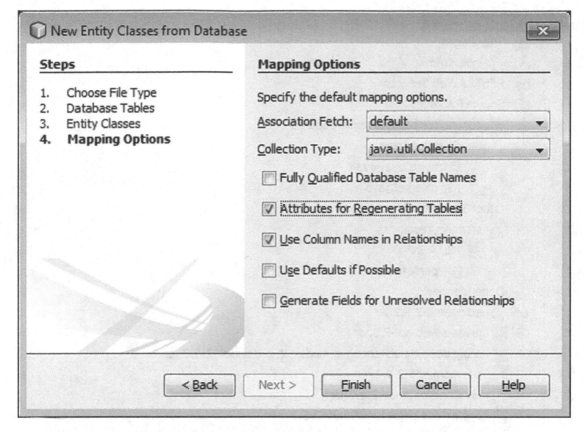

Figure 5-11. *Fine-tuning the settings to define the code to be generated*

When you click Finish, the JPA entity classes are generated, based on the settings you provided in the preceding steps of the wizard.

By default, the persistence unit is also created, as shown in Figure 5-12.

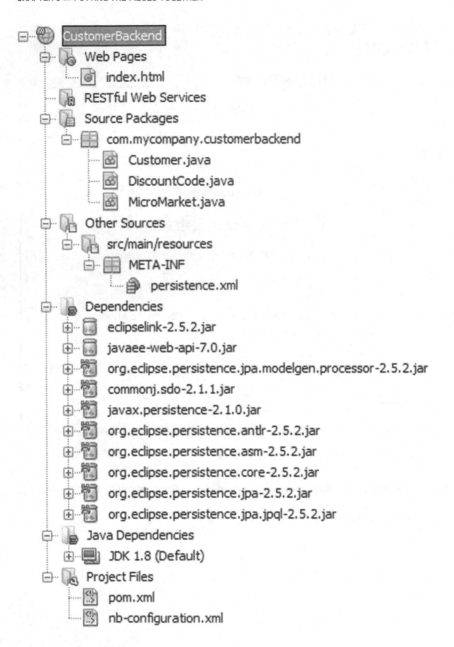

Figure 5-12. Generated JPA entity classes, with related dependencies and persistence unit

All the dependencies that the Maven-based application needs to access are registered in the POM and visualized in the Dependencies node, as shown in Figure 5-12.

Now that you have your JPA entity classes, you can use of a variety of tools in the IDE to access your database and do something with the related data.

Exposing Data to Frontend Clients

The IDE provides tools that support a variety of techniques you can use when providing access to the data in your JPA entity classes.

- Generate JSF pages from entity classes.

- Generate RESTful Web Services from entity classes.

- Generate RESTful JavaScript client from RESTful Web Services.

Generate JSF Pages from Entity Classes

The IDE provides tools for creating JSF pages on top of your JPA entity classes. Moreover, the JSF pages can use the popular PrimeFaces component library, support for which is integrated directly into the IDE.

1. In the IDE, open the New File window (Ctrl+N) and choose Web ➤ JSF Pages from Entity Classes.

2. Click Next, select the entity classes for which you would like to create JSF pages, and click Next again.

3. Figure 5-13 is shown. Specify the templates you would like to use, which can be standard JSF pages or JSF pages that use the PrimeFaces component library.

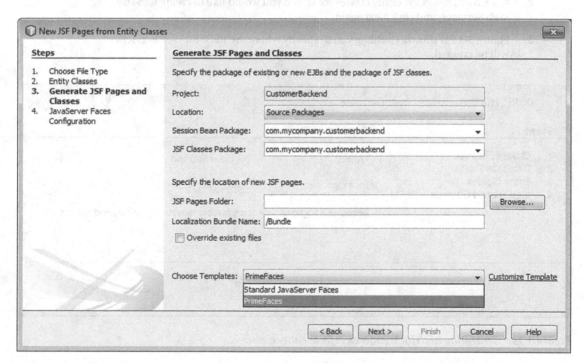

Figure 5-13. Generating PrimeFaces pages from entity classes

Notice that you can customize the templates. For example, you might want to change them so that your style guidelines and company logos are used whenever the IDE creates your JSF pages. If the files to be created already exist, you can override them via the Override existing files checkbox, shown in Figure 5-13.

4.   Click Next, configure JSF as needed, and click Finish.

Your JSF pages will now be created by the IDE, using the templates and other settings you defined in the New JSF Pages from Entity Classes wizard.

Generate RESTful Web Services from Entity Classes

Rather than create a frontend yourself, you can expose the data via RESTful Web Services. RESTful Web Services (JAX-RS) are part of the Java EE platform, just like JPA. Any client can access the XML or JSON payload exposed via your RESTful Web Services, parse the payload, and process it as needed.

For example, you could create a frontend for a mobile device, such as iOS or Android, by parsing the payload provided by a RESTful Web Service. Typically, you'll create a responsive design, by means of which the same code base is used to create different user experiences for different devices. The starting point for all these activities is to create RESTful Web Services that access your data via your JPA entity classes.

The IDE makes it trivial to create your RESTful Web Sevices.

1.   In the IDE, open the New File window (Ctrl+N) and choose Persistence ➤ RESTful Web Services from Entity Classes.

2.   Click Next, select the entity classes for which you would like to create RESTful Web Services, and click Next again.

3.   Figure 5-14 is shown, enabling you to specify where the RESTful Web Services will be created.

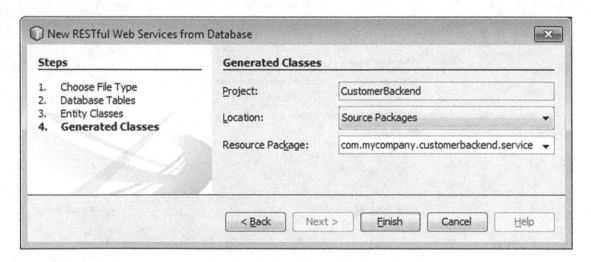

Figure 5-14. *Generating RESTful Web Services from entity classes*

When you click Finish, the RESTful Web Services will be created in the specified package, together with an ApplicationConfig class, which uses the javax.ws.rs.ApplicationPath annotation to specify the URL subroot of the application, which is followed by the paths of each of the RESTful Web Services that you generated using the wizard.

Generate RESTful JavaScript Clients from RESTful Web Services

Another approach is to create a JavaScript frontend. Although JavaScript is not a focus of this book, it is worthwhile to see how easy it is to create a JavaScript frontend on top of your JPA entity classes that you created in the IDE.

Before beginning to create your JavaScript client, you need to have an HTML5 project, that is, a separate and new project, that provides support for HTML5/JavaScript applications.

1. In the IDE, choose File ➤ New Project (Ctrl+Shift+N) and then choose HTML5 ➤ HTML5 Application.

2. For purposes of this scenario, click Next and then click Finish. You now have the basis of a new HTML5 application that has support for technologies such as HTML, JavaScript, and CSS.

3. In the IDE, choose File ➤ New File (Ctrl+N), which brings up the New File window. In the New File window, choose HTML5 ➤ RESTful JavaScript Client and click Next.

4. Figure 5-15 is shown, where you can browse to the RESTful Web Service for which you would like the IDE to create a JavaScript client. By default, the IDE will use the Backbone.js framework to design the JavaScript frontend, although plugins exist for generating an AngularJS or KnockoutJS frontend, instead.

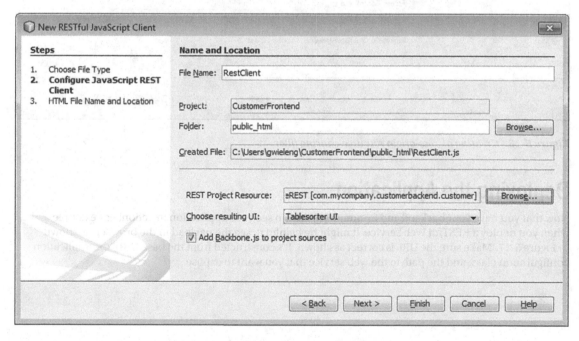

Figure 5-15. *Generating a RESTful JavaScript client from RESTful Web Services*

5. Since you will be interacting with the backend from a different domain in your frontend, you will need a cross-origin resource sharing filter, which the IDE can create for you, as shown in Figure 5-16. This is done in the New File window, via Web Services ➤ Cross-Origin Resource Sharing Filter. Create this filter in your Java EE application, so that your JavaScript frontend will be able to access and use its payload.

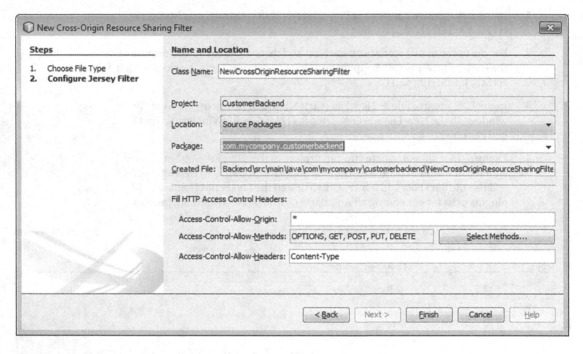

Figure 5-16. *Creating a cross-origin resource-sharing filter*

Deploying the Application

Now that you have your backend and frontend, it's time to see your application in action! For example, when you deploy a RESTful Web Service, it might be helpful to see the payload in the browser, as shown in Figure 5-17. Make sure the URL is correct as shown. It's constructed from the base URL, the application configuration class, and the path to the web service that you want to expose.

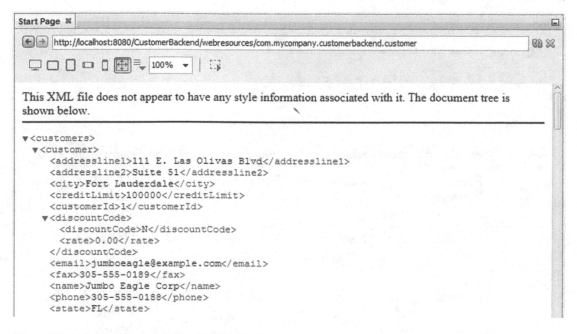

Figure 5-17. Seeing the payload in the browser

By accessing this URL, any client can parse the payload and build a user interface that allows the user to access and manipulate the underlying data.

Instead of deploying a RESTful Web Service, you might want to expose your data via the frontends you have created. By default, the JavaScript frontend, using the Backbone.js framework, is displayed as shown in Figure 5-18. The user can view the data and change it. The deployed application provides full CRUD features, that is, the user can create, read, update, and delete the underlying data. Notice that you did not have to add any code to the application for this basic functionality to be supported.

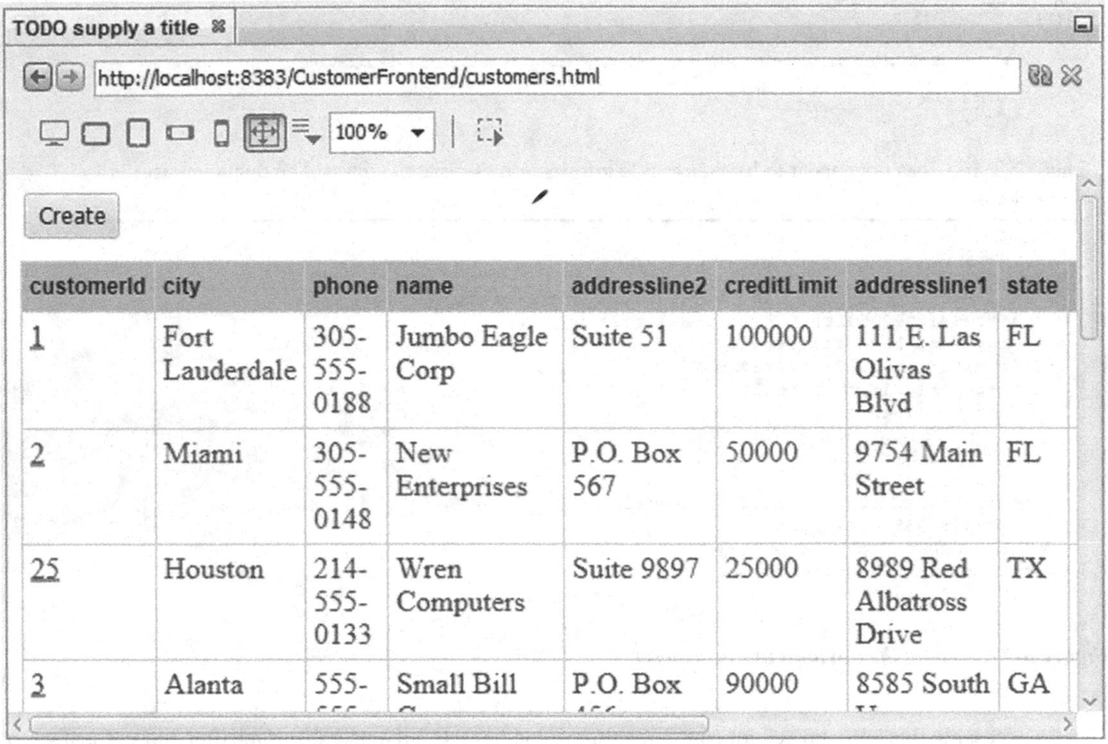

Figure 5-18. *Deployed JavaScript front-end displaying Java EE payload*

Finally, when you look in the Servers node in the Services window, you should see that the Java EE backend application is deployed, as shown in Figure 5-19. Right-click on the deployed node to undeploy the application, if needed.

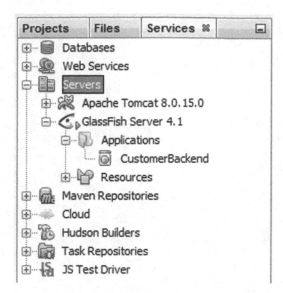

Figure 5-19. *Deployed application shown in Services window*

In this chapter, you have worked through a complete and realistic use case for building a coherent and functional application in the IDE.

The refactoring tools in NetBeans IDE are so good that they've replaced a huge amount of what I used to do with the editor. Using them is not an occasional thing for me.

—James Gosling,
founder of Java

CHAPTER 6

■ ■ ■

Analysis and Refactoring

NetBeans IDE has out-of-the-box tools for refactoring Java code. The term "refactoring" refers to the process of renaming and rearranging code without changing what the code does.

Over the years of its existence, code can become messy and, while it may work as expected, it may not be well structured. This is especially true when it has been developed over many years and release cycles, by various different groups of developers, many of whom may not be working on the application anymore. Methodologies that might have been popular at the time the code was first written may no longer be optimal and your code may, as a result, have been influenced by a variety of different approaches, making it difficult to understand. An application that is not well structured can become increasingly unmaintainable over time.

Reasons for refactoring include the need to restructure the code to be able to separate the API from implementation, to make code easier to read, and to make code easier to reuse.

The IDE's refactoring tools enable you to analyze and update all the code in your applications automatically to reflect changes that you make in other parts of your application. For example, if you rename a class, references to that class in other classes are also updated. The IDE provides batch analyzers that scan through your code to identify patterns, such as anonymous inner classes with single abstract methods, and helps you upgrade all found instances, for example, to Java 8 lambda expressions, as shown in Figure 6-1.

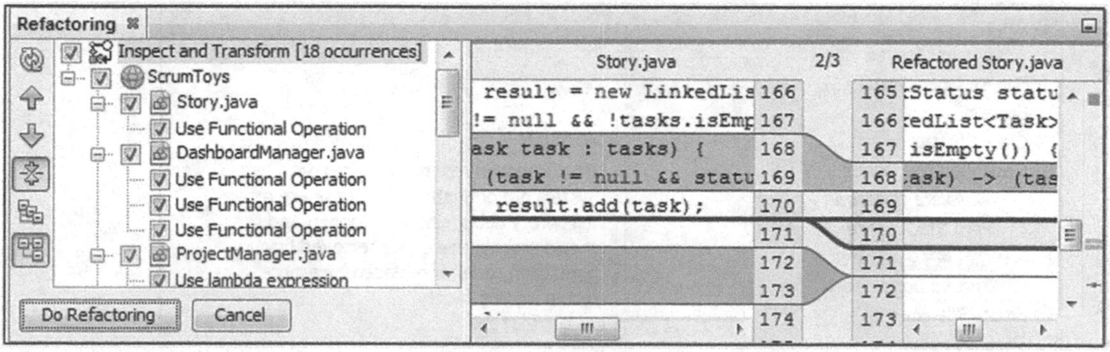

Figure 6-1. Batch refactoring results for Java 8 lambda expressions

The refactoring tools in NetBeans IDE are so good that they've replaced a huge amount of what I used to do with the editor. Using them is not an occasional thing for me.

—James Gosling, Founder of Java

Analysis

Before beginning the process of refactoring problematic areas of your code, it is a good idea to spend some time finding and analyzing your entire application. After all, you need to identify problem areas before you can fix them. Code analysis done in this context is known as "static code analysis" because it takes place in a development environment, such as the IDE. This is compared to analyzing code "dynamically," which entails the analysis of an application while it is running, by means of a Profiler, which is discussed in Chapter 9. Dynamic code analysis is focused on identifying threading problems and other bottlenecks in your code. When these kinds of problems are identified, parts of your application need to be *rewritten*, not *refactored*.

Problems identified by dynamic code analysis imply that there is something wrong with your code, while problems identified by static code analysis do not necessarily mean that your code is wrong. Instead, the problems identified statically imply that you can express your code in a different way, while the application itself will continue to function exactly as before. Although the responsiveness and performance of the application may well improve as a result of refactoring after static code analysis, the way it works and the way that the user interacts with it normally remain unchanged.

A simple example of what static code analysis can do is shown in Figure 6-2. Using the static code analysis tools in the IDE, you can easily identify all the places throughout your code where System.out. println needs to be marked as code. Typically, this statement is not something you want in your production code. While a simple text search would also find these statements in your code, you can use the static code analysis tools in the IDE to group multiple different kinds of pattern searches together and, in a batch process, locate all areas of interest throughout your code.

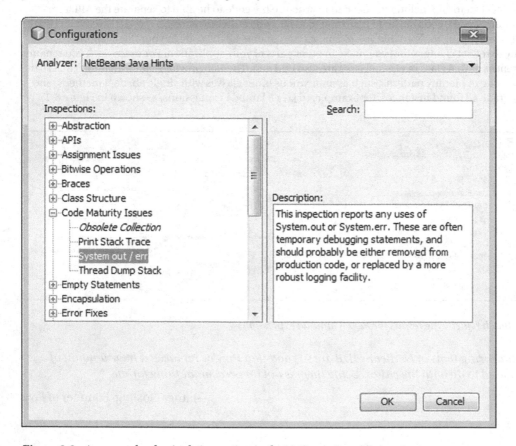

Figure 6-2. An example of a single inspection in the NetBeans Java Hints category

When you run an inspection or a configuration of inspections, yellow light bulb marks are shown in the editor in all lines of code where related problems are identified, as shown in Figure 6-3.

```
84              final File file1 = new File(FILENAME1 TEXT);
85   new de.cismet.custom.visualdiff.Testapplication() may fail to clean up java.io.Reader
86   ----
87   (Alt-Enter shows hints)
⚠            pnlDiff.setLeftAndRight(getLines(new FileReader(file1)),
89               MIMETYPE_TEXT,
90               file1.getName(),
91               getLines(new FileReader(file2)),
92               MIMETYPE_TEXT,
93               file2.getName());
94          getContentPane().add(pnlDiff, BorderLayout.CENTER);
95        }
```

Figure 6-3. An example of a single inspection in the NetBeans Java Hints category

Two types of static code analysis tools are available in the IDE.

- Inspect. These tools help you identify areas of your code that can be improved, without providing automated solutions for solving the identified problems. For example, the Code Metrics tools let you find intertwined code segments and very long blocks of code, which imply a "code smell," that is, an indication that there might be something wrong in your code, without the IDE immediately being able to fix the code for you. Another example of an Inspect tool is FindBugs, which is a popular open source library that is integrated into the IDE. You can switch between Inspect tools at will and choose a scope on which they will be run, that is, project scope, package scope, or file scope. Go to Source ➤ Inspect in the main menubar of the IDE to access these tools.

- Inspect & Transform. These tools not only identify problems but they're also able to fix them. When you're upgrading to the latest version of Java, the Inspect & Transform tools can identify code patterns that can be changed to new constructs. For example, in Java 8, lambda expressions have been introduced and the Inspect & Transform tools can scan throughout all your applications, identify anonymous inner classes with a single abstract method, and refactor all of them simultaneously to use lambda expressions. From Refactor ➤ Inspect and Transform in the main menubar, you can get started using these tools.

The static code analysis tools provide *inspections*, that is, features that search through your code to identify specific patterns for refactoring. The inspections are grouped in the following configurations.

- NetBeans Java Hints. A set of inspections created by the NetBeans team, these are listed in Table 6-1.

Table 6-1. NetBeans Java Hints categories

Category	Inspections
Abstraction	**Type cast is too strong.** Reports type casts that are too strict and casting to a more general type would be sufficient for the actual expression. Sometimes, an instance is casted to a specific subtype, but methods invoked or fields used from the casted instance are actually defined by some supertype. In that case, cast to too specific type introduces an unnecessary coupling to the code and limits its extensibility. This inspection will suggest you use the most general type that would satisfy the expression's needs.
APIs	**Be aware that this API will be optional in Java EE 7 platform.** Warns the user about using APIs from technologies that will be optional in the Java EE 7 specification. These APIs are not deprecated and can be used but because they will be optional they may or may not be available in future Java EE 7-compliant platforms.
	Exporting non-public type through public API. Checks that return types and parameter types of all public methods and all types of public fields are publicly available from other packages. Having private or package private types in a package API is useless.
	Utility class with visible constructor. Finds out classes containing only static elements with public or protected constructors.
	Utility class without constructor. Finds out classes containing only static elements and still being instantiable.
Assignment Issues	**Assignment replaceable with operator-assignment.** Reports instances of assignment operations that can be replaced by operator-assignment. Code using operator-assignment may be clearer and theoretically more performant.
	Assignment to catch-block parameter. Reports any instances of assignment to variable declared as a catch block parameter. While occasionally intentional, this construct can be confusing.
	Assignment to for loop parameter. Reports any instances of assignment to variable declared in a for statement in the body of that statement. It also reports any attempt to increment or decrement the variable. While occasionally intentional, this construct can be extremely confusing and is often the result of a typo.
	Assignment to method parameter. Reports any instances of assignment to a variable declared as a method parameter. It also reports any attempt to increment or decrement the variable. While occasionally intentional, this construct can be extremely confusing and is often the result of a typo.
	Nested assignment. Reports any instances of assignment expressions nested inside other expressions. While admirably terse, such expressions may be confusing and violate the general design principle that a given construct should do only one thing.
	Value of increment/decrement expression used. Reports any instances of increment or decrement expressions nested inside other expressions. While admirably terse, such expressions may be confusing and violate the general design principle that a given construct should do only one thing.

(continued)

Table 6-1. (*continued*)

Category	Inspections
Bitwise Operations	**Incompatible mask.** This inspection reports any instances of bitwise mask expressions that are guaranteed to evaluate to false. Expressions checked are of the form (var & constant1) == constant2 or (var | constant1) == constant2, where constant1 and constant2 are incompatible bitmask constants.
	Pointless bitwise expression. This inspection reports any instances of pointless bitwise expressions. Such expressions include anding with zero, oring by zero, and shifting by zero. Such expressions may be the result of automated refactorings not completely followed through to completion, and in any case are unlikely to be what the developer intended to do.
	Shift operation outside of the reasonable range. This inspection reports any instances of shift operations where the value shifted by is constant and outside of the reasonable range. Integer shift operations outside of the range 0..31 and long shift operations outside of the range 0..63 are reported. Shifting by negative or overly large values is almost certainly a coding error.
Braces	**Do-While loops should use braces.** Identifies Do/While loops that do not use braces.
	For loops should use braces. Warns you when a for loop does not have its body wrapped in curly braces.
	If-Else statements should use braces. Identifies If-Else statements that do not use braces.
	While loops should use braces. Identifies While loops that do not use braces.
Class Structure	**Class may be interface.** Reports any concrete or abstract classes that may be simplified to be interfaces. This occurs if the class has no superclass (other than Object), has no fields declared that are not static, final, and public, has no methods declared that are not public and abstract, and has no inner classes that cannot themselves be interfaces.
	Final class. Reports any instances of classes being declared final. Some coding standards discourage final classes.
	Final method. Reports any instances of methods being declared final. Some coding standards discourage final methods.
	Final method in final class. Reports any instances of methods being declared final in classes that are declared final. This is unnecessary and may be confusing.
	Final private method. Reports any instances of methods being declared final and private. As private methods cannot be meaningfully overridden, declaring them final is redundant.
	Initializer may be static. The initializer does not access any instance variables or methods. It can be static and execute just once, not during each instance creation.
	Marker interface. Reports marker interfaces that have no methods or fields. Such interfaces may be confusing and normally indicate a design failure. Interfaces that extend two or more other interfaces will not be reported.
	Multiple top-level classes in file. Reports any instances of multiple top-level classes in a single Java file. Putting multiple top-level classes in a file can be confusing and may degrade the usefulness of various software tools.
	No-op method in abstract class. Reports any instances of no-op methods in abstract classes. It is usually a better design to make such methods abstract, so that classes that inherit the methods will not forget to provide their own implementations.

(*continued*)

Table 6-1. (*continued*)

Category	Inspections
	Organize members. Checks whether members order corresponds to the specified code style rules.
	Protected member in final class. Reports any instances of members being declared protected in classes that are declared final. Such members may be declared private or package-visible instead.
	Public constructor in non-public class. Reports all constructors in non-public classes that are declared public.
Code Maturity Issues	**Obsolete collection.** This inspection reports any uses of java.util.Vector or java.util. Hashtable. While still supported, these classes were made obsolete by the JDK1.2 collection classes, and should probably not be used in new development.
	Print stack trace. This inspection reports any uses of Throwable.printStackTrace() without arguments. These are often temporary debugging statements and should probably be either removed from production code or replaced by a more robust logging facility.
	System out/err. This inspection reports any uses of System.out or System.err. These are often temporary debugging statements and should probably be either removed from production code or replaced by a more robust logging facility.
	Thread dump stack. This inspection reports any uses of Thread.dumpStack(). These are often temporary debugging statements and should probably be either removed from production code or replaced by a more robust logging facility.
Empty Statements	**Empty statement.** Checks for empty statements in blocks, usually represented as superfluous semicolons.
	Empty statement after 'do'. Checks for empty statement after do in do/while statements.
	Empty statement after 'for'. Checks for empty statement after for, that is, empty for loops.
	Empty statement after 'if/else'. Checks for empty statement after if, that is, empty if/else clauses.
	Empty statement after 'while'. Checks for empty statement after while in while loops.
Encapsulation	**Access of private field of another object.** Warns you about access of private fields of another objects.
	Assignment to array field from parameter. Warns you about assignment of array into fields.
	Assignment to collection field from parameter. Warns you about assignment of java. util.Collection into fields.
	Assignment to date or calendar field from parameter. Warns you about assignment of java.util.Date or java.util.Calendar into fields.
	Package field. Warns you about existence of package visible variables.
	Package visible inner class. Warns you about the existence of package visible inner class.
	Protected field. Warns you about the existence of protected variables.
	Protected inner class. Warns you about the existence of protected visible inner class.
	Public field. Warns you about the existence of public variables.

(*continued*)

Table 6-1. (*continued*)

Category	Inspections
	Public inner class. Warns you about the existence of public visible inner class.
	Return of array field. Warns you about the return of array fields.
	Return of collection field. Warns you about the return of collection fields.
	Return of date or calendar field. Warns you about the return of java.util.Date or java.util.Calendar fields.
Enterprise Java Beans	**@Remote uses value in business interface.** If an interface is annotated with @Remote, then the value attribute must not be specified. In other words, if value is specified for @Remote, then it must be annotating a class (not an interface).
	Annotation @PostConstruct. Checks usage of @PostConstruct annotation, including its return value, singularity per class, parameters, and so on.
	Asynchronous method invocation. Checks usage of @Asynchronous. Tests whether it's used in the supported project and interface type.
	Bean doesn't implement business interface. It is recommended that a bean class implement its business interface.
	Inheritance of session beans. A session bean must not extend another session bean.
	Instantiation replaceable with @EJB injection. Finds instantiations of a bean which can be injected by @EJB annotation
	Local and remote business interface together. The same business interface cannot be both a local and a remote business interface of the bean.
	Method definition in local and remote interface. When a session bean has remote and local business interfaces, there should not be method common to both of them.
	Method not exposed in business interface. Method is not exposed in any business interface.
	Modifiers of the EJB bean. Checks whether the defined EJB beans have correct modifiers—are public, not final, and not abstract.
	No-arg constructor in the EJB bean. EJB class must have a public or protected no-arg constructor.
	Persistent timer within EJB Lite. Persistent timer (@Schedule annotation) can't be used in case of EJB 3.2 Lite and timer can't be used at all within EJB 3.1 Lite targeting project.
	SessionSynchronization implemented by non-SFSB. Only stateful session bean (SFSB) can implement the SessionSynchronization interface.
	Incomplete LBI session bean. If a session bean is annotated as @Local, then it must have a local business interface.
	Incomplete RBI session bean. If a session bean is annotated as @Remote, then it must have a remote business interface.
	WebService must be designated as session bean. If a class is part of ejb-jar and is annotated as @WebService, then it must be designated as a stateless or as a singleton session bean.

(*continued*)

Table 6-1. (*continued*)

Category	Inspections
Error Fixes	**Implementation of EJBContainer is missing on project's classpath.** Find out whether the implementation of EJBContainer necessary for successful execution of unit test is available.
	Java EE API is missing on project classpath. Find out whether Java EE API is available on project classpath. Java EE API is necessary for successful test execution. This hint also warns about incorrect usage of javaee-web-api artifact. That artifact is suitable only for compilation, not for test execution because body of all API methods was removed from the bytecode.
Finalization	**finalize() called explicitly.** Warns about an explicit call of the Object.finalize().
	finalize() declared. Warns about implementations of Object.finalize().
	finalize() does not call super.finalize(). Warns about implementations of Object. finalize() that do not call supertype implementation.
	finalize() not declared protected. Warns about non-protected implementations of Object.finalize().
General	**.equals method not checking type.** Implementation of .equals methods is not checking the type of the input parameter.
	Accessing static via reference. Java language allows access to static fields thru instance variables; however, this is often misleading and harder to read.
	Assignment to itself. Assignment of a variable to itself.
	Comparing strings using == or !=. Checks for usages of == or != operators for comparing strings. String comparisons should generally be done using the equals() method.
	Field hides another field. Declaration of a field in a class can hide declaration of another field in superclasses. Although possible, this is not very good programming style.
	Generates missing hashCode or equals. Checks whether a class that overrides the equals() method also overrides hashCode.
	Local variable hides a field. Declaration of a variable in a method can hide declaration of a field declared in the surrounding class. Although possible, this is not very good programming style.
	Redundant conditional statement. Redundant conditional statement.
	Redundant if statement. Redundant if statement.
	Remove unnecessary continue statement. Remove unnecessary continue statement.
	Remove unnecessary label in break. Remove unnecessary label in break statement.
	Remove unnecessary label in continue. Remove unnecessary label in continue statement.
	Remove unnecessary return statement. Remove unnecessary return statement.
	Unnecessary Throwable.initCause. Finds invocations of Throwable.initCause that can be replaced with simple constructor invocation. When the Never Alter Result of getMessage() checkbox is unchecked, (IllegalStateException) new IllegalStateException(). initCause(ex) will be rewritten as new IllegalStateException(ex), which will alter the value of getMessage(). When the checkbox is checked, the code will become new IllegalStateException(null, ex). A similar rule holds for creating the exception from getMessage() or getLocalizedMessage() of the cause.
	Use functional operations. Use functional operations instead of imperative style loop.
	Wrong package. Java source file is in a package that does not correspond to its import statement.

(*continued*)

Table 6-1. (*continued*)

Category	Inspections
Imports	**Import from the same package.** Imports from the same package. **Import From java.lang package.** Import from java.lang package. **Import from excluded.** Import from package or class that has been labelled "Excluded" in the Code Completer. **Organize imports.** Checks whether import statements correspond to the specified code style rules. **Star import.** Star import. **Unused import.** Unused import.
Initialization	**Passing suspicious parameter in the constructor.** Using this as parameter can be dangerous in the constructor because the object is not fully initialized. **Problematic call in the constructor.** Calling methods that can be overridden can be dangerous in the constructor because at the moment the overridden method is called, the object is not fully initialized. **Static non-final variable used during initialization.** Using static non-final variables can be dangerous in the initialization code because their values may depend on the order of initialization statements.
JDK Migration Support	**AbstractProcessor.getSupportedAnnotationTypes() is overridden.** Overriding Processor.getSupportedAnnotationTypes() may lead to unnecessary class-loading during development, and may prevent important optimization. Consider using @javax.annotation.processing.SupportedAnnotationTypes. **Add @Override annotation.** Add an @Override annotation. **Add underscores.** Add underscores to integer literals to improve their readability. **Can use diamond.** Warns about places where the diamond operator in JDK 7 can be used instead of explicit type parameters. **Convert to lambda or member reference.** Converts anonymous inner classes to lambda expressions or member references. **Convert to try-with-resources.** Converts try-finally block to try-with-resources. **Don't use annotation as super interface.** Despite the compiler permitting such constructs, annotations should not be used as super interfaces. **Join catch sections using multicatch.** Join catch sections using multicatch. **Static imports.** Convert method to static import. **String.indexOf can be replaced with String.contains.** Finds usages of String.indexOf that can be replaced with String.contains. **Too broad 'catch' clause.** Reports catch clauses, which catch a supertype rather than the actually thrown exception type. Such broad catches may provide inappropriate reports or overly general exception handling. Sometimes the method produces more than one exception type, which can be handled by catching their common supertype. The Report Common Supertypes option controls whether such situations will be reported. The generic exceptions configured for the Use Specific Catch hint are always reported. **Unnecessary boxing.** Explicit boxing using new Integer(x) or Integer.valueOf(x) is not necessary in JDK 5 and up. This hint detects such situations and suggestions you remove the boxing call.

(*continued*)

Table 6-1. (*continued*)

Category	Inspections
	Unnecessary unboxing. Explicit unboxing using x.intValue() is not necessary under JDK 5 and up. The hint finds such calls and suggests you remove them.
	Use JDK 5 for loop. Replaces simple uses of Iterator with a corresponding for loop.
	Use specific catch. Converts catch (Throwable) or catch (Exception) to multicatch (when Java source level is 7 and above) or to several catch clauses (for earlier Java platforms) catching the exceptions thrown by the try body. The watched exception types can be configured; fully qualified names must be used.
	Use switch over strings where possible. Marks cascades of ifs that can be converted to strings.
Java Code Metrics	**Anonymous class has too many methods.** Reports anonymous class with many methods. Anonymous classes typically implement a very simple interface and should be very simple. It is recommended to create at least named local class, if the anonymous class' complexity grows.
	Anonymous class is too complex. Reports anonymous classes whose cyclomatic complexity exceeds the configured limit. The complexity of a class is computed as a sum of complexities of its methods. Anonymous classes should have far fewer responsibilities and lower complexity than a regular class.
	Arithmetic expression too complex. Reports arithmetic expressions that include more than the defined number of operations. Expressions with many operands are harder to read and often could be split into several assignment statements to interim result variables.
	Class has too many constructors. Reports classes that define too many constructors.
	Class has too many fields. Reports a class that holds too many fields. The state kept by the class is too large and it should be investigated if the state can be split into several state classes, often also separating manipulation methods and reducing the overall class complexity.
	Class has too many methods. Reports classes that contain too many methods. The option allows you to ignore simple bean property accessors. Lazy getters or setters that fire change events are not considered 'simple'. Implementations of superclass (not implementation of interface methods) abstract methods can be also ignored.
	Class is too complex. Reports classes whose cyclomatic complexity exceeds the configured limit. The complexity of a class is computed as a sum of complexities of its methods.
	Class is too coupled. Reports classes that are too coupled (use too many) to other types. References to Java system libraries (java.** and javax.**) can be ignored.
	Constructor declares too many parameters. Reports constructors that take too many parameters. Constructors typically take more parameters than a regular method, especially when initializing a large object. Large number of parameters indicate a bad design. It's likely that yet more parameters will be added in the future, so creational patterns like Builder should be considered.
	Logical expression too complex. Reports logical expressions that include more than the defined number of operations. Expression with many operands are harder to read and often could be split into several assignment statements to interim result variables.

(*continued*)

Table 6-1. (*continued*)

Category	Inspections
	Method body is too long. Reports methods that have too long a body. Longer methods require scrolling back and forth and typically can be refactored into several methods called from a mediating method. Splitting a long method into several named pieces may also help code reuse. Some coding practices even demand that a method should fit a screen size, so it can be easily scanned and understood by the developer.
	Method declares too many parameters. Reports methods that take too many parameters. Methods with a large number of parameters indicate a bad design. It's likely that yet more parameters will be added in the future, so the parameters should be grouped into a command object, improving maintenance costs. Alternatively, the method could be refactored into several methods, each doing part of the task and requiring fewer parameters at input.
	Method is too complex. The inspection reports method whose cyclomatic complexity exceeds a configurable value. The cyclomatic complexity measures a number of potential branching points (or cycles) in a method. It is believed that methods with high cyclomatic complexity usually do too much and should be split to several, more focused, methods. Such complex methods are also prone to code duplication between their execution paths and are hard to sustain. Usually it is recommended that cyclomatic complexity of a method is 5 or below; less than 10 may be also acceptable for more elaborate algorithms.
	Method or constructor declares too many exceptions. Reports methods that declare many exceptions in their throws clause. Methods that produce a large number of exception types are hard to use, as the caller must handle all the outcomes or complicate its own declaration with exceptions. The error-handling code grows more complex. The inspection also processes constructors.
	Method with multiple loops. Methods that contains multiple loop statements.
	Method with multiple negations. Methods with multiple negated expressions (unary ! or !=) are said to confuse readers, true (non-negated) expressions are considered easier to read and understand. Consider changing the logic to use true instead of false values.
	Method with multiple return points. Reports methods, which exit at multiple places using return statement. Such methods may be confusing and are harder to refactor. The inspection can ignore conditional guard returns such as a return statement that's the sole statement in an if branch. Optionally, all equals methods can be ignored, as contents of equals is traditionally generated using early returns on type or value mismatch.
	Too coupled method. Reports methods that are too coupled. They refer to too many other types. Methods that refer to large number of types are fragile; they tend to fail or require refactoring if the referenced type(s) change. It is also more difficult to move a method that has many dependencies to another module. References to the method class' itself and its superclasses are ignored. With Ignore dependencies on Java Platform, references to java.** and javax.** classes are also ignored.
	Too deep nesting. Reports methods whose bodies contain statements that are nested too deep. Such methods are less readable, contain indent space, and allow less screen space for code reading. Methods can be often refactored and split to improve code readability.
Javadoc	**Create Javadoc.** Create Javadoc.
	Error in Javadoc. Error in Javadoc.

(*continued*)

Table 6-1. (*continued*)

Category	Inspections
Java Persistence API	**Check access types for JPA classes.** JPA classes need to have consistent access types for fields/properties.
	Default public/protected constructor. JPA classes need to have default public/protected no arg constructor.
	Entity implements Serializable verification. If an entity instance is to be passed by value as a detached object (e.g., through a remote interface), the entity class must implement the Serializable interface.
	Entity table name verification. Entity table name must be valid QL identifier.
	JPQL validation. Parse and find errors in a JPQL query.
	Presence of persistence.xml. Check if project with JPA usage contain persistence.xml with persistence unit.
	The IdClass must override equals(Object o) and hashCode() method. The IdClass must override the equals(Object o) and hashCode() methods.
	Verify @IdClass location. Only entity or MappedSuperclass can use IdClass.
	Verify IdClass in entity subclass. An entity subclass cannot have an IdClass because it will result in multiple IDs in the entity hierarchy.
	Verify access level for IdClass. IdClass needs to be public.
	Verify attributes of JPA classes. This validation covers a number of issues like valid column name, valid attribute modifiers, valid basic type, relationships, and so on.
	Verify combinations of JPA annotations. Some JPA annotations may not be applied to the same element at the same time.
	Verify entity have defined primary key. ID is required for entities.
	Verify entity name is unique. Entity names must not be the same in one persistence unit.
	Verify JPA annotations on accessors. JPA annotations should be applied to getter methods only.
	Verify JPA class is top level class. JPA classes must not be inner classes.
	Verify JPA class isn't final. JPA classes must not be final.
	Verify named query location. Named queries can be defined only on an entity or on a MappedSuperclass class.
Java Server Faces	**@FlowScoped bean in the non-CDI capable project.** @FlowScoped bean in the non-CDI capable project.
	Classes of javax.faces.bean are going to be deprecated. Annotations from the package javax.faces.bean will be deprecated in the next JSF version. CDI and Java EE ones are recommended instead.
Logging	**Logger declaration is not static final.** Each class should have one unique logger. If it's declared as a field, it should be static and final.
	Multiple loggers. There are several loggers declared for a single class.
	No loggers. There is no logger declared for a class.
	String concatenation in logger. It is not performance efficient to concatenate strings in logger messages. It is better to use a template message with placeholders that are replaced by concrete values only when the message is really going to be logged.

(*continued*)

Table 6-1. *(continued)*

Category	Inspections
NetBeans Development	**Empty cancel() for cancelable tasks.** Warns about empty cancel() methods for cancelable tasks.
	HelpCtx issues. Warns about misuse of org.openide.util.HelpCtx.
	Illegal use of instanceOf operator. Shows illegal use of instanceof on javax.lang.model.elements, javax.lang.model.type, and com.sun.source.tree.
	Use @NbBundle.Messages. Use @NbBundle.Messages in preference to Bundle.properties and NbBundle.getMessage(...).
Performance	**.getClass() replaceable with .class.** Finds instances of a class directly followed by invocation of .getClass() on the newly constructed object.
	Boxing of already boxed value. Reports boxing of already boxed value. Constructor or valueOf take a primitive parameter, so a boxed value is unboxed first, then boxed again, which may create an extra instance of the wrapper and impact the performance.
	Collections without initial capacity. Looks for instances of collections with missing initial capacity. Only collections backed up with an array are tested.
	Creating new Boolean. Creating a new Boolean is inefficient and typically useless.
	Length one string in String.indexOf. Length one string literal in String.indexOf can be replaced with a character literal.
	Manual array copy. Finds occurrences of manual array copying via for loop.
	Map replaceable with EnumMap. Finds instantiations of maps that can be replaced with EnumMap.
	Redundant String.toString(). Reports calls of String.toString(), which is entirely useless. The string can be used directly.
	Replace StringBuffer/StringBuilder by string. The hint will find and offer to replace instances of StringBuffer or StringBuilder that are accessed using ordinary string methods and are never passed out of the method or assigned to another variable. Keeping such data in StringBuffer/Builder is pointless, and String would be more efficient.
	Set replaceable with EnumSet. Finds instantiations of sets that can be replaced with EnumSet.
	String concatenation in StringBuilder.append. Looks for string concatenation in the parameter of an invocation of the append method of StringBuilder or StringBuffer.
	String constructor. Use of java.lang.String constructor is usually useless.
	String.equals(""). Use of String.equals("") can be replaced with String.length() == 0 (for JDK5 and lower) or String.isEmpty() (for JDK6 and higher).
	String.intern() called on constant. Invocations of String.intern() on compile-time constants are superfluous.
	StringBuilder without initial capacity. Looks for instantiations of StringBuilder or StringBuffer with missing initial capacity.
	Unnecessary temporary during conversion from String. Finds occurrences of new Integer("111").intValue() and similar constructions, where the boxed instance is created just to parse the String parameter. Boxing types have parseXXX methods, which perform the conversion without creating the temporary instance.

(continued)

Table 6-1. (*continued*)

Category	Inspections
	Unnecessary temporary during conversion to string. Finds places like new Integer(11). toString() where a temporary boxed instance is created to just produce a String representation of a primitive. The boxed types have a toString() static method just for that purpose.
	Usage of .size() == 0. Use .isEmpty() or !.isEmpty() instead of .size() == 0 or .size() != 0 where possible.
	Useless use of StringBuffer. Use StringBuilder instead of StringBuffer where possible.
	Zero element array passed to Collection.toArray. Passing zero element array to Collection.toArray may affect performance.
Probable Bugs	**'finally' block suppresses exceptions.** Reports usage of return statements in finally block. Such return discards the exception being thrown and causes the whole method to complete normally, which is usually not the desired outcome. Break and continue statements, which break out of the finally block, are also reported.
	'throw' inside 'finally' block. Throwing an exception inside the finally block will hide the original exception thrown from the associated try or catch blocks from enclosing exception handlers. Note that the exception can be still inspected using Throwable. getSuppressedException(), although it cannot be directly caught by a catch block.
	.equals on Array. .equals on array.
	.equals on incompatible types. .equals on incompatible types.
	.equals(null). Finds invocations of the Object.equals method with literal parameter 'null'.
	@CheckReturnValue. Verifies that a result of method marked with @CheckReturnValue is really checked.
	Annotations without runtime retention. Warns about reflective access to annotations with CLASS or SOURCE retentions.
	Assert with side effects. Identifies assert statements whose condition reportedly causes some side effects. The hint checks assignments to local variables and fields made from within the condition expression. If the expression calls a method, the hint checks whether the method assigns to some fields. Only the directly called methods are checked. For performance reasons, although the called method may resolve to some overrides in subclasses at runtime, only the base class method body is inspected. Calls to interface type methods are ignored completely. Inspection of all possible overrides of a method would greatly hurt performance.
	Boxed value identity comparison. If two boxed values are compared using == or !=, identity of the boxed object's identity is compared instead of the boxed value. The inspection suggests a fix, which performs a null-safe comparison using java.util.Objects. equals().The fix is only available for source level greater or equal to 7, since a conditional expression would require multiple evaluation of one of the operands, which may not be possible because of potential expression's side effects.
	Cloneable class does not implement clone(). Cloneable class should override clone(). If it does not, the clone operation uses the default java.lang.Object.clone(), which is usually not suitable. Lack of overridden clone indicates a possible error.
	Comparator.compare() does not use its parameter {0}. The comparator is expected to compare the arguments to its compare method. If one of the parameters is not used for comparison, it indicates that the other argument might be compared to self or some other error in the implementation.

(*continued*)

Table 6-1. (*continued*)

Category	Inspections
	Confusing indentation. Warns about indentation that suggests possible missing surrounding block.
	Confusing primitive array passed to varargs method. A primitive array passed to variable-argument method will not be unwrapped and its items will not be seen as items of the variable-length argument in the called method. Instead, the array will be passed as a single item.
	Created Throwable not thrown. The hint detects creation of a Throwable, which is then discarded. Throwable creation is rather expensive and not using a created Throwable may indicate an unfinished error-handling code. The Throwable is considered used, if it is thrown, passed to a method as a parameter, returned as a method's result, or assigned to a field. Possible assignments through local variables are also inspected to determine whether the value will be finally used.
	Dead branch. Dead branch.
	Incompatible cast/instanceof. Incompatible cast surrounded with incompatible instanceof.
	Incorrect column index in ResultSet. Reports incorrect column indices passed to various methods of java.sql.ResultSet.
	Infinite recursion. Detects methods that must recurse infinitely and could only terminate by throwing an exception. Only definitively recursions are reported, not possibilities. The recursion only inspected across the single method (so recursion like a -> b -> a is not reported). Recursion through several instances of the class is also not reported. The hint can be disabled when the recursing method could be overriden in subclasses, since subclass implementations could avoid the recursion. However, if some subclass does not override and fix the method, recursion may still happen. By default, the inspection warns even for the overridable case.
	Malformed XPath expression. The hint checks syntax of the XPath expression passed to the JAXP XPath evaluator. The calls checked are: JAXP XPath compile and evaluate calls, Xalan-J XPath creation and XPathAPI usage, Apache Common's JXPath calls.
	Malformed format string. Reports format strings passed to String.format, printf-style methods. Checks that the number of arguments corresponds to the number of % specifiers, and the arguments have the correct type.
	Malformed regular expression. Warns about malformed regular expressions.
	Math.random() casted to int. Math.random produces a double in range 0..1. If the value is immediately cast to int, it is always rounded down to 0, which is probably not intended. The fix will move the cast so the enclosing arithmetic expression is casted and possibly rounded.
	Null pointer dereference. Checks various problems related to dereferencing nulls.
	Possibly missing switch "case" statement. The hint detects a typo made in a switch statement indicating a label without a case statement. While it may be an intended label for the following statement, it could be also an intended case branch with the keyword forgotten.
	Result of new object ignored. Result of new object ignored.
	String.replaceAll(".",). Finds occurrences of calls to String.replaceAll(".", $target), which would replace all characters of the source string with $target.

(continued)

141

Table 6-1. (*continued*)

Category	Inspections
	StringBuffer constructor called with char argument. StringBuffer and StringBuilder constructors accept int as a parameter. If a char is passed, it is silently promoted to int, and the call creates a StringBuffer instance with a defined initial capacity, rather than a StringBuffer that initially contains a single (the passed one) character. The offered fix will add an append that actually adds the character.
	Suspicious Collections.toArray() call. Detects such calls whose array type parameter does not match the Collection's type parameter. The collection's type parameter should be assignable to the array type. For raw collections, the hint checks that the array type is actually assignable to the casted-to array type. The hint offers to change the newly created array type, or to change the toArray parameter to new Type[], but the fix is not available if the collection expression may have some side effects.
	Suspicious names combination. Suspicious names combination.
	Suspicious invocation of System.arraycopy. Finds invocations of System.arraycopy with negative offsets, length or used on non-array objects.
	Suspicious method call. Warns about suspicious calls to Collection.remove/contains and Map.containsKey/containsValue/remove.
	Synchronizing on this in anonymous class. Synchronizing on this in anonymous or local class is probably a result of refactoring and possibly a mistake.
	Throwable method result is ignored. If a Throwable is returned from a method call as a return value (as an opposite to be thrown), it is usually somehow recorded (assigned), further processed (passed to another method call), or thrown. Ignoring such Throwable or using in some simple comparison indicates either a defect in error handling, or that the method should return a different value to save time for Throwable's stacktrace creation.
	Unbalanced read/write with arrays. Unbalanced read/write with arrays.
	Unbalanced read/write with collections. Unbalanced read/write with collections.
	Unused assignment. Unused assignment.
	clone() does not call super.clone(). Cloned instances should be allocated using super. clone() so fields are initialized properly.
	clone() does not throw CloneNotSupportedException. If clone() is not declared to throw CloneNotSupportedException subclasses cannot prohibit cloning using standard Cloneable contract.
	clone() in a non-Cloneable class. The contract for Object.clone() requires that a class must implement Cloneable marker interface. If not, the clone() method will raise CloneNotSupportedException. Declaring a cloneable interface is often overlooked.
	hashCode() used on array instance. hashCode for array instances is inherited from java. lang.Object, and it is based on the array's reference rather than on array's contents. In order to obtain a more reasonable hashCode, which reflects contained objects or values, use Arrays.hashCodeor Arrays.deepHashCode().
	toString() used on array instance. toString() implementation for arrays does not convert array contents to string, rather it will print array's type and hash code (defined as identity hash code). To get string representation of contents of the array, the array could be, for example, wrapped into Arrays.asList(), as collections produce content representation in their toString().

(*continued*)

Table 6-1. (*continued*)

Category	Inspections
Testing	**Inconvertible parameters of Assert.assertEquals.** Inconvertible parameters of Assert.assertEquals.
	Incorrect order of parameters of Assert.assertEquals. Incorrect order of parameters of Assert.assertEquals.
	assertEquals for array parameters. Warns about assertEquals whose parameters are arrays.
Threading	**.notify invoked outside a synchronized context.** .notify invoked outside a synchronized context.
	.wait invoked outside a synchronized context. .wait invoked outside a synchronized context.
	Double-checked locking. Searches for examples of double-checked locking, for example, when a variable is tested before as well as inside a synchronized block.
	Empty synchronized block. Empty synchronized block are usually useless.
	Field can be final. Finds fields that can be made final, which can simplify synchronization and clarity.
	Invoking Condition.notify(). Invoking notify or notifyAll on java.util.concurrent.locks.Condition should probably be replaced with invoking signal or signalAll.
	Invoking Condition.wait(). Invoking wait on java.util.concurrent.locks.Condition is probably unintended.
	Invoking Thread.run(). Invoking run on java.lang.Thread should be probably replaced with invocation of method start().
	Invoking Thread.stop()/suspend()/resume(). Methods stop(), suspend(), and resume() of java.lang.Thread are dangerous and should not be used.
	Invoking Thread.yield(). Invocation of method yield() on java.lang.Thread is usually used to masquerade synchronization problems and should be avoided.
	Lock not unlocked in finally. Finds occurrences of Lock.lock()-Lock.unlock( ) not properly wrapped in a try-finally.
	Nested synchronized blocks. Nesting synchronized blocks is either useless (if they use the same lock object) or dangerous.
	Starting thread in constructor. Starting a new thread in a constructor is dangerous and should be avoided.
	Synchronization on non-final field. Synchronization on non-final field.
	Synchronizing on lock. Synchronizing on java.util.concurrent.locks.Lock is usually unintended and should be replaced with Lock.lock()-Lock.unlock().
	Thread.sleep in loop. Invoking Thread.sleep in loop can cause performance problems.
	Thread.sleep in synchronized context. Invoking Thread.sleep in synchronized context can cause performance problems.
	Volatile array field. Finds declarations of volatile array fields.

- FindBugs. A set of hints provided by the open source FindBugs project, `http://findbugs.sourceforge.net`, integrated into the IDE, these are listed in Table 6-2.

Table 6-2. *FindBugs categories*

Feature	Description
Bad Practice	Violations of recommended and essential coding practice. Examples include hash code and equals problems, cloneable idiom, dropped exceptions, serializable problems, and misuse of finalize. We strive to make this analysis accurate, although some groups may not care about some of the bad practices.
Correctness	Probable bug is an apparent coding mistake resulting in code that was probably not what the developer intended. We strive for a low false positive rate.
Dodgy Code	Code that is confusing, anomalous, or written in a way that leads itself to errors. Examples include dead local stores, switch fall through, unconfirmed casts, and redundant null check of value known to be null. More false positives accepted. In previous versions of FindBugs, this category was known as Style.
Experimental	Experimental and not fully vetted bug patterns.
Internationalization	Code flaws having to do with internationalization and locale.
Malicious Code Vulnerability	Code that is vulnerable to attacks from untrusted code.
Multithreaded correctness	Code flaws having to do with threads, locks, and volatiles.
Performance	Code that is not necessarily incorrect but may be inefficient.
Security	A use of untrusted input in a way that could create a remotely exploitable security vulnerability.

- JRE 8 Profiles Conformance. A configuration aimed at making sure that the JDK classes used in an application are available in the JRE 8 Profile defined for the application.

- Migrate to JDK. A set of configurations providing a subset of the NetBeans Java Hints configuration, focused on migration to a specific release of the JDK. For example, the "Migrate to JDK 8" configuration includes inspections for converting anonymous inner classes with single abstract methods to lambda expressions.

- Organize Imports. A configuration containing a single inspection that checks whether import statements correspond to the specified code style rules.

Each of the configurations provides one or more inspections, which are organized in categories and listed in Tables 6-1 and 6-2.

Manual Refactoring

While the analysis and refactoring tools described in the previous section are focused on batch-automated tasks, you'll often need to do more fine-grained refactoring work. Typical examples of these tasks include moving classes from one package to another and changing method parameters. These tasks need to be done on a case-by-case basis, for which the IDE has a range of small, subtle, and powerful features to help you get started.

You can start using the manual refactoring features from the Refactor menu in the main menubar or by right-clicking in the Source Editor or on a class node in the Projects window and choosing from the Refactor submenu.

Table 6-3 provides a summary of the refactoring features that are available in this context. These features are explained more thoroughly in task-specific topics throughout the remainder of this chapter, starting right after Table 6-3.

Table 6-3. *Refactoring Features*

Feature	Description	Shortcut
Find Usages	Displays all occurrences of the name of a given class, method, or field. See "Finding Occurrences of the Currently Selected Class, Method, or Field Name" in the previous chapter.	Alt+F7
Rename	Renames all occurrences of the selected class, interface, method, or field name. See "Renaming All Occurrences of the Currently Selected Class, Method, or Field Name" in the previous chapter.	Ctrl+R
Safely Delete	Deletes a code element after making sure that no other code references that element. See "Deleting Code Safely" earlier in this chapter.	Alt+Delete
Change Method Parameters	Enables you to change the parameters and the access modifier for the given method. See "Changing a Method's Signature" later in this chapter.	Ctrl+Alt+Shift+C
Encapsulate Fields	Generates accessor methods (getters and setters) for a field and changes code that accesses the field directly so that it uses those new accessor methods instead. See "Encapsulating a Field" later in this chapter.	Ctrl+Alt+Shift+E
Replace Constructor with Factory	Allows you to hide a constructor and replace it with a static method that returns a new instance of a class.	Ctrl+Alt+Shift+F
Replace Constructor with Builder	Helps hide a constructor, replacing its usage with the references to a newly generated builder class or to an existing builder class.	Ctrl+Alt+Shift+B
Invert Boolean	Allows you to change the sense of a Boolean method or variable to its opposite.	Ctrl+Alt+Shift+I
Copy	Copies a class to a different package and enables you to update all references to that class with the new package name.	Alt+C
Move Class	Moves a class to a different package and updates all references to that class with the new package name. See "Moving a Class to a Different Package" later in this chapter.	Ctrl+M
Pull Up	Moves a method, inner class, or field to a class's superclass. You can also use this feature to declare the method in the superclass and keep the method definition in the current class. See "Moving Class Members to Other Classes" later in this chapter.	Ctrl+Alt+Shift+U

(continued)

Table 6-3. (*continued*)

Feature	Description	Shortcut
Push Down	Moves a method, inner class, or field to a class's direct subclasses. You can also use this feature to keep the method declaration in the current class and move the method definition to the subclasses. See "Moving Class Members to Other Classes" later in this chapter.	Ctrl+Alt+Shift+D
Introduce Method	Creates a new method based on a selection of code in the selected class and replaces the extracted statements with a call to the new method. See "Creating a Method from Existing Statements" later in this chapter. Similarly, you can use existing statements to create a variable (Alt+Shift+V), Constant (Alt+Shift+C), Field (Alt+Shift+E), Parameter (Alt+Shift+P), and local extension (Alt+Shift+X).	Alt+Shift+M
Extract Interface	Creates a new interface based on a selection of methods in the selected class and adds the new interface to the class's implements class. See "Creating an Interface from Existing Methods" later in this chapter.	Ctrl+Alt+Shift+T
Extract Superclass	Creates a new superclass based on a selection of methods in the selected class. You can have the class created with just method declarations, or you can have whole method definitions moved into the new class. See "Extracting a Superclass to Consolidate Common Methods" later in this chapter.	Ctrl+Alt+Shift+S
Use Supertype Where Possible	Changes code to reference objects of a superclass (or other type) instead of objects of a superclass. See "Changing References to Use a Supertype" later in this chapter.	Ctrl+Alt+Shift+W
Move Inner Class to Outer Level	Moves a class up one level. If the class is a top-level inner class, it is made into an outer class and moved into its own source file. If the class is nested within the scope of an inner class, method, or variable, it is moved up to the same level as that scope. See "Unnesting Classes" later in this chapter.	Ctrl+Alt+Shift+L
Convert Anonymous Class to Member	Converts an anonymous inner class to a named inner class. See "Unnesting Classes" later in this chapter.	Ctrl+Alt+Shift+A

Deleting Code Safely

Over time, your code tends to gather elements that have limited or no usefulness. To make the code easier to maintain, it is a good idea to remove as much useless code as possible. However, it is often difficult to decide whether you can delete code without causing errors throughout your application.

The Safely Delete feature can help with the process of removing unused code, saving you time and work in doing manual searches and recompilation attempts. When you use this feature, the IDE checks to see if the selected code is referenced anywhere else in your code. If the code is not used, the IDE immediately deletes it. If the code element is used, the IDE can display where the code is used, enabling you to resolve references to the code you want to delete and then try the Safely Delete operation again.

You can use the Safely Delete feature on any type (such as a class, interface, and or enumeration), method, field, or local variable. To safely delete a code element, in the Source Editor or Projects window, right-click the code element that you want to delete and choose Refactor ➤ Safely Delete or press Alt+Delete. The Safely Delete window appears, as shown in Figure 6-4.

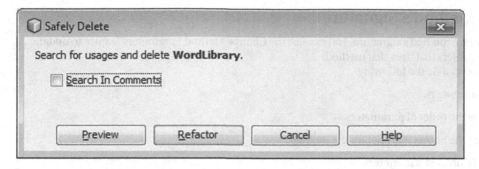

Figure 6-4. Safely Delete window

If you want the IDE to look inside comments for mentions of the code element, select the Search in Comments checkbox. If this checkbox is not selected, comments referring to the code element are not affected if you delete the code element.

Click Refactor. If no references to the code element are found, the Safely Delete window closes and the code element is deleted. If references to the code element are found, no code is deleted and the Safely Delete window remains open.

If you click the Show Usages button, the Usages window opens and displays the references to that code element, as shown in Figure 6-5.

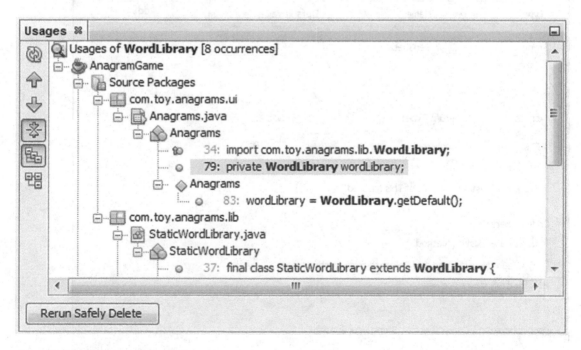

Figure 6-5. Find Usages window

Double-click an item in the list to jump to the line of code that it represents. If you remove the cited references, you can click the Rerun Safely Delete button to repeat the attempt to safely delete the code element.

To undo the refactoring change, choose Edit ➤ Undo Safely Delete (Ctrl+Z).

Changing a Method's Signature

If you want to change a method's signature, you can use the Change Method Parameters feature to update other code in your project that uses that method.

Specifically, you can do the following:

- Add parameters.

- Change the order of parameters.

- Change the access modifier for the method.

- Remove unused parameters.

You cannot use the Change Method Parameters feature to remove a parameter from a method if the parameter is used in your code.

To change a method's signature, right-click the method in the Source Editor and choose Refactor ➤ Change Method Parameters, which opens the Change Method Parameters window, shown in Figure 6-6.

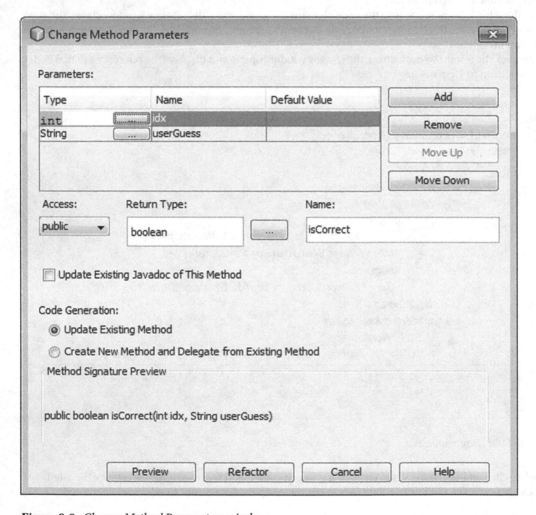

Figure 6-6. *Change Method Parameters window*

Click Add if you want to add parameters to the method. Then edit the Name, Type, and (optionally) the Default Value cells for the parameter. Click a cell to make it editable.

To switch the order of parameters, select a parameter in the Parameters table and click Move Up or Move Down. Select the preferred access modifier from the Access combo box. If you click Refactor, the changes are applied immediately. If you click Preview, the Refactoring window appears with a preview of the changes, as shown in Figure 6-7.

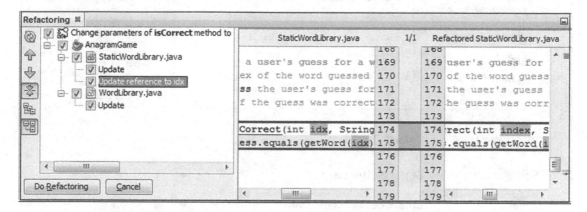

Figure 6-7. Refactoring window

In the Refactoring window, look at the preview of the code to be changed. If there is a modification that you do not want to be made, deselect the checkbox next to the line for that change. Click Do Refactoring.

If you later find that the refactoring has had some consequences that you want to reverse, you can choose Edit ➤ Undo Safely Delete (Ctrl+Z).

Encapsulating a Field

One common design pattern in Java programs is to make fields accessible and changeable only by methods in the defining class. In the convention used by JavaBeans components, the field is given private access and accessor methods are written for the field with broader access privileges. The names of the accessor methods are created by prefixing get and set to the field's name. If you have fields that are visible to other classes and want to better control access to those fields, you can use the Encapsulate Fields feature to automate the necessary code modifications.

The Encapsulate Fields feature does the following:

- Generates getter and setter methods for the desired fields.

- Enables you to change the access modifier for the fields and accessor methods.

- Changes code elsewhere in your project that accesses the fields directly to instead use the newly generated accessor methods.

To encapsulate fields in a class, right-click the field or the whole class in the Source Editor or the Projects window and choose Refactor ➤ Encapsulate Fields. The Encapsulate Fields window opens, as shown in Figure 6-8.

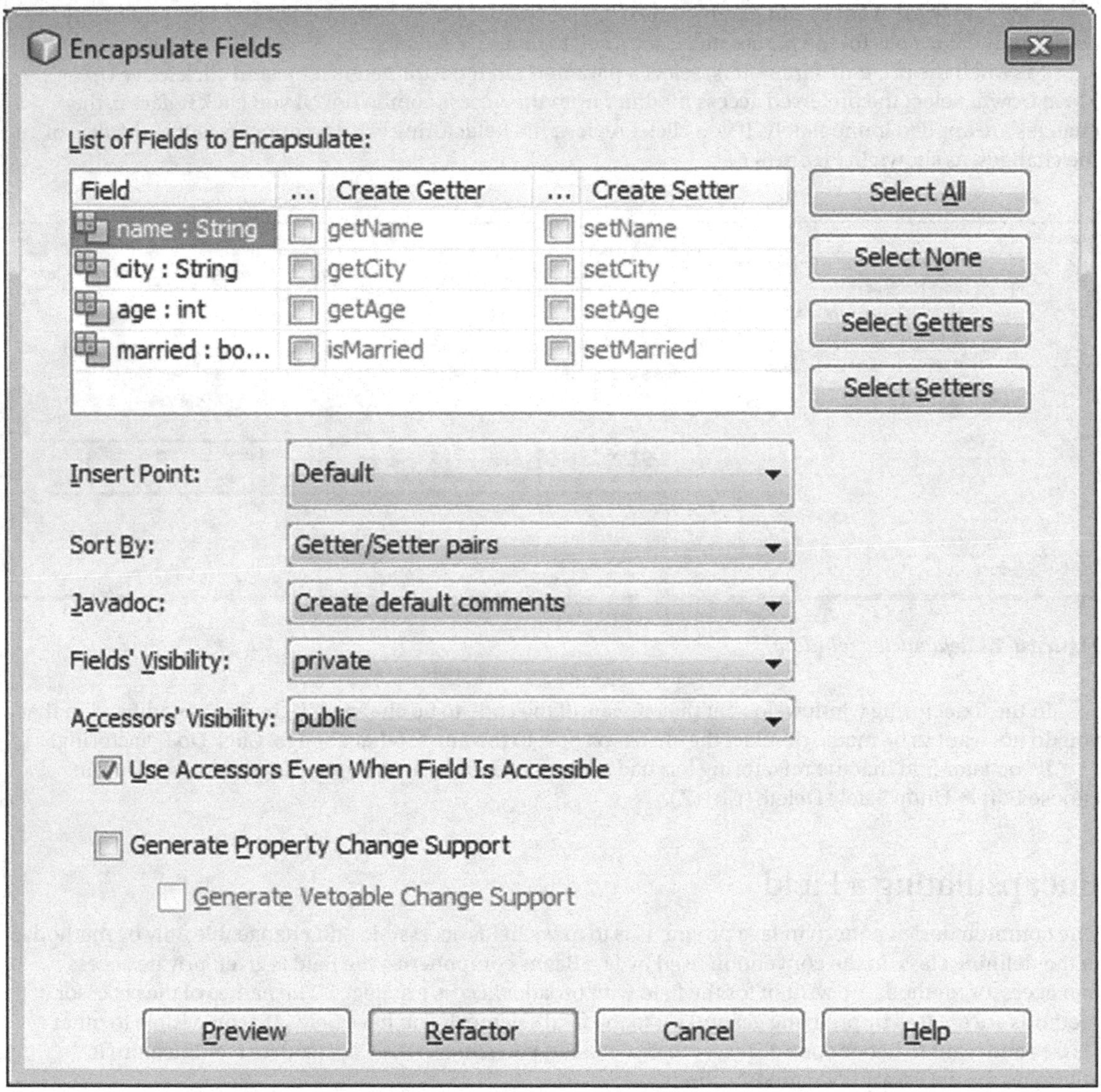

Figure 6-8. *Encapsulate Fields window*

In the Encapsulate Fields window, select the Create Getter and Create Setter checkboxes for each field that you want to have encapsulated. If you have selected a specific field, the checkboxes for just that field should be selected by default. If you have selected the whole class, the checkboxes for all of the class' fields should be selected by default. In the Fields' Visibility drop-down list, set the access modifier to use for the fields that you are encapsulating. Typically, you would select private here. If you select a different visibility level, other classes will still have direct access to the fields for which you are generating accessor methods.

In the Accessors' Visibility drop-down list, set the access modifier to use for the generated getters and setters. If you decide to leave the fields visible to other classes but you want to have current references to the field replaced with references to the accessor methods, select the Use Accessors Even When Field Is Accessible checkbox. Otherwise, those direct references to the field will remain in the code. This checkbox is only relevant if you decide to leave the fields accessible to other classes and there is code in those classes that accesses the fields directly.

If you click Refactor, the changes are applied immediately. If you click Preview, the Refactoring window appears with a preview of the changes, as shown in Figure 6-9.

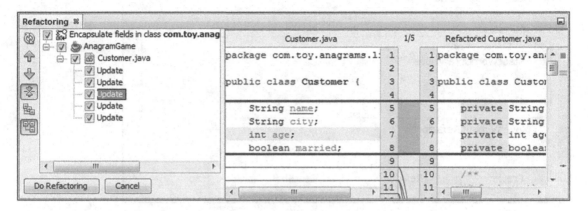

Figure 6-9. *Refactoring window*

In the Refactoring window, verify the changes that are about to be made and click Do Refactoring.

If you later find that the refactoring has had some effects that you want to reverse you can choose Edit ➤ Undo Safely Delete (Ctrl+Z).

Moving a Class to a Different Package

If you want to put a class into a different package, you can use the Move feature to move the class and then update all the references to that class automatically throughout your project.

To move one or more classes in the Projects window, drag the class from its current package to the package you want to place it in. You can also use the Cut and Paste commands in the contextual menus or the corresponding Ctrl+X and Ctrl+V keyboard shortcuts. The Move Class(es) window opens, as shown in Figure 6-10.

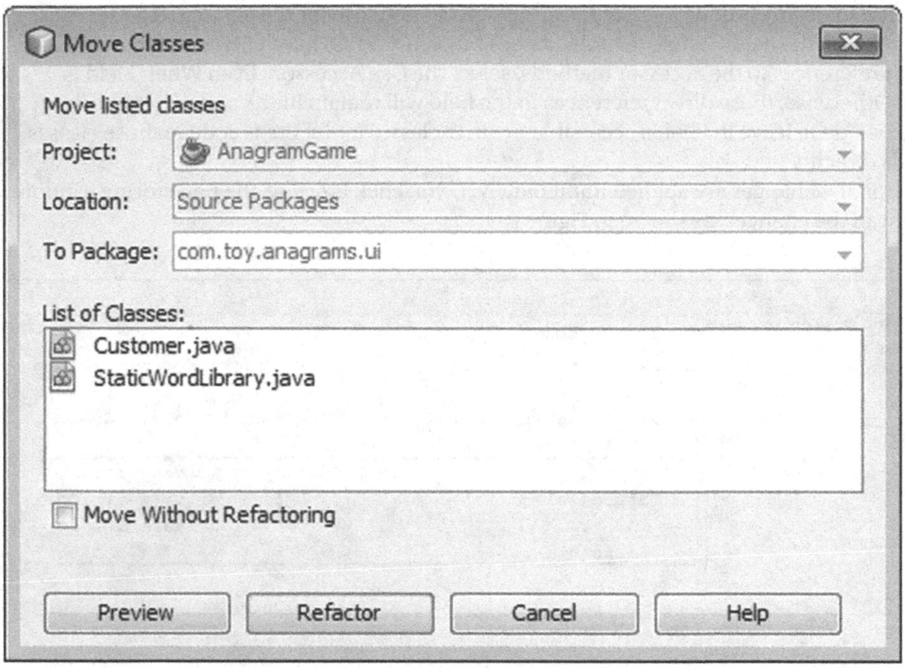

Figure 6-10. *Move Classes window*

In the Move Class(es) window, click Preview or Refactor after verifying that the To Package field reflects the destination package of the class you are moving. If you move multiple classes, a List of Classes text area is shown, displaying all the classes that will be moved.

If you click the Refactor button, the changes are applied immediately. If click the Preview button, the Refactoring window appears with a preview of the changes, as shown in Figure 6-11.

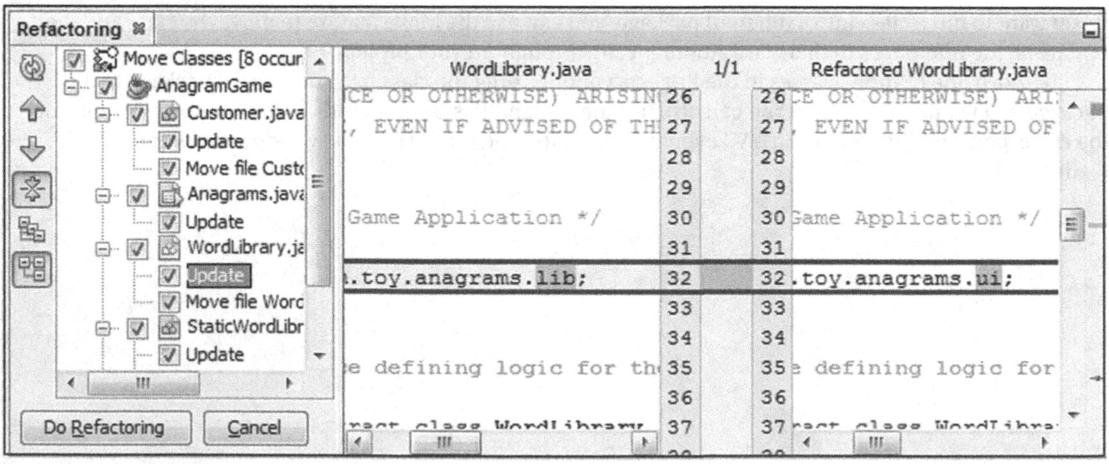

Figure 6-11. *Refactoring window*

In the Refactoring window, look at the preview of the code to be changed. If there is a modification that you do not want to be made, deselect the checkbox next to the line for that change. Click Do Refactoring.

If you later find that the refactoring has had some consequences that you want to reverse, you can choose Edit ➤ Undo Move or, if you want to move multiple classes back to where they came from, choose Edit ➤ Undo Move Classes.

If you want to create a new package and move all of the classes in the old package to the new package, you can do an in-place rename of a package in the Projects window or of a folder in the Files window.

Moving Class Members to Other Classes

The Pull Up and Push Down features help you move methods and fields to other classes and interfaces. When you use these features to move class members, the IDE updates references to those members throughout your project. These features are useful for improving the inheritance structure of your code.

You can do the following:

- Move methods and fields to a superclass or super-interface.

- Leave method implementations in the current class but create abstract declarations for those methods in a superclass.

- Move methods and fields to the class's subclasses or sub-interfaces.

- Move the implementations of methods to subclasses while leaving abstract method declarations in the current class.

- Move the interface name from the implements clause of a class to the implements clause of another class.

Moving Code to a Superclass

To move a member, a method's declaration, or a current class to a superclass, in the Source Editor or the Projects window, select the class or interface that contains the member or members that you want to move. Choose Refactor ➤ Pull Up to open the Pull Up window, as shown in Figure 6-12.

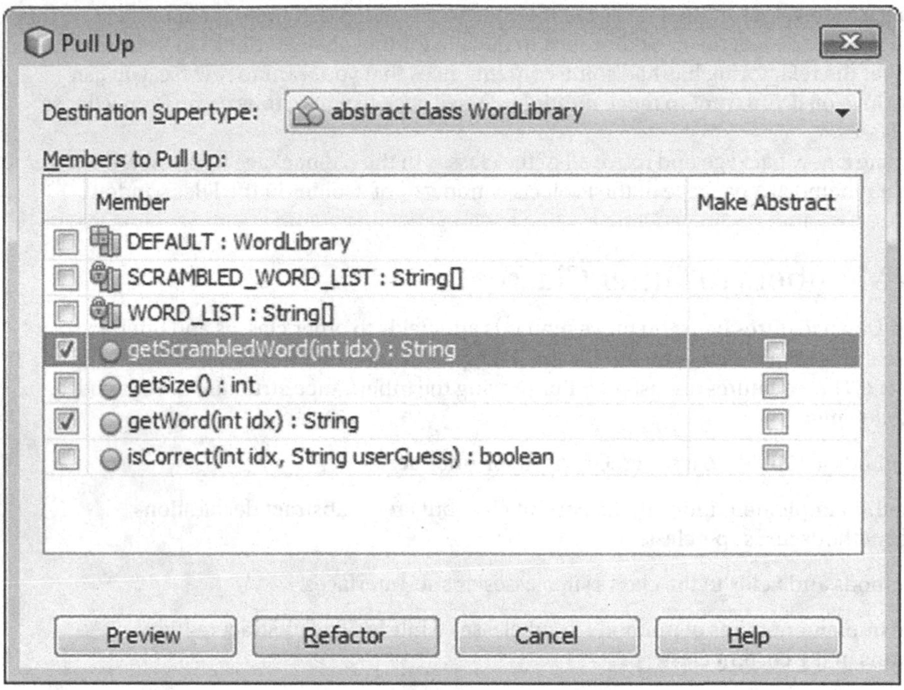

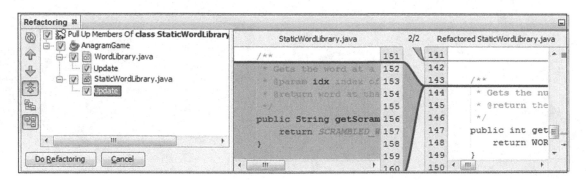

Figure 6-12. *Pull Up window*

In the Destination Supertype drop-down, select the superclass or interface that you want to move the members to. Select the checkbox for each member that you want to move.

If you want to leave the method implementation in the current class and create an abstract declaration for the method in the superclass, select the Make Abstract checkbox for the method.

If the class from which you are moving members implements an interface, a checkbox for that interface is included in the dialog box. If you select the checkbox for that interface, the interface is removed from the implements clause of the current class and moved to the implements clause of the class to which you are moving members. If you select a checkbox for an interface, be sure that all the checkboxes for the methods declared in that interface are also selected.

If you click Refactor, the changes are applied immediately. If you click Preview, the Refactoring window appears with a preview of the changes, as shown in Figure 6-13.

Figure 6-13. *Refactoring window*

In the Refactoring window, look at the preview of the code to be changed. If there is a modification that you do not want to be made, deselect the checkbox next to the line for that change.

Click Do Refactoring.

If you later find that the refactoring activity had some effects that you want to reverse, you can choose Edit ➤ Undo (Ctrl+Z).

Moving Code to Subclasses

To move a member, a method's implementation, or the current class to that class's subclasses, in the Source Editor or the Projects window, select the class or interface that contains the members that you want to move. Choose Refactor ➤ Push Down to open the Push Down window, as shown in Figure 6-14.

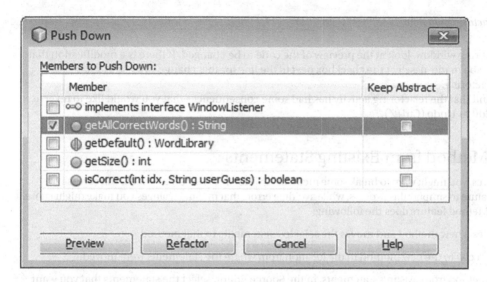

Figure 6-14. Push Down window

Select the checkbox for each member you want to move to the subclasses.

If you want to leave an abstract declaration for the method in the current class and move the implementation to the subclasses, select the Keep Abstract checkbox for the method.

If the class from which you are moving members implements an interface, a checkbox for that interface is included in the window. If you select the checkbox for that interface, the interface is removed from the implements clause of the current class and moved to the implements clause of the class to which you are moving members.

If you click Refactor, the changes are applied immediately. If you click Preview, the Refactoring window appears with a preview of the changes, as shown in Figure 6-15.

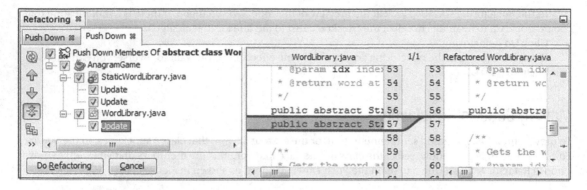

Figure 6-15. *Refactoring window*

In the Refactoring window, look at the preview of the code to be changed. If there is a modification that you do not want to be made, deselect the checkbox next to the line for that change.

Click Do Refactoring.

If you later find that the refactoring activity has had some consequences that you would like to reverse, you can choose Edit ➤ Undo (Ctrl+Z).

Creating a Method from Existing Statements

As your code evolves, you might want to break some methods up into multiple new methods. You can use the Extract Method feature to simplify this process, while avoiding errors that manual changes you make might cause.

The Extract Method feature does the following:

- Creates a new method and moves the selected statements to that method.

- Adds a call to the new method in the location from where the statements were moved.

To extract a method from existing statements, in the Source Editor, select the statements that you want to be extracted into the new method and press Alt+Shift+M. Alternatively, instead of using the keyboard shortcut, right-click the selection and choose Refactor ➤ Introduce ➤ Method. The Introduce Method window opens, as shown in Figure 6-16.

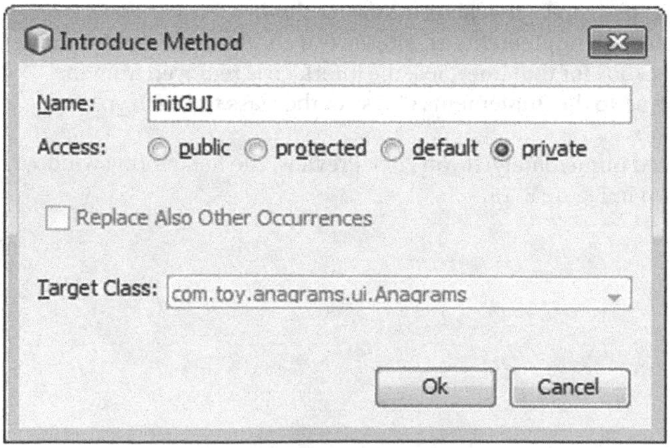

Figure 6-16. *Introduce Method window*

In the Introduce Method window, enter a name for the method and select an access level.

If you click OK, the method is immediately extracted.

If you later find that the refactoring activity has had some consequences that you want to reverse, you can choose Edit ➤ Undo (Ctrl+Z).

Similarly, you can introduce a variable (Alt+Shift+V), a constant (Alt+Shift+C), a field (Alt+Shift+E), a parameter (Alt+Shift+P), and a local extension (Alt+Shift+X).

Creating an Interface from Existing Methods

If you decide to divide your code into API and implementation layers, you can get started on that conversion by using the Extract Interface feature to create an interface from methods in an existing class. The Extract Interface feature does the following:

- Creates a new interface containing declarations for selected public methods.

- Adds the name of the created interface to the implements clause of the class from which the interface is extracted. If the interface is extracted from another interface, the name of the newly created interface is added to the extends clause of the other interface.

To extract an interface from existing methods, in the Source Editor or the Projects window, select the class that contains the methods that you want to be extracted into the new interface. Choose Refactor ➤ Extract Interface. The Extract Interface window opens, as shown in Figure 6-17.

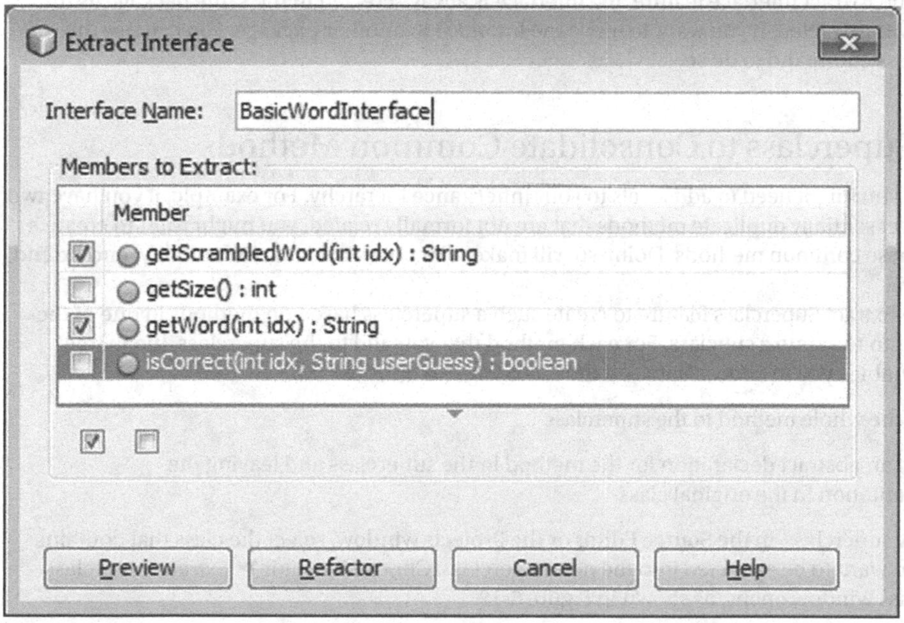

Figure 6-17. *Extract Interface window*

In the Extract Interface window, select the checkbox for each method that you want to be declared in the new interface. If the class from which you are extracting an interface already implements an interface, a checkbox for that interface is included in the Extract Interface window. If you select the checkbox for that interface, the interface is removed from the implements clause of the previously implementing interface and moved to the extends clause of the new interface.

If you click Refactor, the changes are applied immediately. If you click Preview, the Refactoring window appears with a preview of the changes, as shown in Figure 6-18.

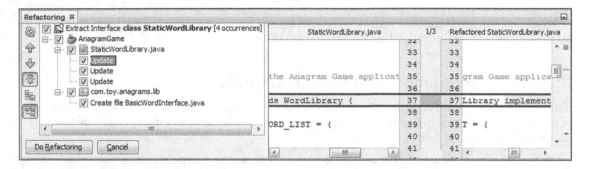

Figure 6-18. *Refactoring window*

In the Refactoring window, look at the preview of the code to be changed. If there is a modification that you do not want to be made, deselect the checkbox next to the line for that change.

Click Do Refactoring.

If you later find that the refactoring activity has made some changes that you want to reverse, you can choose Edit ➤ Undo (Ctrl+Z).

When you use the Extract Interface feature, the interface is always created in the same package as the class from which it was extracted. If you want to move the interface to another package, you can use the Refactor ➤ Move Class command to do so.

Extracting a Superclass to Consolidate Common Methods

As a project evolves, you might need to add levels to your inheritance hierarchy. For example, if you have two or more classes with essentially duplicate methods that are not formally related, you might want to create a superclass to hold these common methods. Doing so will make your code easier to read, modify, and extend, now and in the future.

You can use the Extract Superclass feature to create such a superclass based on methods in one of the classes that you want to turn into a subclass. For each method that you add to the superclass, the Extract Superclass feature enables you to choose between the following two options:

- Moving the whole method to the superclass

- Creating an abstract declaration for the method in the superclass and leaving the implementation in the original class

To extract a new superclass, in the Source Editor or the Projects window, select the class that contains the methods that you want to be extracted into the new superclass. Choose Refactor ➤ Extract Superclass. The Extract Superclass window opens, as shown in Figure 6-19.

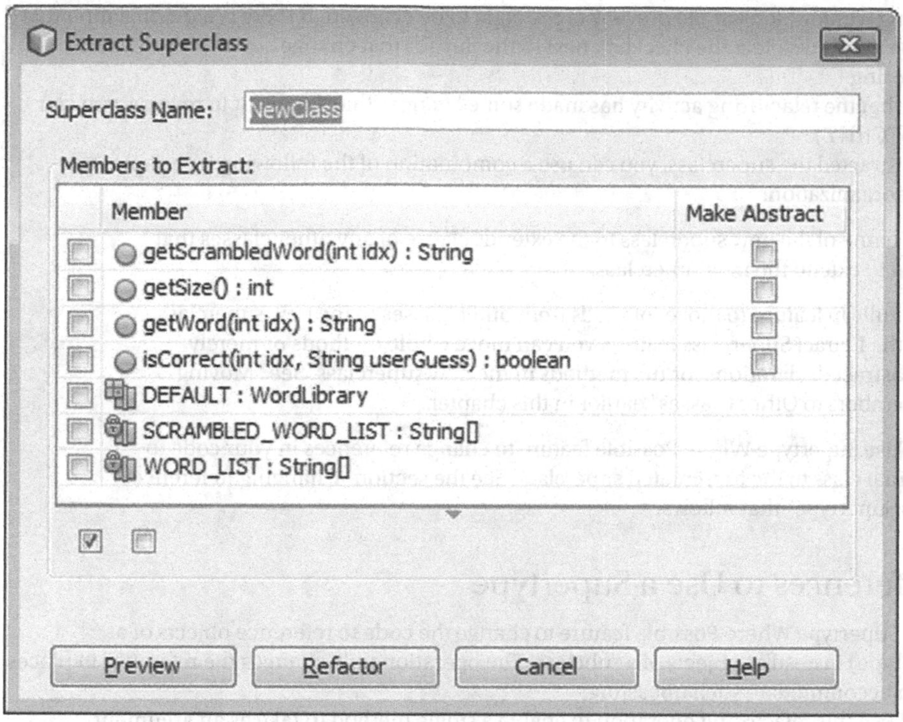

Figure 6-19. *Extract Superclass window*

In the Extract Superclass window, select the checkbox for each method and field that you want to be moved to the new superclass. Private methods and private fields are not included. If you want to leave a method implementation in the current class and create an abstract declaration for the method in the superclass, select the Make Abstract checkbox for the method.

If the class from which you are extracting a superclass implements an interface, a checkbox for that interface is included in the Extract Superclass window. If you select the checkbox for that interface, the interface is removed from the implements clause of the class that you are extracting from and moved to the implements clause of the new superclass.

If you click Refactor, the changes are applied immediately. If you click Preview, the Refactoring window appears with a preview of the changes, as shown in Figure 6-20.

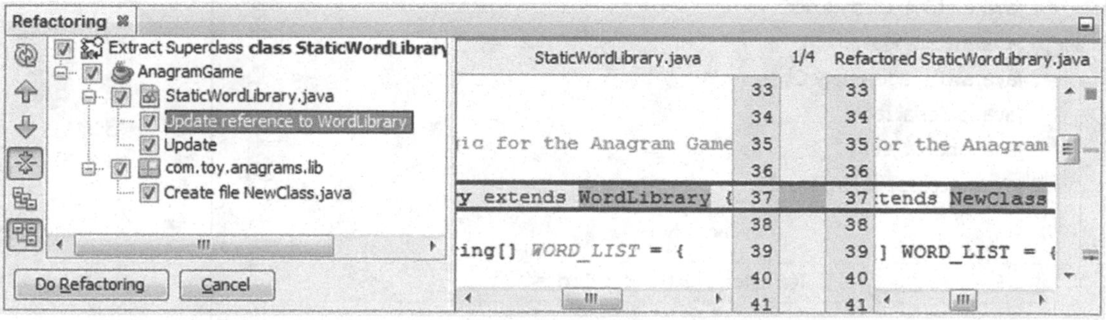

Figure 6-20. *Refactoring window*

In the Refactoring window, look at the preview of the code to be changed. If there is a modification that you do not want to be made, deselect the checkbox next to the line for that change.

Click Do Refactoring.

If you later find that the refactoring activity has made some changes that you want to reverse, you can choose Edit ➤ Undo (Ctrl+Z).

After you have extracted the superclass, you can use a combination of the following techniques to complete the code reorganization:

- Add the name of the new superclass to the extends clause of any other classes that you want to extend the new superclass.

- Use the Pull Up feature to move methods from other classes to the new superclass. As with the Extract Superclass feature, you can move whole methods or merely create abstract declarations for the methods in the new superclass. See "Moving Class Members to Other Classes" earlier in this chapter.

- Use the Use Supertype Where Possible feature to change references in your code to the original class to the just created superclass. See the section "Changing References to Use a Supertype" that follows.

Changing References to Use a Supertype

You can use the Use Supertype Where Possible feature to change the code to reference objects of a superclass (or other type) instead of objects of a subclass. The operation only changes the reference in places where your code can accommodate such upcasting.

Typically, you'll use this refactoring operation to enable a single method to take as an argument different types of objects (all deriving from the same superclass).

This operation might be particularly useful after you have used the Extract Superclass feature.

To change references to a supertype, select the class to which you want to replace references and choose Refactor ➤ Use Supertype Where Possible. The Use Supertype Where Possible window opens, shown in Figure 6-21.

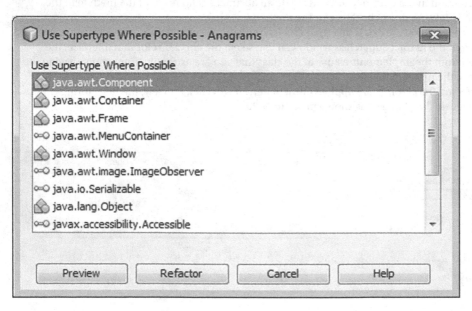

Figure 6-21. *Use Supertype Where Possible window*

In the list, select the class or other type that should be referenced instead of the type currently referenced.

If you click Refactor, the changes are applied immediately. If you click Preview, the Refactoring window appears with a preview of the changes, shown in Figure 6-22.

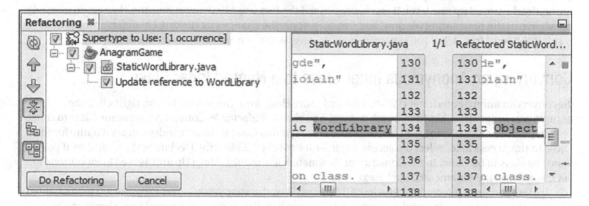

Figure 6-22. Refactoring window

In the Refactoring window, look at the preview of the code to be changed. If there is a modification that you do not want to be made, deselect the checkbox next to the line for that change.

Click Do Refactoring.

If you later find that the refactoring activity has done something that you want to reverse, you can choose Edit ➤ Undo (Ctrl+Z).

Unnesting Classes

As a project grows, you might find that some classes become tangled with a dense structure of inner classes that are hard to read and cannot be elegantly modified or extended. If this is the case, you might want to simplify the nesting structure and move some classes into their own source files.

The IDE has useful features for simplifying your code's nesting structure:

- Move Inner to Outer Level. This feature moves a class up one level. If the class is a top-level inner class, it is made an outer class and moved into its own source file. If the class is nested within an inner class, method, or variable scope, it is moved up one level.

- Convert Anonymous Class to Inner. This feature converts an anonymous inner class (that is, a class that is unnamed and has no constructor) into a named inner class (inner class that has a name and a constructor). This also makes it possible for other code to reference this class.

Moving an Inner Class Up One Level

To move an inner class up one level, in the Source Editor, right-click the inner class that you want to move and choose Refactor ➤ Move Inner to Outer Level.

In the Class Name field of the Move Inner to Outer Level window, set the name of the class. Select the Declare Field for the Current Outer Class checkbox if you want to generate a field in the moved inner class to hold the outer class instance and include a reference to that instance as a parameter in the moved class' constructor. If you select this option, fill in the Field Name text field with a name for the outer class' instance field. Click Next.

If you have deselected the Preview All Changes checkbox, the changes are applied immediately. If you leave the Preview All Changes checkbox selected, the Refactoring window appears with a preview of the changes.

In the Refactoring window, look at the preview of the code to be changed.

If you later find that the refactoring activity has done something that you want to reverse, you can choose Edit ➤ Undo (Ctrl+Z). Unless you have selected the Preview All Changes box, the inner class is immediately moved up one level. If you have selected the Preview All Changes box, the changes to be made are shown in the Refactoring window. You can then apply the changes by clicking Do Refactoring. If the result is different from what you expected, you can reverse the command by choosing Edit ➤ Undo.

Converting an Anonymous Inner Class to a Named Inner Class

To convert an anonymous inner class to a named inner class, from the Source Editor, right-click the anonymous inner class that you want to convert and choose Refactor ➤ Convert Anonymous Class to Inner.

In the Inner Class Name field of the Convert Anonymous Class to Inner window, enter a name for the class. In the Access field, select the access modifier for the class. Select the Declare Static checkbox if you want the class to be static. In the Constructor Parameters list, use the Move Up and Move Down buttons to set the order of the parameters. Click Next.

Unless you have selected the Preview All Changes box, the anonymous class is converted to the named inner class. If you have selected the Preview All Changes box, the changes to be made are shown in the Refactoring window. You can then apply the changes by clicking Do Refactoring.

If you later find that the refactoring activity did something you would like to reverse, you can choose Edit ➤ Undo (Ctrl+Z).

Quick Access to Keyboard Shortcuts

While Table 6-3 lists the keyboard shortcuts applicable to the refactoring tools, you can quickly access them all by right-clicking in the Java Editor and going to the Refactor menu, as shown in Figure 6-23.

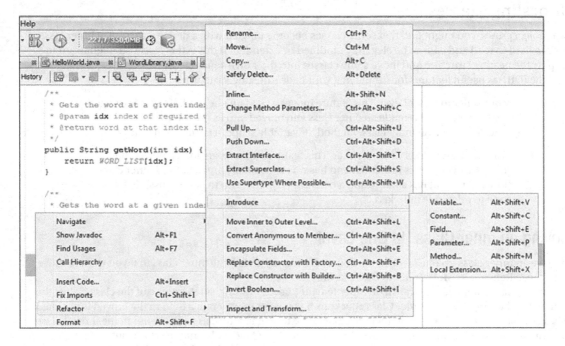

Figure 6-23. *Keyboard shortcuts for refactoring*

In the Options window, use the Keymap tab to change any of the keyboard shortcuts for the refactoring tools, as shown in Figure 6-24.

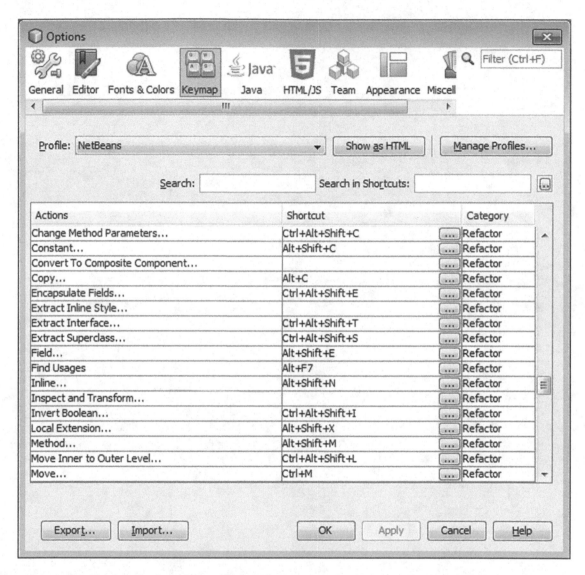

Figure 6-24. *Changing keyboard shortcuts for refactoring*

NetBeans presents quality issues and test results in a simple and detailed way, which allows me to stay focused on my primary task—writing code. I rarely ever need to use other tools besides NetBeans.

—Sven Reimers,
System Engineer, Airbus Defence & Space

CHAPTER 7

■■■

Testing and Code Quality

Testing an application is an integral part of the development cycle, while writing and maintaining tests can help ensure the quality of the individual methods and the code of the application as a whole. NetBeans IDE's integrated support for test-related frameworks, libraries, and related code-quality solutions is the focus of this chapter.

It is outside the scope of this book to compare the testing solutions. You will be introduced to different solutions in this chapter and learn how to work with them in the IDE. It is up to you to decide whether those solutions are applicable to the projects you're working on and determine how the solutions compare with each other. Also, be aware that you should read Chapter 6, "Analysis and Refactoring," in combination with this chapter, since code quality via testing described in this chapter and the analysis tools described in Chapter 6 have a certain amount of synergy and overlap.

Table 7-1 lists the solutions related to testing and code quality that you will learn about in the context of the IDE.

Table 7-1. *Frameworks Related to Testing and Code Quality*

Framework	Description
JUnit	The most widely established unit testing framework. If your requirements are limited to finely detailed unit tests with no dependencies between them, JUnit is an appropriate unit testing framework.
TestNG	A unit testing framework created some years after JUnit, enabling its developers to benefit from insights gained from JUnit. In particular, consider using TestNG if your requirements include dependencies and sharing of data (in this context known as "parameters") between unit tests.
Selenium	Selenium automates browsers. It is a testing framework centrally focused on automating web applications for testing purposes; for example, it provides lifecycle management for testing services.
Arquillian	Specifically focused on being an integration testing solution for Java EE applications, Arquillian picks up where other testing frameworks leave off. Arquillian handles the plumbing of container management, together with deployment and framework initialization. As opposed to "simple" module tests, Arquillian aims at testing projects in their runtimes with all the necessary resources available, specifically for Java EE environments, while tightly integrating with various other testing frameworks, such as those listed above.
Cobertura	A Java code coverage solution that informs you of the percentage of your application that is under test.
JaCoCo	A Java code coverage solution that informs you of the percentage of your application that is under test.
SonarQube	An open source platform to manage code quality. It was previously known as "Sonar".

Of course, many other testing frameworks and other related solutions exist in the Java ecosystem. However, the ones listed in Table 7-1 are most commonly used in combination with projects that are developed in the IDE. To explore testing frameworks and code quality beyond the scope of this chapter, you are recommended to investigate the Software Quality Environment (`sqe-team.github.io`), which aims to be a one-stop shop for a variety of code quality frameworks, as well as the EasyPmd (`github.com/giancosta86/ EasyPmd`) plugin, which was mentioned in Chapter 4.

JUnit and TestNG

In the IDE, the tools provided to help you with JUnit and TestNG are identical, so you will learn about them in this same section. Both are applicable to unit testing, that is, one or the other should be used when you are testing the individual methods in your applications.

In both cases, the starting point for working with these frameworks is to select a project in the Projects window and then go to the New File window (Ctrl+N). In the Unit Tests category, you'll find templates for getting started with JUnit and TestNG, as shown in Figure 7-1.

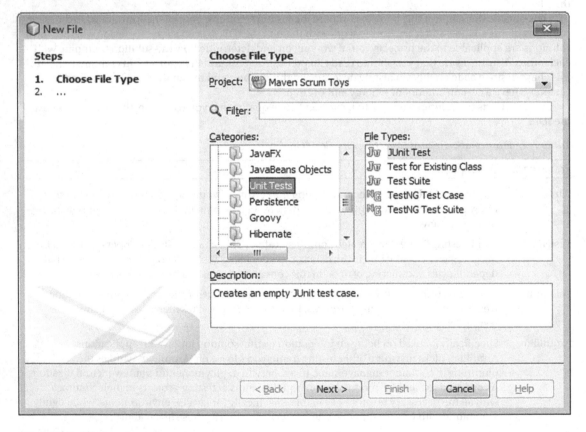

Figure 7-1. *File templates for unit tests*

Alternatively, right-click a Java file in the Projects window and choose Tools ➤ Create/Update Tests (Ctrl+Shift+U). The Create Tests window opens for the currently selected file, enabling you to choose either JUnit or TestNG. You can also use all the other settings found in the wizards in the Unit Tests category shown in Figure 7-1.

As shown in Figure 7-2, the wizards in the Unit Tests category are detailed and help generate exactly the kind of tests that you need. For detailed information on JUnit and TestNG, see their online documentation, at junit.org and testng.org, respectively.

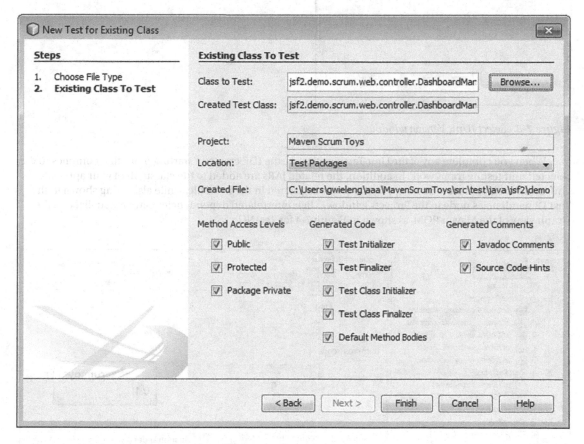

Figure 7-2. New Test for Existing Class wizard

For JUnit, when you click Finish in Figure 7-2, you are prompted to select whether the generated tests should be based on JUnit 3 or JUnit 4, as shown in Figure 7-3. With JUnit 4, your tests can use Java features introduced in JDK 5, such as generics and annotations. In order to use JUnit 4, the version of the JDK used by your application should at least be JDK 5.

Figure 7-3. *Select JUnit Version window*

When you complete any of the Unit Testing wizards, the IDE creates a starting point that complies to the selected unit testing framework. In addition, the related JARs are added to the classpath of your application and, in the case of Maven-based applications, are registered in the POM file, while also being shown in the Test Dependencies node in the Projects window. Their interrelated dependencies can be visualized in the Graph view of the Maven POM, as shown in Figure 7-4 for TestNG.

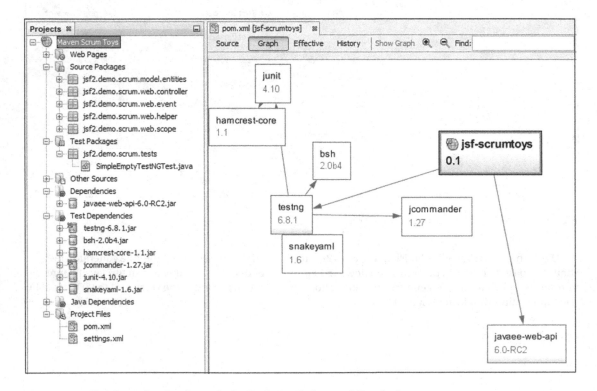

Figure 7-4. *Test dependencies shown in the Projects window and Graph view*

A useful related hint is that you can easily find a Java file's unit test file. Open the Java file in the editor, such as by double-clicking on it, and then press Ctrl+Alt+T. If a related test file exists, it will be opened. If the file does not exist, you will be prompted to create it.

Once you have written your tests, you can run them. To run all the tests in a project, right-click the project and choose Test (Alt+F6). To run the test file for a specific Java file, right-click the Java file and choose Test (Ctrl+F6). To run a specific test method, open the test file in the Source Editor, right-click in the signature of the method you want to test, and choose Run Focused Test Method.

The Test Results window (Alt+Shift+R) opens to show the results of the tests, as shown in Figure 7-5.

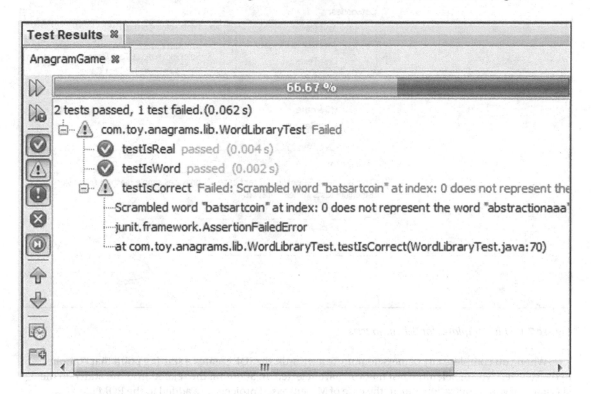

Figure 7-5. *Test Results window*

In the Test Results window, double-click an entry to jump to the related source code that defines the test method. The buttons along the left of the Test Results window let you rerun test methods and filter out items from the test Results window.

More features can be incorporated into your unit tests. For example, when you use the JUnitReport Ant task or the Maven surefire-report plugin, reports can automatically be generated in various formats during the testing process.

Selenium

Selenium (seleniumhq.org) automates browsers. It is a testing framework centrally focused on automating web applications for testing purposes, for example, it provides lifecycle management for testing services.

The starting point for working with Selenium is to select a project in the Projects window and then go to the New File window (Ctrl+N). In the Selenium Tests category, you'll find templates for getting started with Selenium, as shown in Figure 7-6.

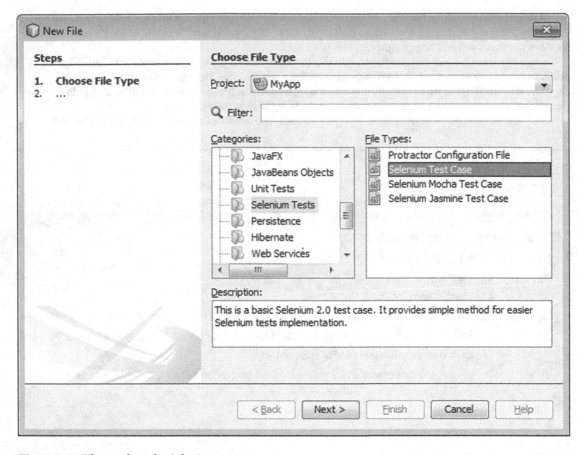

Figure 7-6. *File templates for Selenium tests*

When you complete any of the Selenium Test wizards, the IDE creates a starting point that complies to the selected type of Selenium test that you have selected. In addition, the related JARs are added to the classpath of your application and, in the case of Maven-based projects, are added to the POM file.

As is the case with unit tests discussed in the previous section, the Test Results window (Alt+Shift+R), shown in Figure 7-5, opens to show the results of the tests.

Arquillian

Arquillian (`arquillian.org`) is a testing framework of relevance to applications that use the Java EE platform. Arquillian is a community-oriented project started at and sponsored by Red Hat. It originated from the JBoss Test Harness, a utility created by Pete Muir from Red Hat, as the foundation of the test-related kits for JSR-299 (CDI 1.0) and JSR-303 (Bean Validation 1.0).

The basic idea behind Arquillian is that writing tests via JUnit and TestNG in a Java EE environment is a challenge. In Java EE environments, a variety of Java EE containers are available, such as WebLogic, GlassFish, JBoss, and WildFly. Each of the Java EE containers provide a variety of libraries and facilities. Arquillian enables you to seamlessly use the resources made available by specific Java EE containers and lets you switch between them easily. While part of its benefit is that it is container-agnostic, more generally Arquillian has as its focus server-side integration testing, while plain JUnit and TestNG were not created with server-side concerns in mind at all.

As with the other solutions discussed in this chapter, I don't provide more than the cursory introduction you have received thus far because there are a variety of other books and online articles available if you're interested in learning about Arquillian. The focus here is, as always, how to work with Arquillian in the IDE.

A useful starting point for writing tests for Java EE applications in Arquillian is the "hello world" Arquillian project by Aslak Knutsen, the Arquillian project lead, available at this location:

github.com/aslakknutsen/arquillian-example-helloworld

When you use Git to check out this project, you will have a Maven project. Go to File ➤ Open in the IDE and browse to the folder that contains the POM file. The IDE will let you open the project. Explore the project and notice the following characteristics common to all Java EE applications that use Arquillian:

- An `arquillian.xml` file is found in the `src/test/resources` folder.

- The POM file has a `dependency-management` section that registers dependencies for `arquillian-bom` and `jboss-javaee-7.0`.

- The POM file has a number of dependencies registered in the `dependencies` section, including `org.jboss.arquillian.junit`, `org.arquillian.container`, and `junit`.

- The `GreetingServiceTestCase.java` file shows that typical Java EE constructs such as the `@Inject` annotation can be used, while Arquillian annotations such as `@RunWith` and `@Deployment` help you to set up and initialize the lifecycle of your tests.

In the IDE, tests defined via Arquillian can be run in the same way as described in earlier sections, with the same kinds of results, as shown in Figure 7-7.

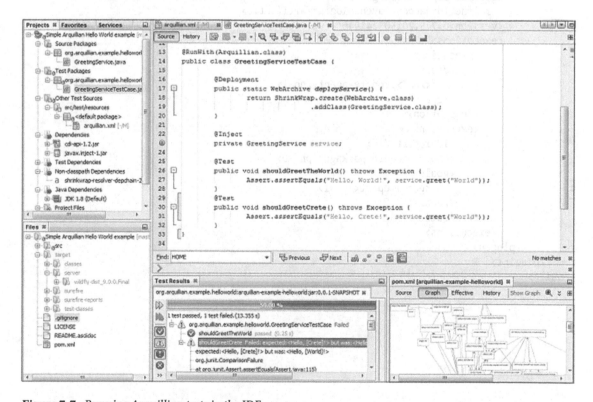

Figure 7-7. *Running Arquillian tests in the IDE*

In summary, the IDE is a natural environment for setting up, developing, and running tests with Arquillian.

Java Code Coverage

JaCoCo (eclemma.org/jacoco) and Cobertura (cobertura.github.io/cobertura) are free Java code coverage libraries for Java. The aim of these projects is to provide standard technologies for code coverage analysis in Java VM based environments. Their focus is on providing lightweight, flexible, and well documented libraries for integration with various build and development tools.

Features in Java code coverage libraries include code analysis of instructions, branches, lines, methods, types, and cyclomatic complexity. In the case of JaCoCo, analysis is based on Java byte code and therefore works without source files. Integration is simple and painless because everything is done via a Java agent based on on-the-fly instrumentation. Moreover, these solutions are framework agnostic in that they smoothly integrate with Java VM-based applications, such as plain Java applications, OSGi frameworks, web containers, and EJB servers. Various reporting formats are supported, including HTML, XML, and CSV.

In the IDE, integration with JaCoCo and Cobertura is included out-of-the-box for Maven applications. Setting up Java code coverage in a Maven application is as simple as adding the Maven plugin for JaCoCo to the POM:

```
<build>
    <plugins>
        <plugin>
            <groupId>org.jacoco</groupId>
            <artifactId>jacoco-maven-plugin</artifactId>
            <version>0.7.5.201505241946 </version>
            <executions>
                <execution>
                    <goals>
                        <goal>prepare-agent</goal>
                    </goals>
                </execution>
                <execution>
                    <id>report</id>
                    <phase>prepare-package</phase>
                    <goals>
                        <goal>report</goal>
                    </goals>
                </execution>
            </executions>
        </plugin>
    </plugins>
</build>
```

In the case of Cobertura, the Maven Cobertura plugin is registered as follows in the POM:

```
<reporting>
  <plugins>
    <plugin>
      <groupId>org.codehaus.mojo</groupId>
      <artifactId>cobertura-maven-plugin</artifactId>
      <version>2.7</version>
    </plugin>
  </plugins>
</reporting>
```

When one of the Java code coverage plugins (and not more than one!) has been registered in the POM of a project, the IDE immediately detects that the plugin has been added. Immediately, new menu items are made available for checking the code coverage of your Maven-based project. These menu items are available when you right-click a project to which the Java code coverage Maven plugin has been added to the POM, as shown in Figure 7-8.

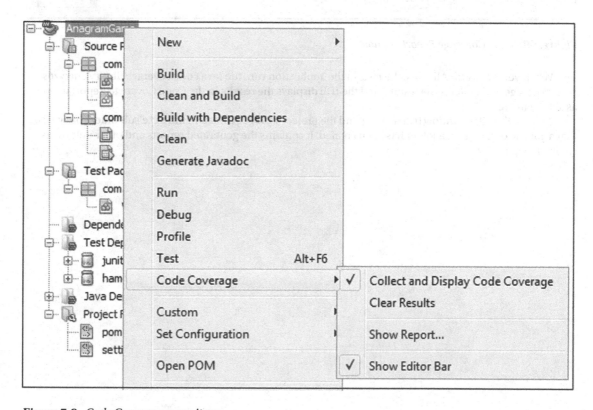

Figure 7-8. *Code Coverage menu items*

Select the Show Report menu item to open the Code Coverage Report window, as shown in Figure 7-9.

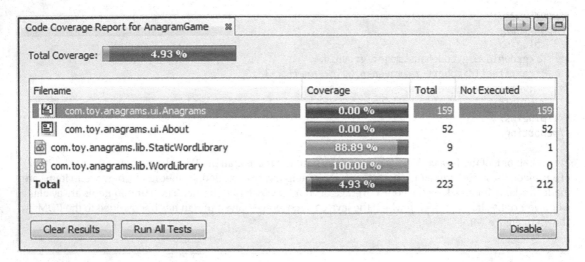

Figure 7-9. Code Coverage Report window

When you click Run All Tests, the tests in the application run, the Java code coverage library analyzes code coverage and collects the results, and the IDE displays the results in the Code Coverage Report window, as shown in Figure 7-9.

Next, in the Files window (Ctrl+2), expand the project's `target` folder. In the `site` subfolder you will see that a `jacoco` or `cobertura` folder has been created. It contains the generated reports and other output, as shown in Figure 7-10.

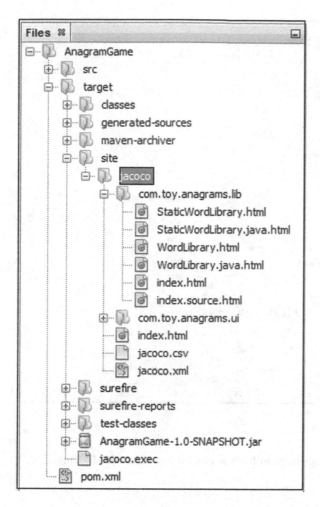

Figure 7-10. *JaCoCo reports and output in the Files window*

Each Java file, when opened in the editor, shows the statements that are being tested (green) and are not (red), as shown in Figure 7-11. The combination of Java code coverage libraries and the IDE helps to support test driven development because the green/red markings in the editor are continually updated, while you're writing new tests for the statements defined in the class.

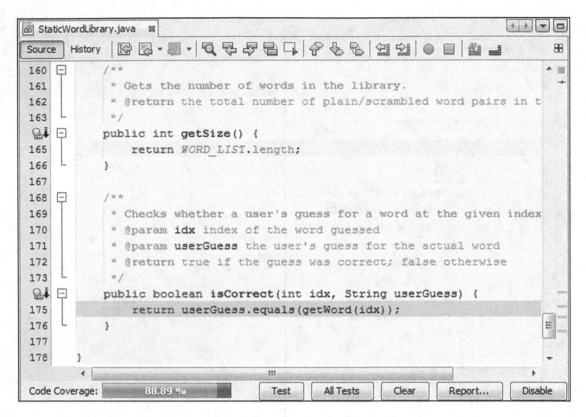

Figure 7-11. *Code coverage shown in Java source file*

To use comparable features for Ant-based projects, go to Tools ➤ Plugins and install the TikiOne JaCoCoverage plugin, as shown in Figure 7-12.

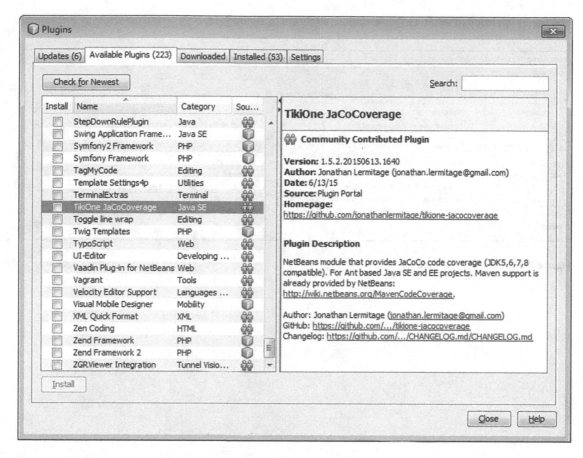

Figure 7-12. *Code coverage for Ant-based Java projects*

SonarQube

SonarQube (sonarqube.org) is an online open platform to manage code quality. It covers a range of areas of code quality, with a particular focus on code analysis relating to architecture, design, duplications, unit tests, complexity, potential bugs, coding rules, and comments.

In the IDE, integration with SonarQube is made available by the Radar plugin, which can be downloaded from the following URL: `github.com/hmvictor/radar-netbeans`. The source code of the plugin is found at the following URL: `github.com/hmvictor/radar-netbeans`. With the Radar plugin, you can retrieve issues from a SonarQube server or you can run a local analysis.

Once you have installed the Radar plugin, your access points to SonarQube are available when you right-click a Maven project and choose Get Issues from Server or Get Issues with Sonar Runner.

Issues are listed in the SonarQube window, as shown in Figure 7-13.

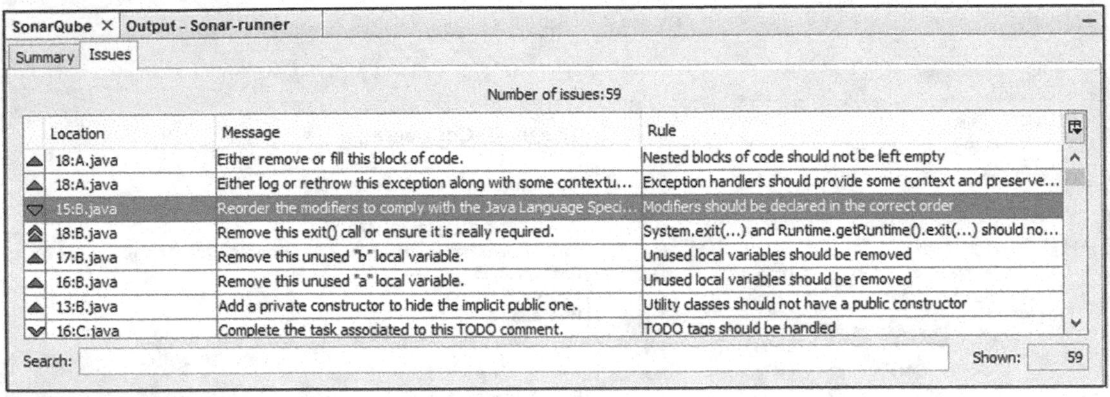

Location	Message	Rule
▲ 18:A.java	Either remove or fill this block of code.	Nested blocks of code should not be left empty
▲ 18:A.java	Either log or rethrow this exception along with some contextu…	Exception handlers should provide some context and preserve…
▽ 15:B.java	Reorder the modifiers to comply with the Java Language Speci…	Modifiers should be declared in the correct order
⬔ 18:B.java	Remove this exit() call or ensure it is really required.	System.exit(…) and Runtime.getRuntime().exit(…) should no…
▲ 17:B.java	Remove this unused "b" local variable.	Unused local variables should be removed
▲ 16:B.java	Remove this unused "a" local variable.	Unused local variables should be removed
▲ 13:B.java	Add a private constructor to hide the implicit public one.	Utility classes should not have a public constructor
⌄ 16:C.java	Complete the task associated to this TODO comment.	TODO tags should be handled

SonarQube × Output - Sonar-runner

Summary Issues

Number of issues: 59

Search: _____   Shown: 59

Figure 7-13. *SonarQube window*

Something I like about NetBeans is the continual striving for innovation. The NetBeans Debugger was the first to to deliver mixed language support (e.g., Java/JavaScript) and will soon help to deliver out-of-the-box debugging for any language built on top of the new Truffle framework by Oracle Labs, e.g., JRuby, FastR, Python, etc!

—Jaroslav Tulach,
founder of NetBeans

CHAPTER 8

■ ■ ■

Debugging

NetBeans IDE provides a rich environment for identifying bugs, troubleshooting bottlenecks, and optimizing the code in your Java applications. The built-in Java debugger lets you step through your Java code incrementally, while it is executing, enabling you to monitor aspects of the running application, such as the values of its variables, the current sequence of its method calls, the status of its threads, and the creation of its objects.

When using the Debugger, shown in Figure 8-1, there is no reason for you to litter your code with `System.out.println` statements to diagnose problems that occur in your application. (Use the "Inspect & Transform" functionality described in an earlier chapter to identify and delete all your `System.out.println` statements.) Instead, you can use the Debugger to designate "points of interest" in your code with breakpoints (which are not stored in your code, but in the IDE), pause your program at those breakpoints, and use the debugging tools in the IDE to evaluate the current state of the running program.

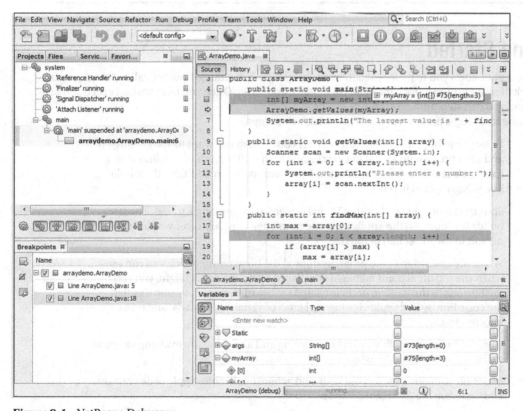

Figure 8-1. *NetBeans Debugger*

In addition, you can change code while debugging and dynamically reload classes into the Debugger without needing to restart the debugging session.

Table 8-1 lists the activities you can perform with the Debugger.

Table 8-1. Debugger Activities

Activity	Description
Step	Step through application code line by line, including JDK source code. When needed, you can step back to the beginning of a previously called method ("pop" a call) in the current call stack.
Execute	Execute specific chunks of code at a time, using breakpoints as delimiters.
Suspend	Suspend execution when a condition that you have specified is met, such as when an iterator reaches a certain value or suspend execution at an exception, either at the line of code that causes the exception or in the exception itself. When monitoring threads, you can suspend them individually or collectively.
Track	Track the value of a variable or expression or the object referenced by a variable by means of the "watch" feature.
Apply	Apply code changes on the fly and continue the debugging session.
Identify	Identify and analyze deadlocks.
Run	Individual or multiple debugging sessions can be run simultaneously.

Getting Started

The Debugger enables you to pause execution of your program at strategic points, called "breakpoints," and check the values of variables, the status of threads, and so on. Once you have paused execution at a breakpoint, you can step through code line by line.

Starting to debug a program consists of the following steps.

1. Determine the "point of interest" in your code where you want to start debugging and set a breakpoint at that line by clicking in the left margin of that line. A red icon appears in the left margin to mark the breakpoint. In addition, the whole line is highlighted in red.

2. Start the Debugger by choosing Debug Project or by pressing Ctrl+F5. The IDE builds (or rebuilds) the application and then opens up Debugger windows, by default in the lower half of the IDE.

3. When the execution of the program stops at the breakpoint, which you can see when the red breakpoint highlight is replaced by the green highlight, you can use the buttons in the toolbar, or their related keyboard shortcuts, to step through the code line by line while viewing the status of variables, threads, and other information.

4. Observe the program flow, while monitoring and analyzing the evolving values of variables in the Variables window.

5. Based on your analysis, fix your code and, where applicable, apply code changes and continue the debugging session.

Alternatively, instead of setting breakpoints, you can start to debug a program using two other tools that may be helpful in specific circumstances.

- Run To Cursor. In the Source Editor, click in the line where you want execution to initially suspend and click Run To Cursor in the toolbar. This command works for starting a debugging session only if you select a line of code in the project's main class or a class directly called by the main class in the main project.

- Debug File. If you have multiple executable classes in your project, there might be times when you want to start the debugger from a class different than the one that is specified as the project's main class. To start the debugger on a class other than the project's main class, right-click the file's node in the Projects window or Files window and choose Debug File. You can only start the debugger on a file if it has a main method.

Debugger Windows

When you start debugging a program, a variety of Debugger windows appear. The Debugger windows log the execution status of the debugged program, such as whether the code has stopped at a breakpoint. Tabs open in the Output window to log any application output, as well the output from the scripts the IDE uses when running the command.

The Debugger windows, such as Watches, Variables, and Call Stack, open as tabs and provide current information on the debugging session, such as the current values of variables and a list of current method calls. They are described in Table 8-2. You can also open individual debugging windows by choosing from the Window ➤ Debugging menu.

Table 8-2. *Debugger Windows*

Tool	Open With	Description
Variables	Alt+Shift+1	Displays all fields and local variables in the Debugger's current context and their current values. Fields are listed under this node.
Watches	Alt+Shift+2	Displays the names of fields, local variables, or expressions that you have placed a watch on. Although all of your watches are displayed no matter the current context, the value displayed is the value for that context (not for the context that the watch was set in). For example, if you have a watch on the this keyword, the this referred to in the Watches window will always correspond to the object referred to from the current method call.
Call Stack	Alt+Shift+3	Displays all method calls in the current chain of calls. The Call Stack window enables you to jump directly to code of a method call, back up the program's execution to a previous method call, or select a context for viewing local variable values.
Classes	Alt+Shift+4	Provides a tree view of classes for the currently debugged application grouped by classloader.
Breakpoints	Alt+Shift+5	Displays all breakpoints that you have set in all running debugging sessions.
Threads	Alt+Shift+6	Displays the threads in the current session. In this window, you can switch the context by designating another thread as the current thread.
Sessions	Alt+Shift+7	Displays a node for each debugging session in the IDE. From this window, you can switch the current session.
Sources	Alt+Shift+8	Displays sources that are available for debugging and enables you to specify which ones to use. For example, you can use this window to enable debugging with JDK sources.

Most of the Debugger windows display values according to the debugger's current context. In general, the current context corresponds to one method call in one thread in one session. You can change the context (for example, designate a different current thread in the Threads window) without affecting the way the debugged program runs.

Steps

Once the program is paused, you have several ways of resuming execution of the code. You can step through code line by line (Step In) or in greater increments, as shown in Table 8-3.

Table 8-3. *Debugger Steps*

Step Command	Shortcut	Description
Step Into	F7	Executes the current line. If the line is a call to a method or constructor and there is source available for the called code, the program counter moves to the declaration of the method or constructor. Otherwise, the program counter moves to the next line in the file.
Step Over	F8	Executes the current line and moves the program counter to the next line in the file. If the executed line is a call to a method or constructor, the code in the method or constructor is also executed.
Step Out	Ctrl+F7	Executes the rest of the code in the current method or constructor and moves the program counter to the line after the caller of the method or constructor. This command is useful if you have stepped into a method that you do not need to analyze.
Run to Cursor	F4	Executes all of the lines in the program between the current line and the insertion point in the Source Editor.
Pause	-	Stops all threads in the current session.
Continue	Ctrl+F5	Resumes execution of the program until the next breakpoint.

Executing Code Line By Line

You can have the debugger step a line at a time by choosing Debug ➤ Step Into (F7).

If you use the Step Into command on a method call, the debugger enters the method and pauses at the first line, unless the method is part of a library that you have not specified for use in the debugger.

Executing a Method Without Stepping Into It

You can execute a method without having the debugger pause within the method by choosing Debug ➤ Step Over (F8).

After you use the Step Over command, the debugger pauses again at the line after the method call.

Resuming Execution Through the End of a Method

If you have stepped into a method that you do not need to continue analyzing, you can have the debugger complete execution of the method and then pause again at the line after the method call.

To complete execution of a method in this way, choose Debug ➤ Step Out Of (Ctrl+F7).

Continuing to the Next Breakpoint

If you do not need to observe every line of code while you are debugging, you can continue execution until the next point or until execution is otherwise suspended.

To continue execution of a program that has been suspended at a breakpoint, choose Debug ➤ Continue or press F5.

Continuing to the Cursor Position

When execution is suspended, you can continue to a specific line without setting a breakpoint by placing the cursor in that line and choosing Debug ➤ Run to Cursor (F4).

Stepping Into the JDK and Other Libraries

When you are debugging, you can step into the code for the JDK and any other libraries if you have the source code that is associated with them registered in the IDE's Library Manager.

By default, the IDE does not step into JDK sources when you are debugging. If you use the Step In command on a JDK method call, the IDE executes the method and returns the program counter to the line after the method call (as if you used the Step Over command).

To enable stepping into JDK sources for a debugged application, start the debugger for the application and then open the Sources window by choosing Sources from the Debugging menu within the Window menu or by pressing Alt-Shift+8. Select the Use For Debugging checkbox for the JDK.

Limiting the Classes that You Can Step Into for a Library

If you are using a library for debugging, you can set a filter to exclude some of the sources from being used.

To exclude classes from being used in the debugger, begin by starting the debugger for the application. Open the Sources window by choosing Sources from the Debugging menu within the Window menu or by pressing Alt-Shift+8. Right-click the line for the library that you want to create an exclusion filter for and choose Add Class Exclusion Filter.

Type a filter in the Add Class Exclusion Filter dialog box. The filter can be one or more of the following:

- A fully-qualified class name.

- A package name or class name with an asterisk (*) at the end to create a wildcard. For example, you could type the following to exclude all classes in the `javax.swing` package: `javax.swing.*`

An expression with a wildcard at the beginning. For example, to exclude all classes that have `Test` at the end of their names, you could use `*Test`.

You can create multiple class exclusion filters.

To disable the filter, deselect the Use in Debugging checkbox next to the filter in the Sources window.

To delete a class exclusion filter, right-click the filter and choose Delete.

Backing Up from a Method to its Call

Under some circumstances, it might be useful for you to step back in your code. For example, if you hit a breakpoint and would like to see how the code leading up to that breakpoint works, you can remove ("pop") the current call from the call stack to re-execute the method.

You can open the Call Stack window to view all of the method calls within the current chain of method calls in the current thread. The current call is marked with the icon. Other calls in the stack are marked with the icon.

To back up to a previous method call, open the Call Stack window (Alt+Shift+3), right-click the line in the Call Stack window that represents the place in the code that you want to return to, and choose Pop to Here. The program counter returns to the line where the call was made. You can then re-execute the method. To back up to the most recent method call, you can also choose Pop Topmost Call from the Stack menu within the Debug menu.

Breakpoints

A breakpoint, shown in Figure 8-2, is a marker that you can set to specify where execution should pause while you are running your application in the debugger.

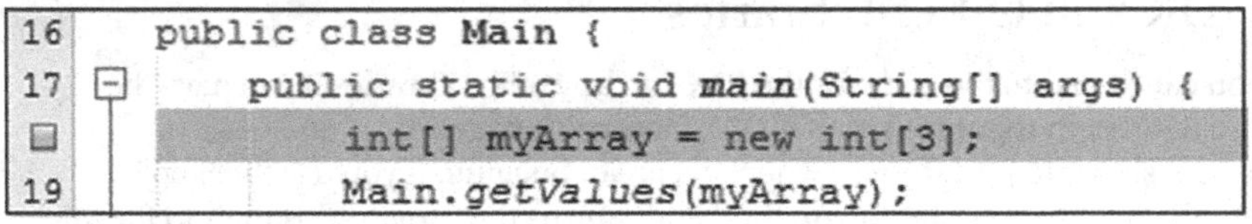

```
16      public class Main {
17          public static void main(String[] args) {
                int[] myArray = new int[3];
19              Main.getValues(myArray);
```

Figure 8-2. *Breakpoint*

Breakpoints are stored in the IDE, not in your application's code, and persist between debugging sessions and IDE sessions.

Setting Breakpoints

When execution pauses on a breakpoint, the line where execution has paused is highlighted in green in the Source Editor, as shown in Figure 8-3.

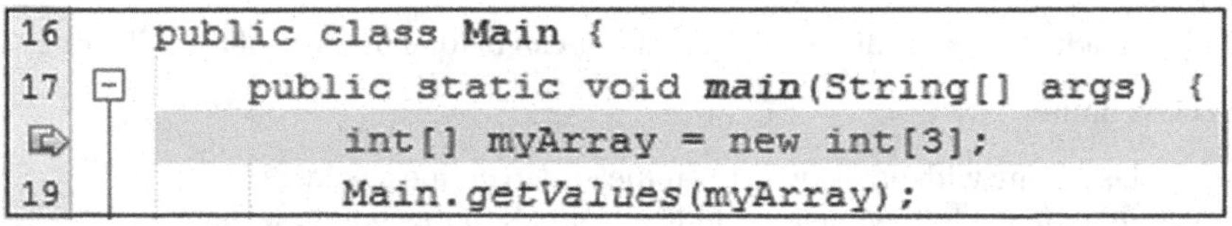

```
16      public class Main {
17          public static void main(String[] args) {
                int[] myArray = new int[3];
19              Main.getValues(myArray);
```

Figure 8-3. *Paused execution*

A message is printed in the Debugger Console, as shown in Figure 8-4, with information on the breakpoint that has been reached.

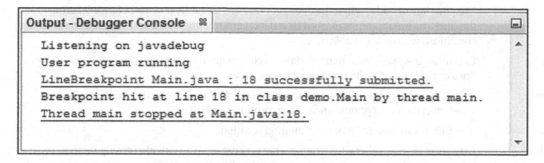

Output - Debugger Console
```
Listening on javadebug
User program running
LineBreakpoint Main.java : 18 successfully submitted.
Breakpoint hit at line 18 in class demo.Main by thread main.
Thread main stopped at Main.java:18.
```

Figure 8-4. *Message printed in the Debugger Console*

In their simplest form, breakpoints provide a way for you to pause the running program at a specific point. When the program reaches a breakpoint, you can perform the activities and diagnostic tasks listed in Table 8-4.

Table 8-4. *Breakpoint Tasks*

Task	Description
Monitor	Monitors the values of variables at that point in the program's execution.
Take Control	Takes control of program execution by stepping through code line by line or method by method.
Detect Change	Detects when the value of a field or local variable is changed (which, for example, can help you determine what part of code assigned an inappropriate value to a field).
Detect Creation	Detects when an object is created (which might, for example, be useful when trying to track down a memory leak).

You can set multiple breakpoints and you can set different types of breakpoints.

The simplest type of breakpoint is a line breakpoint, where execution of the program stops at a specific line. You can also set breakpoints on other situations, such as the calling of a method, the throwing of an exception, or the changing of a variable's value. In addition, you can set conditions in some types of breakpoints so that they suspend execution of the program only under specific circumstances.

See Table 8-5 for a summary of the types of breakpoints.

Table 8-5. *Breakpoint Types*

Type	Description
Line	Sets on a line of code. When the debugger reaches that line, it stops before executing the line. The breakpoint is marked by red background highlighting. You can also specify conditions for line breakpoints.
Class	Execution is suspended when the class is referenced from another class and before any lines of the class with the breakpoint are executed.
Exception	Execution is suspended when an exception occurs. You can specify whether execution stops on caught exceptions, uncaught exceptions, or both.
Method	Execution is suspended when the method is called.
Variable	Execution is suspended when the variable is accessed. You can also configure the breakpoint to have execution suspended only when the variable is modified.
Thread	Execution is suspended whenever a thread is started or terminated. You can also set the breakpoint on the thread's death (or both the start and death of the thread).

Line

To set a line breakpoint, as shown in Figure 8-5, click the left margin of the line where you want to set the breakpoint. Alternatively, click anywhere in the line in the editor and press Ctrl+F8.

```
16      public class Main {
17        public static void main(String[] args) {
            int[] myArray = new int[3];
19          Main.getValues(myArray);
```

Figure 8-5. *Line breakpoint*

When a breakpoint is created, it is automatically registered in the Breakpoints window (Alt+Shift+5), as shown in Figure 8-6.

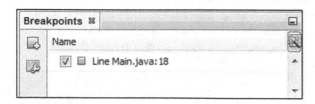

Figure 8-6. *Line breakpoint registered in the Breakpoints window*

To delete the breakpoint, click the left margin of the line where the breakpoint is defined or click in the line and press Ctrl+F8. You can toggle between a line breakpoint and delete by clicking Ctrl+F8 repeatedly. You can also use the Breakpoints window to delete breakpoints.

To customize a line breakpoint, right-click on the red icon in the left margin and choose Breakpoint ➤ Properties. Alternatively, use the Breakpoints window (Alt+Shift+5). In the Breakpoints window, right-click the breakpoint and choose Properties. The Breakpoint Properties window opens, as shown in Figure 8-7.

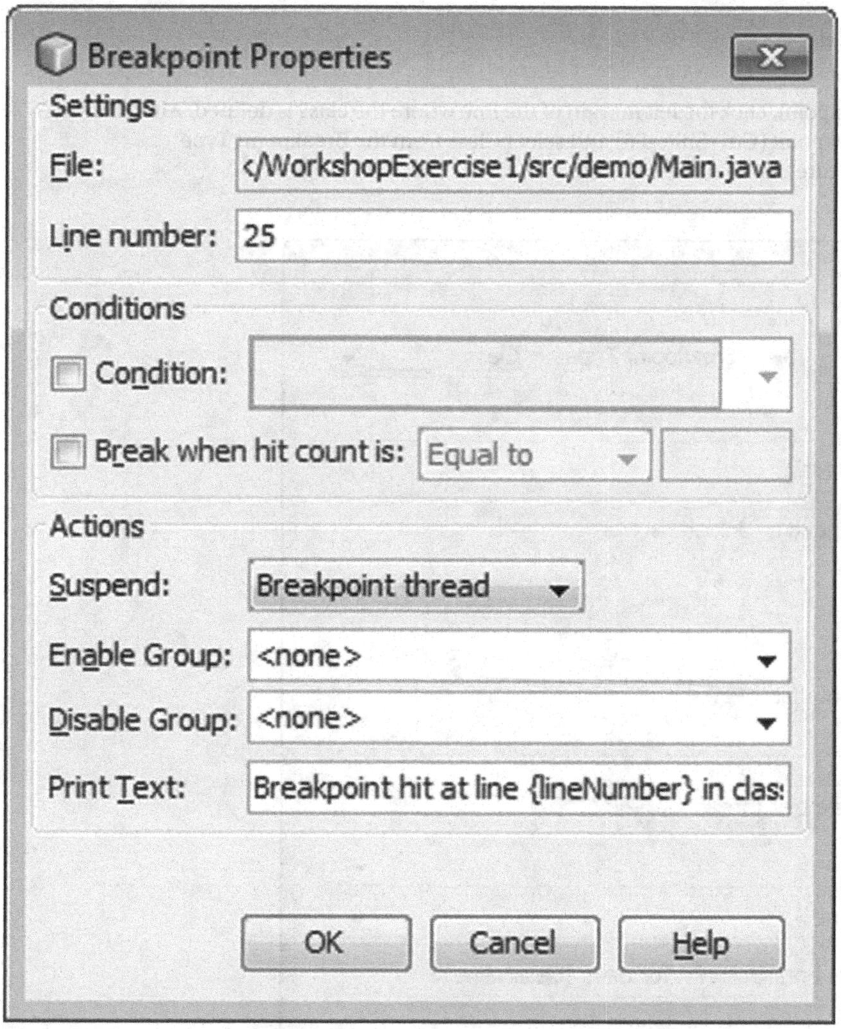

Figure 8-7. *Breakpoint Properties window*

Class

You can set a breakpoint on a class, as shown in Figure 8-8, so that the debugger pauses when code from the class is about to be accessed or when the class is unloaded from memory.

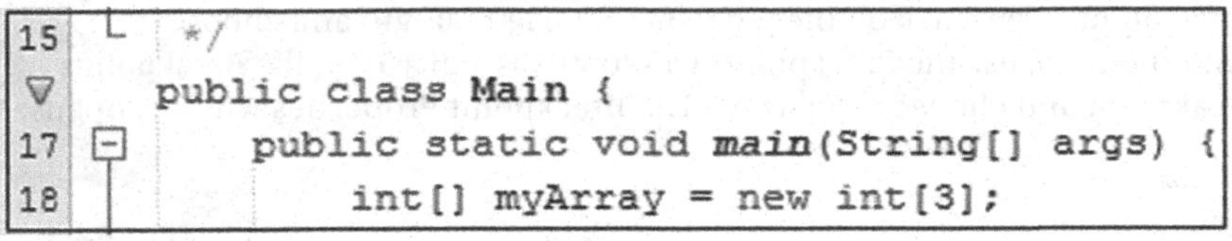

```
15  └   */
▽       public class Main {
17  ⊟        public static void main(String[] args) {
18                 int[] myArray = new int[3];
```

Figure 8-8. *Class breakpoint*

To set a class call breakpoint, click the left margin of the line where the class is defined. Alternatively, choose Debug ➤ New Breakpoint (Ctrl+Shift+F8) and select Class from the Breakpoint Type drop-down, as shown in Figure 8-9.

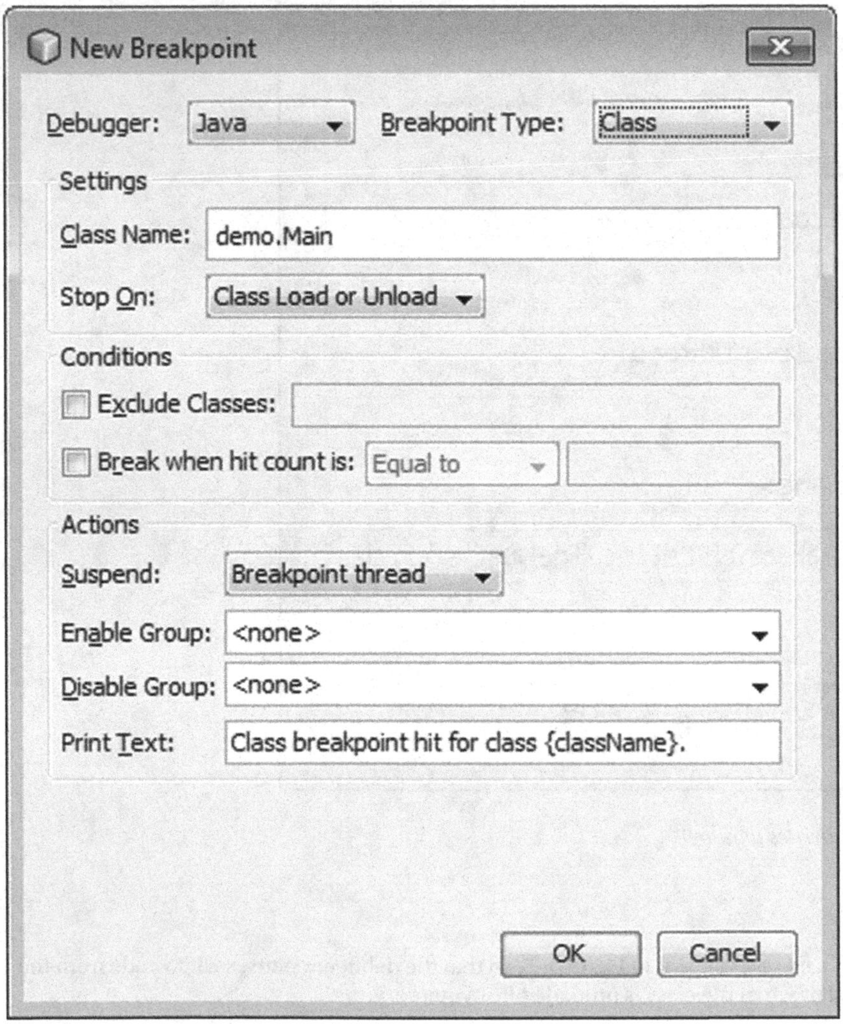

Figure 8-9. *Class breakpoint type in the New Breakpoint window*

The Breakpoints window displays class call breakpoints as shown in Figure 8-10.

Breakpoints
Name
Class Main load / unload

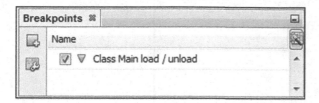

Figure 8-10. Class breakpoint registered in the Breakpoints window

Method

You can set a breakpoint so that the debugger pauses when a method or constructor is called, before any lines of the method or constructor are executed, as shown in Figure 8-11.

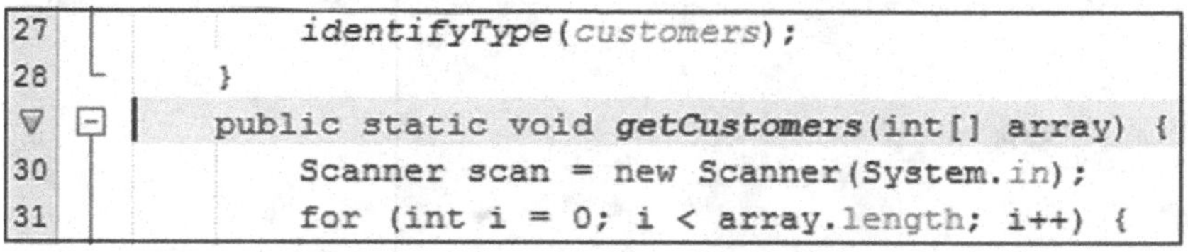

27 identifyType(customers);
28 }
public static void getCustomers(int[] array) {
30 Scanner scan = new Scanner(System.in);
31 for (int i = 0; i < array.length; i++) {

Figure 8-11. Method breakpoint

To set a breakpoint on a method or a constructor, click the left margin of the line where the method is defined. Alternatively, choose Debug ➤ New Breakpoint (Ctrl+Shift+F8) and select Method from the Breakpoint Type drop-down. The Breakpoint Properties window opens, with the Stop On drop-down set to Method Entry, as shown in Figure 8-12.

Figure 8-12. *Stop On Method Entry in the Breakpoint Properties window*

You can make the breakpoint apply to all methods and constructors in the class by selecting the All Methods for Given Class checkbox, which will cause the Breakpoints window to register all the methods in the class. The Breakpoints window displays method call breakpoints, as shown in Figure 8-13.

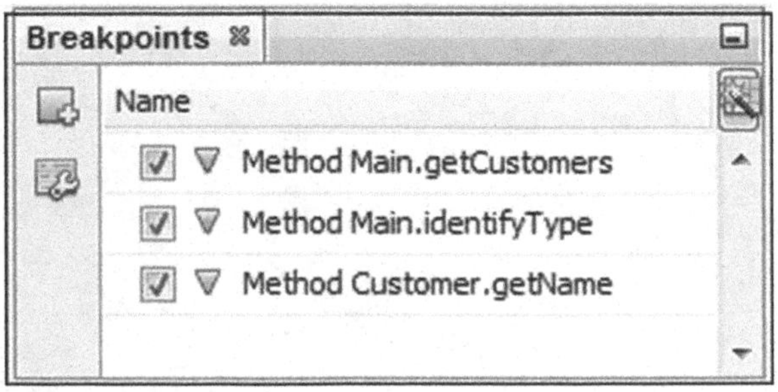

Figure 8-13. *All methods in class registered in the Breakpoints window*

Exception

You can set a breakpoint so that the debugger pauses when an exception is thrown in your program. To set a breakpoint on an exception, choose Debug ➤ New Breakpoint (Ctrl+Shift+F8) and select Exception from the Breakpoint Type drop-down. The New Breakpoint window opens, with the Breakpoint Type drop-down set to Exception, shown in Figure 8-14.

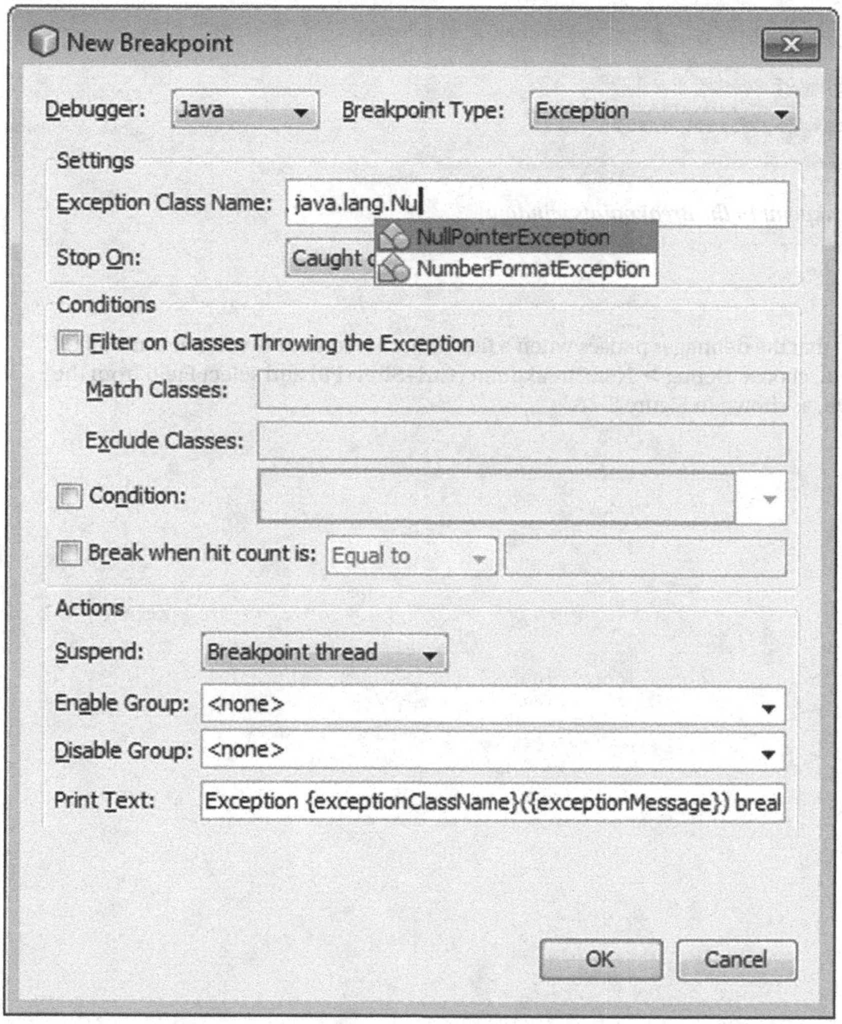

Figure 8-14. Exception breakpoint type in the New Breakpoint window

In the Exception Class Name field, type the exception class that you would like to set the breakpoint on. You can press Ctrl+Space to let the code completion feature help you complete the class name, as shown in Figure 8-14. In the Stop On drop-down, select whether you want the breakpoint to apply to caught exceptions, uncaught exceptions, or both.

The Breakpoints window displays exception breakpoints, as shown in Figure 8-15.

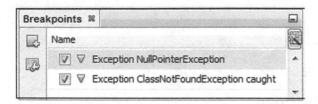

Figure 8-15. *Exception breakpoint in the Breakpoints window*

Field

You can set a breakpoint so that the debugger pauses when a field is accessed or only when it is modified. To set a breakpoint on a field, choose Debug ➤ New Breakpoint (Ctrl+Shift+F8) and select Field from the Breakpoint Type drop-down, as shown in Figure 8-16.

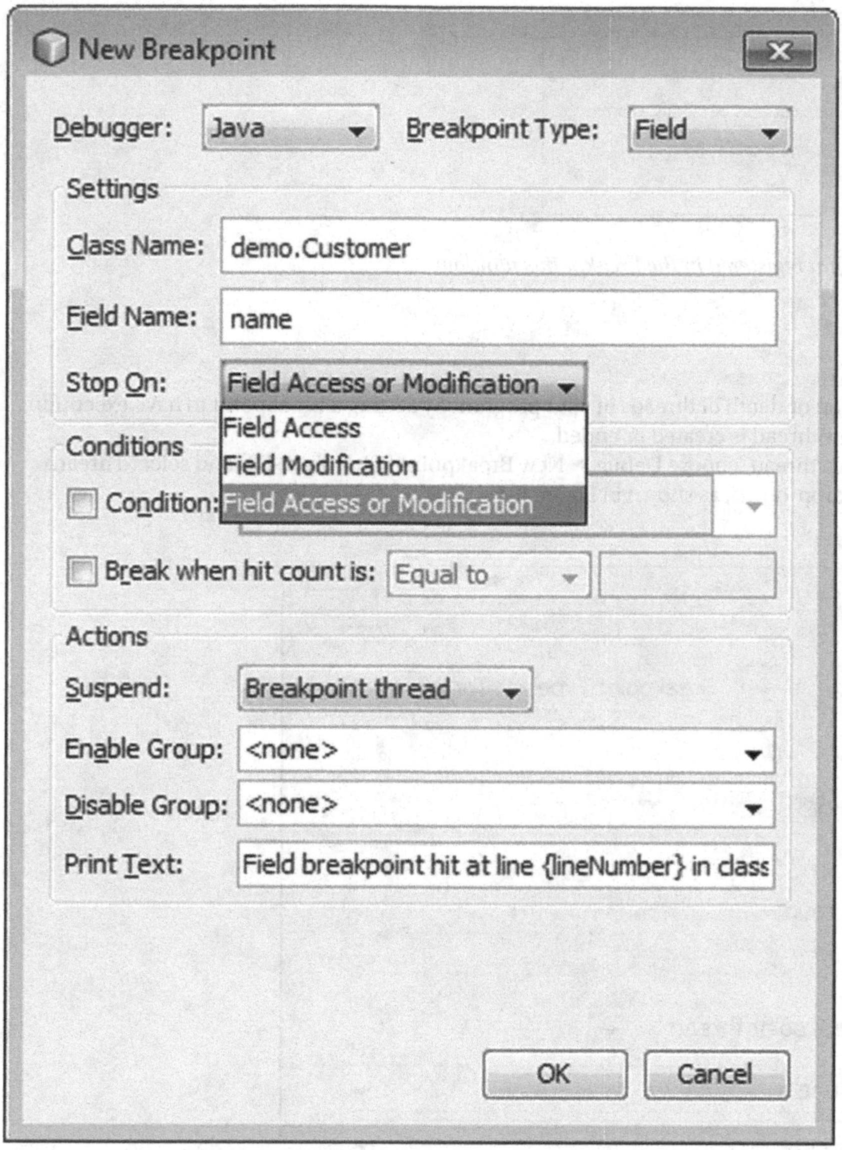

Figure 8-16. *Field breakpoint in the New Breakpoint window*

Fill in the Class Name and Field Name fields. Select an option from the Stop On drop-down. If you select Field Access or Modification, execution is suspended every time that field is accessed in the code. If you select Field Modification, execution is suspended only if the field is modified.

Most of the fields of the New Breakpoint window are correctly filled in for you if you have the variable selected when you press Ctrl+Shift+F8.

The Breakpoints window displays field breakpoints, as shown in Figure 8-17.

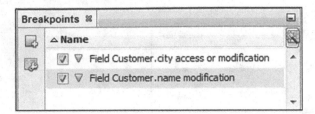

Figure 8-17. *Field breakpoint registered in the Breakpoints window*

Thread

You can monitor the creation or death of threads in your program by setting a breakpoint to have execution suspended every time a new thread is created or ended.

To set a breakpoint on a thread, choose Debug ➤ New Breakpoint (Ctrl+Shift+F8) and select Thread from the Breakpoint Type drop-down, as shown in Figure 8-18.

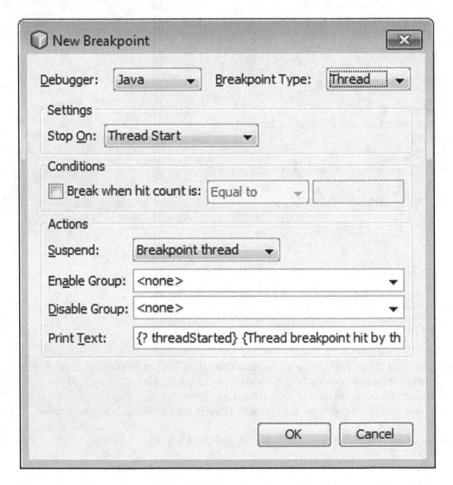

Figure 8-18. *Thread breakpoint in the New Breakpoint window*

In the Stop On drop-down, select Thread Start, Thread Death, or Thread Start or Death. The Breakpoints window displays thread breakpoints, as shown in Figure 8-19.

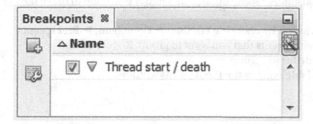

Figure 8-19. *Thread breakpoint registered in the Breakpoints window*

Managing Breakpoints

You can use the Breakpoints window as shown in Figure 8-19 and earlier figures to manage breakpoints in one place. You can define conditions on breakpoints and put breakpoints in groups, which can be very useful for testing designated sets of functionality. You can also temporarily disable breakpoints, as well as provide other customizations to the breakpoints from this window.

To open the Breakpoints window, choose Window ➤ Debugging ➤ Breakpoints or press Alt+Shift+5.

Conditions

You can set up a breakpoint to suspend execution only if a certain condition is met. For example, if you have a long *For* loop and you want to see what happens just before the loop finishes, you can make the breakpoint contingent on the iterator reaching a certain value.

Table 8-6 lists examples of conditions you can define on a breakpoint.

Table 8-6. *Example Breakpoint Conditions*

Task	Description
i==4	Execution will only stop on the breakpoint if the variable i equals 4 in the current scope.
ObjectVariable!=null	Execution will not stop at the breakpoint until ObjectVariable is assigned a value.
MethodName	If Method has a Boolean return type, execution will stop at the breakpoint only if Method returns true.
CollectionX.contains(ObjectX)	Execution will only stop at a breakpoint if ObjectX is in the collection.

To make a breakpoint conditional, open the Breakpoints window (Alt+Shift+5). In the Breakpoints window, right-click the breakpoint that you want to place a condition on and choose Properties.

In the Breakpoint Properties window, fill in the Condition field with the condition that needs to be satisfied for execution to be suspended at the breakpoint.

Groups

In some cases, you might have a several related breakpoints that you would like to be able enable, disable, or delete together. Or maybe you merely want to consolidate some breakpoints under one node to make the Breakpoints window less cluttered.

To group breakpoints, open the Breakpoints window by choosing Window ➤ Debugging ➤ Breakpoints (Alt+Shift+5). Shift-click or Ctrl-click to select the breakpoints that you want to group. Right-click the selection, choose Set Group Name, and enter a name for the group.

The breakpoints are grouped under an expandable node in the Breakpoints window.

Enablement

You might find it useful to keep breakpoints set throughout your application, but you might not want to have all of the breakpoints active at all times. If this is the case, you can disable a breakpoint or breakpoint group and preserve it for later use.

To disable a breakpoint or breakpoint group, open the Breakpoints window by choosing Window ➤ Debugging ➤ Breakpoints (or by pressing Alt+Shift+5). In the Breakpoints window, right-click the breakpoint or breakpoint group and choose Disable.

To delete a line breakpoint, click the left margin of the line that has the breakpoint or click in the line and press Ctrl+F8. To delete another type of breakpoint, open the Breakpoints window by choosing Window ➤ Debugging ➤ Breakpoints (or by pressing Alt+Shift+5). In the Breakpoints window, right-click the breakpoint and choose Delete.

Logging

If you would like to monitor when a breakpoint is hit without suspending execution each time the breakpoint is hit, you can configure the breakpoint to not cause suspension of execution. When the program reaches such a breakpoint in the code, a message is printed in the Debugger Console window.

To turn off suspension of execution when a breakpoint is hit, open the Breakpoints window by choosing Window ➤ Debugging ➤ Breakpoints (Alt+Shift+5). In the Breakpoints window, right-click the breakpoint and choose Properties to open the Breakpoint Properties window. In the Action combo box, select No Thread (Continue).

Messages

You can customize the text that is printed to the console when a breakpoint is hit in your code.

To customize the console message that is printed when a breakpoint is reached, open the Breakpoints window by choosing Window ➤ Debugging ➤ Breakpoints (Alt+Shift+5). In the Breakpoints window, right-click the breakpoint and choose Properties to open the Breakpoint Properties window. In the Print Text combo box, modify the text that you want printed. To make the printed text more meaningful, you can use substitution codes to have, for example, the thread name and the line number printed.

Table 8-7 lists the substitution codes.

Table 8-7. *Example Messages and Substitution Codes*

Substitution Code	Prints
{className}	The name of the class where the breakpoint is hit. This code does not apply to thread breakpoints.
{lineNumber}	The line number at which execution is suspended. This code does not apply to thread breakpoints.
{methodName}	The method in which execution is suspended. This code does not apply to thread breakpoints.
{threadName}	The thread in which the breakpoint is hit.
{variableValue}	The value of the variable (for breakpoints set on variables) or the value of the exception (for exception breakpoints).
{variableType}	The variable type (for breakpoints set on variables) or the exception type (for exception breakpoints).

Watches

As you step through a program, you can monitor the running values of fields and local variables.

The Variables window (Alt+Shift+1), shown in Figure 8-20, displays all variables that are in the current execution context of the program and lists their types and values.

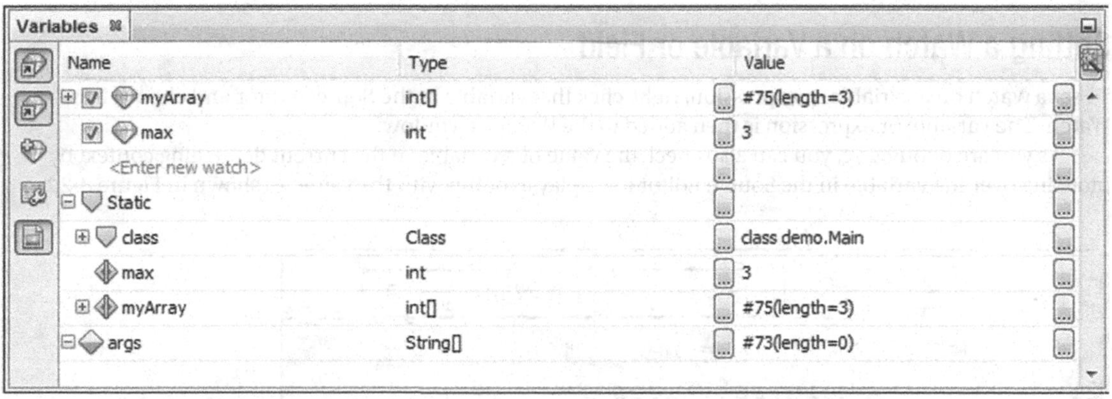

Figure 8-20. *Variables window*

If the value of a variable is an object reference, the value is given with the pound sign (#) and a number, which serves as an identifier of the object's instance.

You can jump to the source code of a variable by double-clicking the variable name.

You can also create a customized view of the variables and expressions that are relevant to your analysis by setting watches and viewing them in the Watches window (Alt+Shift+2), shown in Figure 8-21, which is distinct from the Variables window.

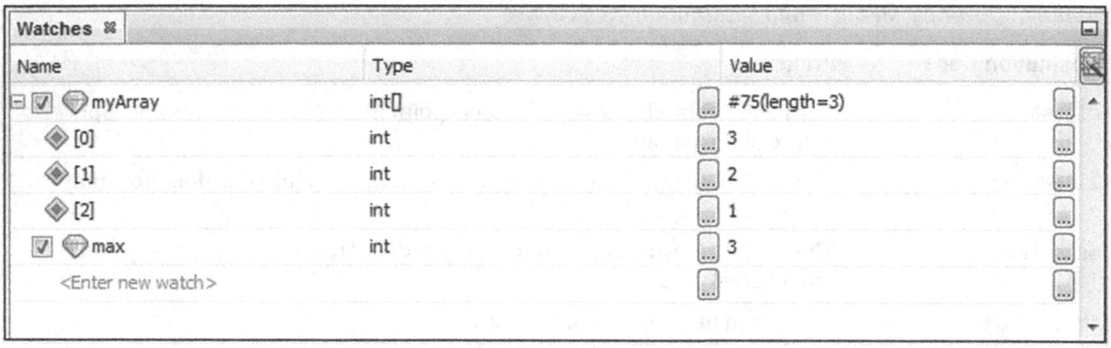

Watches
Name
Type
Value
myArray
int[]
#75(length=3)
[0]
int
3
[1]
int
2
[2]
int
1
max
int
3
<Enter new watch>

***Figure 8-21.** Watches window*

The Watches window is different than the Variables window in three ways.

- The Watches window shows values for variables or expressions that you specify, which keeps the window uncluttered.
- The Watches window displays all watches that you have set, whether or not the variables are in context. If the variable exists separately in different contexts, the value given in the Watches window applies to the value in the current context (not necessarily the context in which the watch was set).
- Watches persist across debugging sessions.

Setting a Watch on a Variable or Field

To set a watch on a variable or expression, right-click that variable in the Source Editor and choose New Watch. The variable or expression is then added to the Watches window.

As you are debugging, you can also check the value of a variable in the current debugging context by mousing over the variable in the Source Editor to display a tooltip with the value, as shown in Figure 8-22.

18
19
21
myArray = (int[]) #75(length=3)
myArray = new int[3];
Main.getValues(myArray);

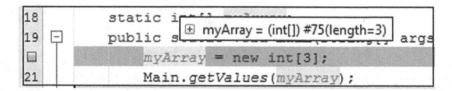

***Figure 8-22.** Tooltip showing value of current variable*

Monitoring the Object Assigned to a Variable

You can create a so-called "fixed watch" to monitor an object that is assigned to a variable, rather than the value of the variable itself.

To create a fixed watch, start a debug session and open the Variables window (Alt+Shift+1). In the editor, right-click the variable that you want to set the fixed watch for and choose Create Fixed Watch.

A fixed watch is then added to the Watches window. Since a fixed watch applies to a specific object instance created during the debugging session, the fixed watch is removed when the debugging session is finished.

Displaying the Value of a Class's toString Method

You can add a column to the Local Variables and Watches windows to display the results of an object's toString method. Doing so provides a way to get more useful information (such as the values of currently assigned fields) on an object than the numeric identifier of the object's instance from the Value column provides.

To display the toString() column in one of those windows, open the Local Variables window (Alt+Shift+1) or the Watches window (Alt+Shift+2). Click the button in the upper-right corner of the window. In the Change Visible Columns dialog box, select the toString() checkbox.

Changing Values of Variables or Expressions

As you debug a program, you can change the value of a variable or expression that is displayed in the Local Variables or Watches window. For example, you might increase the value of an iterator to get to the end of a loop faster.

To change the value of a variable, open the Watches window or Variables window. In the Value field of the variable or expression, type in the new value and press Enter.

Displaying Variables from Previous Method Calls

The Call Stack window (Alt+Shift+3) displays all of the calls within the current chain of method calls, as shown in Figure 8-23.

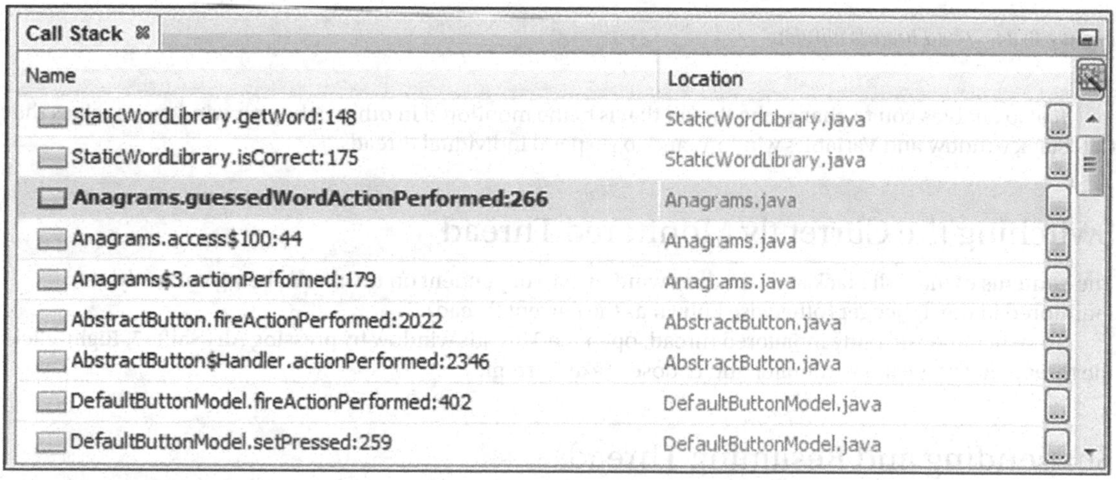

Name	Location	
StaticWordLibrary.getWord:148	StaticWordLibrary.java	
StaticWordLibrary.isCorrect:175	StaticWordLibrary.java	
Anagrams.guessedWordActionPerformed:266	Anagrams.java	
Anagrams.access$100:44	Anagrams.java	
Anagrams$3.actionPerformed:179	Anagrams.java	
AbstractButton.fireActionPerformed:2022	AbstractButton.java	
AbstractButton$Handler.actionPerformed:2346	AbstractButton.java	
DefaultButtonModel.fireActionPerformed:402	DefaultButtonModel.java	
DefaultButtonModel.setPressed:259	DefaultButtonModel.java	

Figure 8-23. *Call Stack window*

If you want to view the status of variables at another call in the chain, you can open the Call Stack window, right-click the method's node, and choose Make Current. You can also double-click on a method to make it current.

You can navigate through items in the call stack using the Make Callee Current (Ctrl+Alt+Up) and Make Caller Current (Ctrl+Alt+Down) commands.

Making a different method current does not change the location of the program counter. If you continue execution with one of the step commands or the Continue command, the program will resume from where execution was suspended.

Threads

The IDE's Threads window (Alt+Shift+7) enables you to view the status of threads in the currently debugged program, as shown in Figure 8-24.

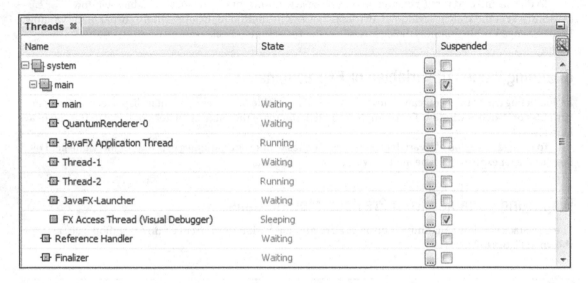

Figure 8-24. *The Threads window*

It also enables you to change the thread that is being monitored in other debugger windows, such as the Call Stack window and Variables window, and to suspend individual threads.

Switching the Currently Monitored Thread

The contents of the Call Stack and Variables windows are dependent on the thread being currently monitored in the debugger (otherwise known as the current thread).

To switch the currently monitored thread, open the Threads window by pressing Alt+Shift+7. Right-click the thread that you want to monitor and choose Make Current.

Suspending and Resuming Threads

You can suspend execution of a thread by right-clicking its node in the Threads window and choosing Suspend.

You can resume execution of a suspended thread by right-clicking its node and choosing Resume.

Suspending a Single Thread at a Breakpoint

By default, when your program hits a breakpoint, all threads are suspended. However, you can configure a breakpoint so that only its thread is suspended when the breakpoint is hit. Open the Breakpoints window by pressing Alt+Shift+5. In the Breakpoints window, right-click the breakpoint and choose Properties. In the Breakpoint Properties window, select Current from the Suspend combo box.

Isolating Debugging to a Single Thread

By default, all threads in the application are executed in the debugger.

If you would like to isolate the debugging so that only one thread is run in the debugger, make sure that the thread that you want debugged is designated as the current thread in the Threads window (Alt+Shift+7). The current thread is marked with the icon. Open the Sessions window by pressing Alt+Shift+6. In the Sessions window, right-click the session's node and choose Scope ➤ Debug Current Thread.

Identifying Deadlocks

The IDE can help you identify potential deadlock situations by automatically searching for deadlocks among all suspended threads. When a deadlock is detected, the IDE displays a notification in the Debugging window and identifies the involved threads, as shown in Figure 8-25.

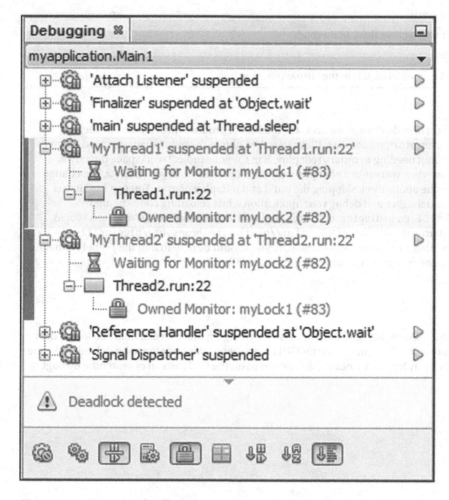

Figure 8-25. *Detecting deadlocks*

While you are debugging an application, choose Debug ➤ Check for Deadlock from the main menu to check the suspended threads for deadlocks.

Code Changes

Using the Apply Code Changes feature, it is possible to fine-tune code in the middle of a debugging session and continue debugging without starting a new debugging session. This can save you a lot of time that would otherwise be spent waiting for sources to be rebuilt and restarting your debugging session.

The Apply Code Changes functionality is useful for a specific set of scenarios, listed in Table 8-8.

Table 8-8. *Scenarios for "Apply Code Changes"*

Scenario	Supported?
Fine-tune the appearance of a visual component that you have created.	Yes
Change the logic within a method.	Yes
Add or remove methods or fields.	No
Change the access modifiers of a class, field, or method.	No
Refactor the class hierarchy.	No
Change code that has not yet been loaded into the virtual machine.	No

For a more advanced set of code change features, see the JRebel products provided by NetBeans partner ZeroTurnaround at `zeroturnaround.com`. JRebel is a JVM plugin that allows you to reload changes you make to your code without needing to restart/redeploy. It maps your project workspace directly to a running application, so that when you make a change to any class or resource in your project, the change is immediately reflected in the application, skipping the build and redeploy phases. You can use JRebel together with the NetBeans debugger and debug your application while reloading code changes.

To install JRebel in the IDE, go to `plugins.netbeans.org`, and look for the JRebel NetBeans Plugin, which can be downloaded from the following URL: `http://plugins.netbeans.org/plugin/22254/jrebel-netbeans-plugin`. Also, in most releases of the IDE, you should be able to find the JRebel NetBeans Plugins in the Plugin Manager, by going to Tools ➤ Plugins in the IDE.

GUI Snapshot

The GUI Snapshot, shown in Figures 8-26 and 8-27, is a visual debugging tool that can help you locate the source code for GUI components. The source code for GUI components can sometimes be difficult to locate and the snapshot provides a way for you to locate the code based on the GUI instead of searching through the code.

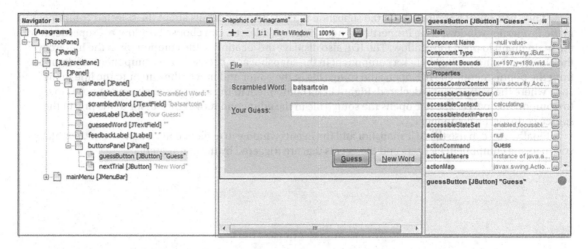

Figure 8-26. *GUI Snapshot for Java Swing components*

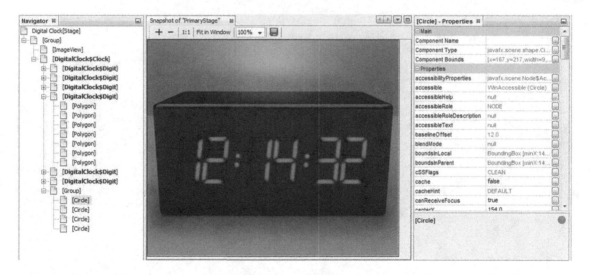

Figure 8-27. *GUI Snapshot for JavaFX components*

Once you have made a snapshot of the GUI, as explained in this section, you can select components in the snapshot and invoke tasks from a popup menu to view the source code for the component, show the listeners, and set breakpoints on components.

To make a GUI snapshot, choose Debug ➤ Take GUI Snapshot from the main menu while you are debugging a Java Swing or JavaFX application. When you choose Take GUI Snapshot, the IDE will take a snapshot of the GUI and will open the snapshot in the main window.

When you select a component in the snapshot, the IDE displays details about the selected component in the Properties window. If the Properties window is not visible, you can choose Window ➤ Properties from the main menu to open the window. The IDE also displays the location of the component in the hierarchy in the Navigator window. Right-click a component in the snapshot and choose Go to Component Declaration from the popup menu. The IDE opens the source file in the editor and moves the cursor to the line in the code where the component is declared. Right-click a component in the snapshot again and choose Go to Component Source. The IDE opens the source file in the editor and moves the cursor to the line in the source code for the component.

Finally, you can use the GUI snapshot and the Events window to explore component events, enabling you to locate component listeners and the events that are triggered by the components.

The memory profiler contained in NetBeans is the only profiler that gives you a true generational count. That one feature on its own is worth many, many times more than the free price of admission. Everything just works so I'm thinking about the code, not about the IDE.

—Kirk Pepperdine,
Java performance expert

CHAPTER 9

■ ■ ■

Profiling and Tuning

Imagine that your application, after months of development time and lots of testing, is finally ready for production deployment. The application goes live, and for the first few minutes everything seems a success. Suddenly you receive a phone call from one of your users telling you that he can't access the application because it appears to load indefinitely. Moments later you receive another call, and yet another. It seems as though your application doesn't allow concurrent access to enough users.

This is a nightmare scenario in which the application development team must make critical performance tuning decisions under extreme pressure, and they must make each of the changes to the production environment directly. Where do you begin in this situation? What could be wrong? Is the server configuration preventing enough connections for your production environment, or does the application code contain a bottleneck that forces the users to wait?

Many applications are not tuned for performance until after they're put into production. Unfortunately, many organizations do not deem performance tuning to be an essential part of their development lifecycle, but, rather, treat it as a triage step when things go wrong. To make matters worse, Java performance tuning can be like finding a needle in a haystack. The cause of performance issues can lie just about anywhere, from the application source code to a server configuration.

In this chapter, you learn about the profiling and tuning processes, in particular when related to the built-in NetBeans IDE Profiler, shown in Figure 9-1, and the Apache JMeter. You can use these processes when profiling and tuning your Java applications proactively, so that you can avoid the nightmare scenarios that can arise when applications have not been tuned or have been tuned incorrectly.

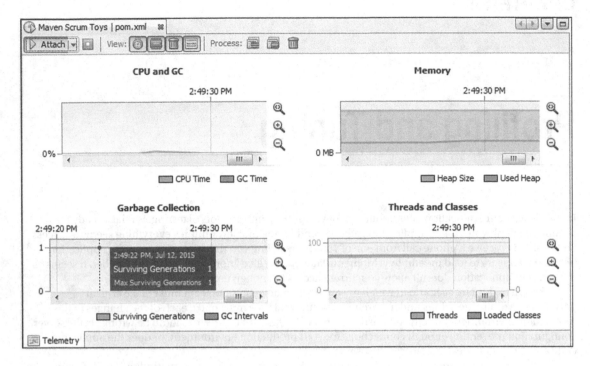

Figure 9-1. NetBeans Profiler

Performance Tuning

Performance tuning should be a standard part of your development lifecycle. Applications should be designed from the ground up with performance in mind. To be forward thinking about performance means to consider carefully all approaches for implementing application solutions, not simply the fastest approach or the one that is easiest to implement.

In particular, Java EE applications can be difficult to develop with performance in mind, especially because several points of contention in a Java EE environment can add performance burdens to an application. The top performance issues experienced in Java EE application environments tend to be related to configuration and environment issues. More often than not, the application itself is coded fine, while the application server to which it is deployed is not tuned correctly or is configured inappropriately for the application or the intended user capacity.

To properly tune for a production employment, perform the following steps in the order listed:

1. Application tuning

2. Server tuning

3. Java runtime tuning

4. Server operating system and platform tuning

Coding for Performance

There are many coding situations that might lead to performance overhead in a Java application. Because Java EE applications, in particular, are executed concurrently, they can lead to bottlenecks. Users might be competing for resources, such as web services and databases. Each remote call can add latency, while processes such as serialization can be CPU-intensive, causing further performance degradation.

With these kinds of issues in mind, you need to craft Java EE applications carefully, ensuring that proper resource handling is used. An application's performance tuning should begin with its source code. Even though the top causes of performance issues in Java EE applications point to the environment, proper coding can still play a key role in an application that performs well.

The following poor coding practices, among others, can lead to performance issues:

- Over-serialization and deserialization

- Overuse of finalizers

- Too much synchronization

- Not discarding unused variables

- Too many dynamic variables

- Rampant use of `System.out.println`

- Sessions that are not released when they are no longer needed

- Failing to close resources (for example, database and network connections)

Chapter 6, which discusses analysis and refactoring, should be helpful in identifying the areas of your code where poor coding practices such as the one listed here are found.

Performing code reviews is imperative for reducing problems that inhibit an application's performance. While poorly crafted code can slip past multiple developers, the more eyes that examine it, the better. In addition to code reviews, more than one individual should run performance and load tests against an application and compare the results of current tests to ones run previously.

Tuning the Environment

Many environmental factors can make a difference in the performance of an application. You should learn to understand the administrative console and command-line utilities for your application server, because you will spend a lot of time using them. For example, for GlassFish 4, the default domain is configured appropriately for testing purposes, while it is more than likely not appropriate for a production environment, at least not without further configuration.

Ensure that the deployment settings are configured appropriately for your application. If your application server allows auto-deployment or dynamic application reloading, be sure to disable those settings in a production environment, because they can have a significant impact on performance. Also take note of how often logs are written, because frequent logging can cause untimely performance issues. Consider the application server configuration settings for enterprise components, such as the Enterprise JavaBeans (EJB) container, Java Message Service (JMS), and Java Transaction Service (JTS). Always review default configuration settings and modify them to support a production environment. Configure server clustering to provide high availability through load balancing, when appropriate.

Remember to not treat your database as a black box for your data. Database access can become a point of contention for applications, either when querying a large dataset or when performing too many small queries. Whatever the case, have a contact number for your database administrator (DBA), who might be able to create an index on a database table, or perhaps even incorporate application logic into the database when it makes sense.

Planning for Capacity

Many tools can help you prepare an application for production release. Profiling tools can play a key role in an application's development lifecycle. Such tools can be used to forecast how an application will perform after it has been released into production under normal or heavy load.

In the context of NetBeans IDE, two such tools are the built-in NetBeans Profiler (henceforth referred to as "the Profiler") and the Apache JMeter plugin. Both of these features help you detect important runtime information about your application before it deploys to production, by giving you the ability to monitor data in relation to thread state, CPU performance, memory usage, and lock contention.

Getting Started with the Profiler

The Profiler is built into NetBeans IDE. No separate installation or enablement process is needed.

By using the Profiler, you can perform a specific set of profiling tasks against a project or file in the IDE. The profiling tasks that the Profiler performs are as follows:

- **Telemetry**: Application monitoring with graphs of CPU and memory usage

- **Methods**: Profiling method executions and times, also known as CPU profiling

- **Objects**: Profiling object allocations and sizes, also known as memory profiling

- **Threads**: Monitoring and visualizing thread states in a timeline

- **Locks**: Profiling and visualization of lock contention

Figure 9-2 shows the Configure and Start Profiling window, which is new in NetBeans IDE 8.1. It lists the profiling tasks discussed previously and gives you easy access points to getting started with them.

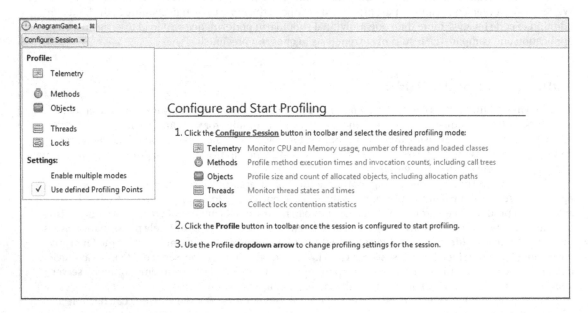

Figure 9-2. *Configure and Start Profiling window*

In the sections that follow, you will learn about each of the profiling tasks in turn.

Basic Profiling Terminology

Before continuing, let's quickly go through a set of terms you need to be familiar with when using a profiler. Though the NetBeans Profiler makes it easy for you to profile your applications even if you have never used a profiling tool before, it certainly helps to understand the basic terminology common to all profilers.

- *Profiler*. A tool that shows you the behavior of an application as it runs in the Java Virtual Machine (JVM).

- *Instrumentation*. The insertion of profiling methods (counters, timers, and so on) into the Java bytecode of your application. These methods do not change the logic of your program and are removed when profiling is stopped.

- *Profiling Overhead*. The time spent executing profiling methods instead of your application code.

- *Heap*. The memory pool used by the JVM for all objects allocated in your program by the new operator.

- *Garbage Collection*. The removal of objects from memory that your application is no longer using. Garbage collection is performed periodically by the JVM.

- *Memory Leak*. An object that is no longer in use by your application but that cannot be garbage collected by the JVM because there are one or more inadvertent references to it.

- *Self Time*. The amount of time needed to execute the instructions in a method. This does not include the time spent in any other methods that were called by the method.

- *Hot Spot*. A method that has a relatively large self time.

- *Profiling Root*. A class or method selected for performance profiling.

- *Call Tree*. All methods reachable from a profiling root.

Telemetry

The Telemetry task is useful for monitoring high-level statistics as your application runs. The Telemetry task does not perform instrumentation and, as a result, starts up fast because it imposes no profiling overhead.

To use the Telemetry task, right-click an application and choose Profile. In the Configure and Start Profiling window, click the Configure Session button and choose Telemetry. Click Profile. Alternatively, you can attach to an already running process via the Profile ➤ Attach menu items in the main menubar. The profiling session begins.

The Telemetry window opens, as shown in Figure 9-3.

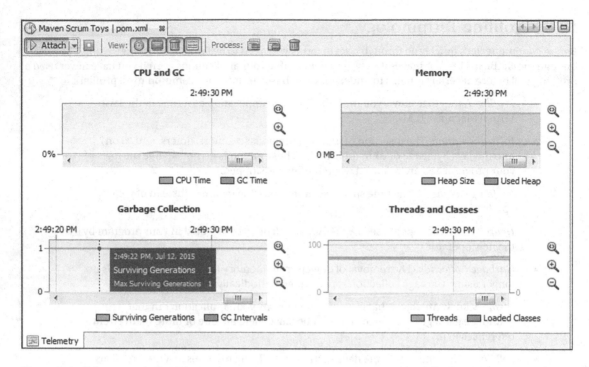

Figure 9-3. *Telemetry window*

The Telemetry task displays basic information about your application:

- Heap memory allocated

- Heap memory in use

- Percentage of time spent doing garbage collection

- Number of threads and classes that are running

The Telemetry window also displays the surviving generations on the heap. For an explanation of surviving generations, refer to the "Understanding Surviving Generations" section that follows.

Understanding Surviving Generations

To understand surviving generations, think about the JVM's garbage collection process. Every time the garbage collector runs, each object either survives and continues to occupy heap memory or is removed and its memory is freed. If an object survives, its age increases by a value of 1. In other words, the age of an object is simply the number of garbage collections that it has survived. The value of surviving generations is the number of different objects' ages.

For example, assume there are several objects that were all allocated when your application started. Further, there is another group of objects that were allocated at the midpoint of your application's run. And finally, there are some objects that have just been allocated and have only survived one garbage collection. If the garbage collector has run 80 times, all of the objects in the first group will have an age of 80; all of the objects in the second group will have an age of 40; and all of the objects in the third group will have an age of 1. In this example, the value of surviving generations is 3, because there are three different ages among all the objects on the heap: 80, 40, and 1.

In most Java applications, the value for surviving generations will eventually stabilize. This is because the application has reached a point where all long-lived objects have been allocated. Objects that are intended to have a shorter life span will not impact the surviving generations count because they will eventually be garbage collected.

If the surviving generations value for your application continues to increase as the application runs, it could be an indication of a memory leak. In other words, your application is continuing to allocate objects over time, and each object has a different age because it has survived a different number of garbage collections. If the objects were being properly garbage collected, the number of different object ages would not be increasing.

Methods

Use the Methods task when you want to obtain detailed information about which methods in your application are using the most CPU time. By means of the Methods task, you are analyzing the performance of your application. The Methods task will also tell you how many times each method has been invoked.

You can profile the entire application for performance of its methods or just parts of it. With the Methods task, the All Classes and Project Classes modes use sampling with very low overhead, thus they are the ideal choice for the initial performance analysis of a large application. (The same is true for the Objects task.) Choosing to profile the entire application means that all called methods will be instrumented. A large amount of instrumentation can slow performance dramatically, so this option is best used on smaller applications. An additional factor is that profiling your entire application will create a large amount of profiling information that you will have to interpret. The more you need to interpret, the greater the likelihood that something will be misinterpreted.

If you suspect that certain parts of your application are causing performance problems, profiling just those parts may be the best approach. If you choose to profile only part of your application, you must select one or more profiling roots.

Viewing Live Results

To use the Methods task, right-click an application and choose Profile. In the Configure and Start Profiling window, click the Configure Session button and choose Methods. Click Profile. Alternatively, you can attach to an already running process via the Profile ➤ Attach menu items in the main menubar. The profiling session begins.

The Methods window opens, as shown in Figure 9-4.

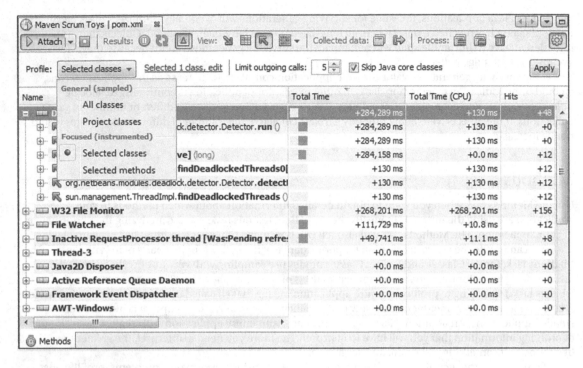

Figure 9-4. *Methods window*

This window displays all the methods that have been invoked at least once. The default sort order is by descending self time. The methods in your application that are using the most time are displayed at the top of the list. The amount of time used is displayed in two columns, one with a graph to show the percentage of time spent in each method and the other with text that displays the raw time value and the percentage. The number of invocations is also shown in the Hits column. The Profiler will update these values as your application runs.

To change the sort order, click a column header. This will sort the table in descending order using the values from the column. Click again to sort in ascending order. Click the Hot Spots button in the toolbar and the column will sort the table by package, class, and method name.

To find a specific method more quickly, right-click in the window and choose Filter or Find. Enter the method name and press Enter. The window displays the items that match your criteria.

Taking a Snapshot of Results

To see more detailed information, select Profile ➤ Take Snapshot of Collected Results (Alt+F2). The CPU snapshot window is displayed with the time of the snapshot as its title.

The CPU Snapshot window opens, as shown in Figure 9-5.

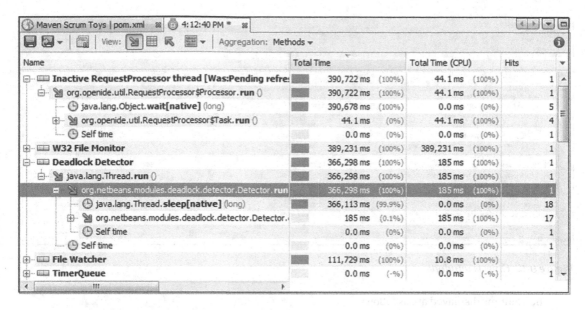

Figure 9-5. *CPU Snapshot window*

The CPU snapshot window shows the call trees organized by thread. To switch to the Hot Spots view, click the Hot Spot button in the toolbar.

When you click the Info icon in the top-right side of the tab, you will see a window showing a summary of the snapshot information: date, time, filter settings, and so on. The icons along the top of the snapshot window allow you to save the snapshot, control the granularity of the snapshot (method, classes, or packages), and search the snapshot.

Objects

Use the Objects task to track the heap memory used by your application. If the JVM is reporting an OutOfMemoryError while running your application, the Profiler can help you determine the cause of the problem.

Viewing Live Results

To use the Objects task, right-click an application and choose Profile. In the Configure and Start Profiling window, click the Configure Session button and choose Objects. Click Profile. Alternatively, you can attach to an already running process via the Profile ➤ Attach menu items in the main menubar. The profiling session begins.

The Objects window opens, as shown in Figure 9-6.

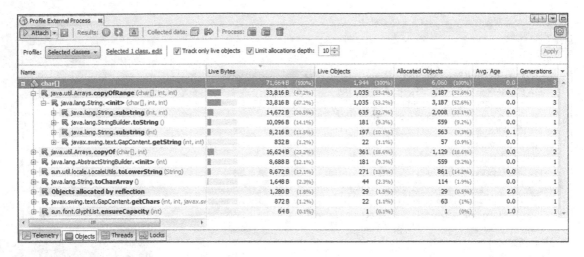

Figure 9-6. *Objects window*

The columns displayed are as follows:

- *Allocated Objects.* The number of objects that the Profiler is tracking. By default this number will be approximately 10% of the objects actually allocated by your application. Use the Limit Allocations Depth checkbox in the Profiler toolbar to change the default. By monitoring only a subset of the created objects, the Profiler can dramatically reduce the overhead it places on the JVM, which then allows your application to run at close to full speed.

- *Live Objects.* The number of the allocated objects that are currently on the heap and are therefore taking up memory.

- *Live Bytes.* The amount of heap memory being used by the live objects.

- *Avg. Age.* Average age of the live objects. The age of each object is the number of garbage collections that it has survived. The sum of the ages divided by the number of live objects is the avg. age.

- *Generations Calculated Using the Live Objects.* The age of an object is the number of garbage collections it has survived. The Generations value is the number of different ages for the live objects. For details on surviving generations, see the earlier section on this topic.

To change the sort order, click a column header. This will sort the table in descending order using the values from the column. Click again to sort in ascending order. Sorting the table by generations can frequently help identify classes that are the source of memory leaks. This is because an increasing value for generations typically indicates a memory leak.

Taking a Snapshot of Results

In order to see which methods in your application are allocating objects, you must take a snapshot. You also can compare snapshots with each other to identify differences and other areas of interest.

Use Profile ➤ Take Snapshot of Collected Results (Alt+F2). The CPU snapshot window is displayed with the time of the snapshot as its title.

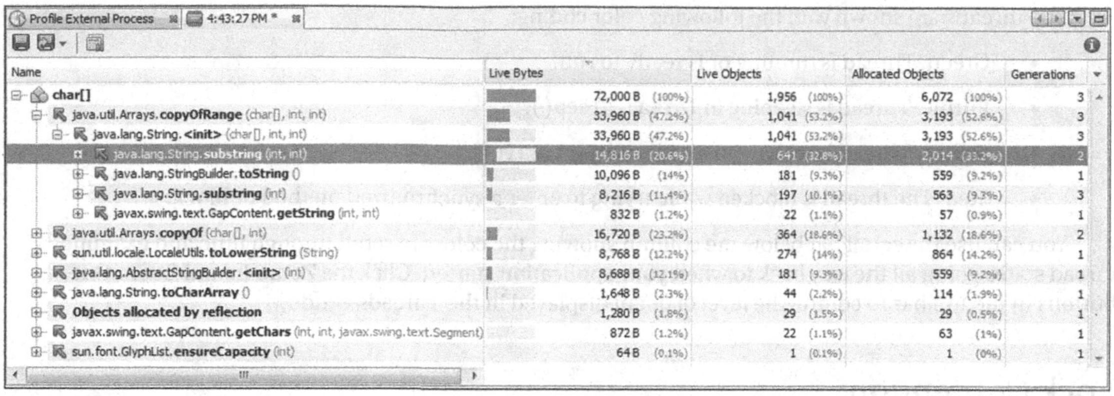

Figure 9-7. *CPU Snaphot window*

Threads

The Threads task is useful for monitoring the state of each thread as your application runs.

To monitor threads, right-click an application and choose Profile. In the Configure and Start Profiling window, click the Configure Session button and choose Threads. Click Profile. Alternatively, you can attach to an already running process via the Profile ➤ Attach menu items in the main menubar. The profiling session begins.

The Threads window is shown in Figure 9-8.

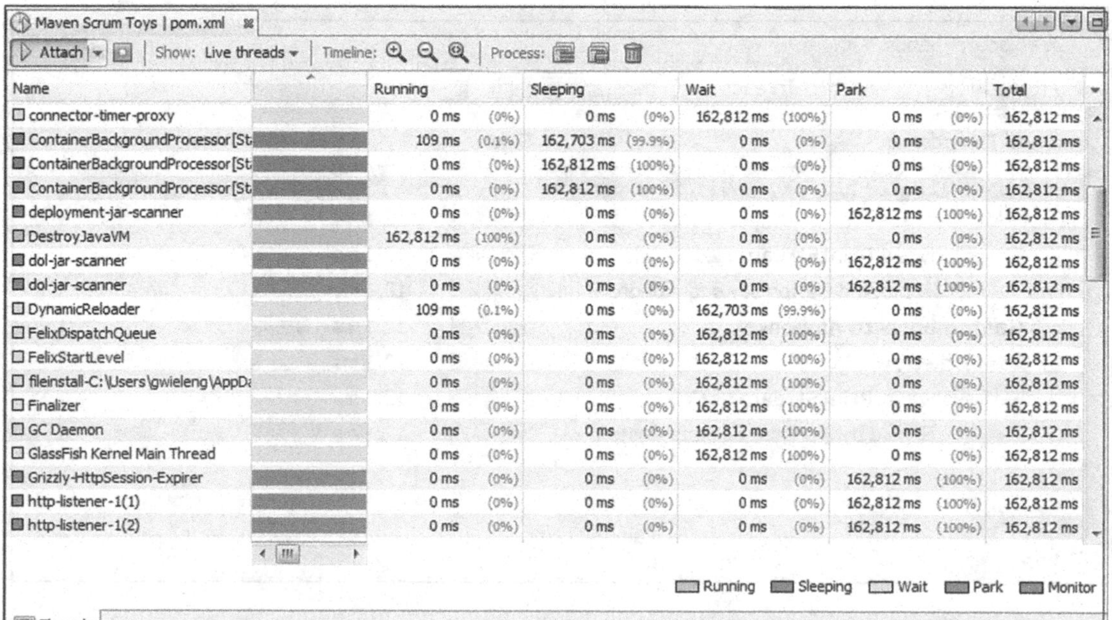

Figure 9-8. *The Threads window*

The threads are shown with the following color coding:

- Green. Thread is running or is ready to run.

- Purple. Thread is sleeping in `Thread.sleep()`.

- Yellow. Thread is waiting in a call to `Object.wait()`.

- Red. The thread is blocked while trying to enter a synchronized method or block.

You can use the scroll bar below the column showing the colors to scroll through time and examine thread states going all the way back to when your application started. Click the Zoom In and Zoom Out buttons in the toolbar to control the level of detail displayed in the Threads window.

Lock Contention

Lock contentions occur when a thread tries to acquire a lock while another thread is holding it, forcing it to wait.

Lock contentions kill any possible performance gains you may have made by using multiple cores in parallel, since you are organizing the work sequentially by using locks. In a worst-case scenario, only one thread will run.

The Lock Contention window displays detailed information about lock contention. It displays an analysis of performance bottlenecks, which can help you identify the responsible thread.

To identify lock contentions, right-click an application and choose Profile. In the Configure and Start Profiling window, click the Configure Session button and choose Lock Contention. Click Profile. Alternatively, you can attach to an already running process via the Profile ➤ Attach menu items in the main menubar. The profiling session begins.

The Lock Contention window is shown in Figure 9-9.

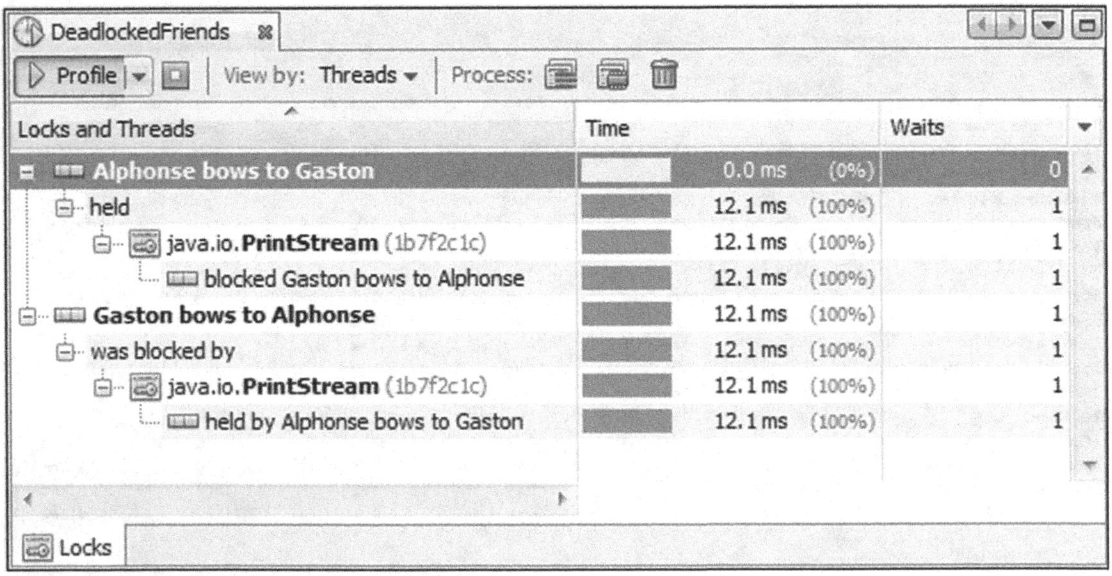

Figure 9-9. Lock Contention window

The lock contention analysis shown in Figure 9-9 applies to the Deadlock example discussed at this URL in the *Java Tutorial*: docs.oracle.com/javase/tutorial/essential/concurrency/deadlock.html.

Attaching the Profiler to External Processes

The NetBeans Profiler can profile applications that are not started by the IDE. In other words, it can be attached to a JVM. To use this feature, select Profile ➤ Attach to External Process and click Attach in the Profile External Process. The Attach Settings window opens, as shown in Figure 9-10.

Figure 9-10. *The Attach Settings window*

The Attach Settings window lets you select a running application for profiling. Alternatively, you can attach the Profiler to a manually started Java process, either locally or remotely.

Getting Started with Apache JMeter

One of the most problematic performance concerns in the Java EE application environment is user capacity. How many users can access the application at the same time? In the development environment, this question is impossible to answer because so many variables are at play. Even if the development environment is configured in exactly the same way as the production environment, inconsistencies between the production and development environments almost always occur. More often than not, user capacity testing can become a game of chance.

The Apache JMeter tool (jmeter.apache.org) can be helpful in this context. Apache JMeter is a Java application that measures performance and load testing. The IDE integrates well with Apache JMeter and, once you have installed the Apache JMeter plugin, you will not need to install Apache JMeter, nor will you need to open it manually.

To get started with Apache JMeter in the IDE, go to Tools ➤ Plugins and install the plugin, as shown in Figure 9-11.

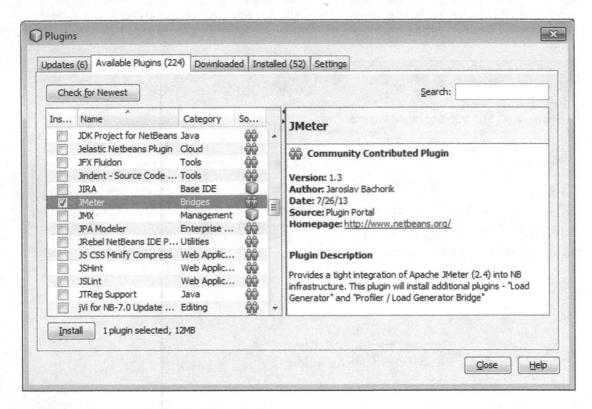

Figure 9-11. *Installing the Apache JMeter plugin*

Using Apache JMeter

Once you have installed the Apache JMeter plugin in the IDE, use the New File window (Ctrl+N) to create JMeter plans, as shown in Figure 9-12.

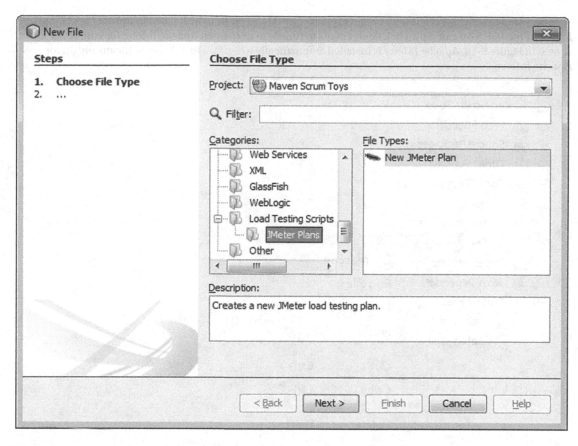

Figure 9-12. *JMeter Plan in the New File window*

To run JMeter tests as part of the build, you can register the Maven JMeter plugin (jmeter.lazerycode.com) in your POM, using the XML entries shown here.

```
<build>
    <plugins>
        <plugin>
            <groupId>com.lazerycode.jmeter</groupId>
            <artifactId>jmeter-maven-plugin</artifactId>
            <version>1.10.1</version>
            <executions>
                <execution>
                    <id>jmeter-tests</id>
                    <phase>verify</phase>
                    <goals>
                        <goal>jmeter</goal>
                    </goals>
                </execution>
            </executions>
        </plugin>
    </plugins>
</build>
```

Be aware that the Maven JMeter plugin expects your JMeter plans to be located in the `src/test/jmeter` folder. In the IDE, you can right-click JMeter plans to run them or to open Apache JMeter for editing, as shown in Figure 9-13. Apache JMeter is installed automatically when you install the NetBeans plugin for Apache JMeter.

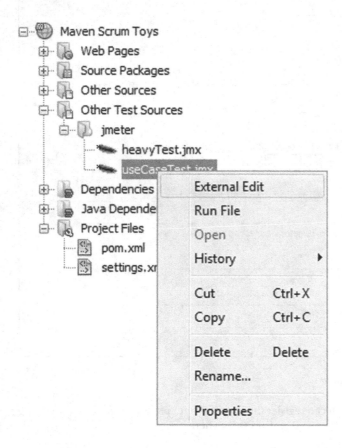

Figure 9-13. Menu items for editing and running JMeter plans

You can perform basic editing of JMeter plans without starting up Apache JMeter. Simply click Properties, which is the last menu item in the list as shown in Figure 9-13. This will open a Properties window, where you can change basic settings such as the number of users and the target server.

Versioning control systems such as Git can appear as complex as a programming language. The integration of Git into NetBeans reduces the complexity so the programmer and my students can get the job done.

—Ken Fogel,
Chair, Computer Science Technology, Dawson College, Canada

CHAPTER 10

■ ■ ■

Versioning

Using a version control system (VCS) to share your projects and integrate contributions from multiple developers is one of the most important parts of working in a group development environment. In NetBeans IDE, version control functionality is integrated right into your daily workflow, so that you do not have to keep switching to the command line or an external tool to perform updates and commit local changes.

You can choose to share just your sources or to share the complete NetBeans projects with which you are working. When you check the NetBeans project, that is, NetBeans metadata, into the repository, other developers who are working on the project in the IDE do not have to go through the trouble of setting up the projects themselves. They can just check out the projects and start working immediately.

Version control support in the IDE provides:

- Display of versioning status in the IDE.

- Ability to run versioning commands on files from within the IDE.

- Tools to help you check in changes to the repository and merge between branches.

- Advanced tools for searching file version history and viewing differences between file revisions.

The IDE provides its most comprehensive support for Git (`git-scm.com`), which is currently the most popular and widely used versioning system. Its support for Mercurial and Subversion is comparable to its support for Git, while plugins exist for CVS, ClearCase, and Perforce. The focus of this chapter is on Git, but if you are using Mercurial, Subversion, CVS, ClearCase, or Perforce, in most cases the commands and settings described here are similar.

Git is a free and open source distributed version control system designed to handle everything from small to large projects with speed and efficiency. Every Git clone is a full-fledged repository with complete history and full revision tracking capabilities, not dependent on network access or a central server. Branching and merging are fast and easy to do and Git is used for version control of files and groups of folders and files, such as NetBeans projects.

Setting Up Git in the IDE

No setup is necessary to work with files in Git. No additional plugins are required to be installed, though the Git Toolbar plugin can be very useful in providing access to the frequently used Git actions: `plugins.netbeans.org/plugin/51604/git-toolbar`.

Whenever you access files that are in a Git repository, the IDE offers the full range of Git commands and status display for the files. You can tell that a directory or project is in a Git working directory by right-clicking the project and choosing Git. Projects that are in a Git repository also display a blue repository icon next to the project name.

The IDE helps you with every step of working with Git repositories. However, the assumption is that you have an actual Git repository created somewhere, such as at GitHub (github.com). Once you have created a Git repository—on the Internet such as GitHub or locally—you're ready to get started with the instructions that follow.

Initializing a Git Repository

To initialize a Git repository from existing files that are not in source control yet, you need to go to the Projects window, select an unversioned project, and right-click the project name. In the right-click popup menu, choose Versioning ➤ Initialize Git Repository, as shown in Figure 10-1.

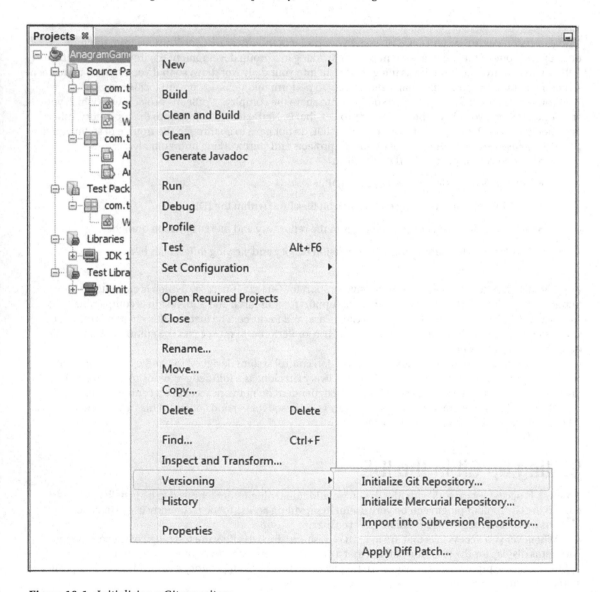

Figure 10-1. *Initializing a Git repository*

Alternatively, in the main menu, choose Team ➤ Git ➤ Initialize.

Specify the path to the repository where you are going to store your versioned files. You can do this by using the Initialize a Git Repository window or by clicking Browse and then browsing for the directory required.

A .git subfolder is created in the folder you specify, which is your NetBeans project folder by default. This is your local Git repository where all the data of your project snapshots are stored. Git starts versioning all files in the folder you specified. You can open Window ➤ Output ➤ Output to view the IDE's report about the progress of the repository creation under your local working directory, as shown in Figure 10-2.

```
Output - AnagramGame - C:\Users\gwieleng\aaa\AnagramGame  ✖           ▬

==[IDE]== Jul 15, 2015 10:49:03 PM Initializing ...          ▲
Initializing repository
Creating git C:\Users\gwieleng\aaa\AnagramGame/.git directory
git init C:\Users\gwieleng\aaa\AnagramGame
==[IDE]== Jul 15, 2015 10:49:03 PM Initializing ... finished.
                                                              ▼
```

Figure 10-2. *Output window showing initialization process*

All the project files are marked Added in Your Working Tree. To view a file's status, place the cursor over the filename in the Projects window. In a tooltip, the status of the file in the Working Tree displays in green to the right of the slash, as shown in Figure 10-3.

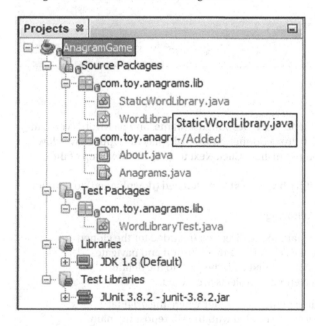

Figure 10-3. *Versioning status in tooltip*

After you have initialized the Git repository, you can either add files or directly commit them to the Git repository.

Cloning a Git Repository

To get a copy of an already existing Git repository, such as on GitHub, you "clone" it. Make sure you know the Git repository URL before take the next steps that help you work through the Clone Repository wizard in the IDE.

Also make sure you do not have a versioned project open in the IDE when you take the next step because the IDE is context-sensitive and if a versioned project is currently selected, the IDE will assume you want to perform versioning tasks on that project. Therefore, when no versioned project is selected in the Projects window, choose Team ➤ Git ➤ Clone from the main menu. The Clone Repository wizard opens, as shown in Figure 10-4.

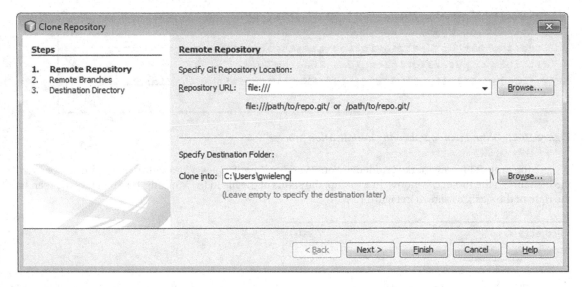

Figure 10-4. *Clone Repository wizard*

In the Repository step, specify the path to a Git repository location, username, and password (you can save them for the future if required). Optionally, click Proxy Configuration to display the Options window and set the proxy server settings. Click OK when you're finished. Click Next to go to the next step of the wizard.

In the Remote Branches page, select the repository branch(es) to be fetched (downloaded) to your local repository. Click Next.

In the Destination Directory page, specify the following:

- In the Parent Directory field, specify the path to the directory intended for the cloned repository on your hard drive (alternatively, click the Browse button and navigate to the directory). The Parent Directory field is filled with the path to the default NetBeansProjects directory, where all NetBeans projects are stored.

- In the Clone Name field, specify the name of the local folder where the original project will be cloned. By default, Clone Name is filled with the Git repository name.

- In the Checkout Branch field, select the branch to be checked out into the Working Tree.

- In the Remote Name field, the name that represents the original repository being cloned. `origin` is the default alias of the repository being cloned. It is a recommended value.

- Leave the Scan for NetBeans Projects after Clone checkbox selected to activate after-scanning right after the clone finishes. That will enable a search for NetBeans projects in the cloned resources and the IDE will offer to open the found projects.

Click Finish. After a Git repository is cloned, the metadata `.git` folder is created inside the folder you selected in the wizard.

Adding Files to a Git Repository

To start tracking a new file and stage changes to an already tracked file in the Git repository, you need to add it to the Git repository. When adding files to a Git repository, the IDE composes and saves snapshots of your project first in the Index. After you perform the commit, the IDE saves those snapshots in the HEAD in your local Git repository.

The IDE allows you to choose between the two workflows, described next.

- Explicitly add new or modified files to the Index and then commit only those that are staged in the Index to the HEAD. To start doing this, open the Projects window and right-click the file you want to add. In the context menu, choose Git ➤ Add. This adds the file's contents to the Index before you commit it. In the Projects window, right-click the file you want to commit. In the Commit window, select the Changes Between HEAD and Index toggle button. This displays the list of files that are already staged. Commit the file(s) as described in the "Committing Sources to a Repository" section that follows.

- Skip adding new or modified files to the Index and commit the required files directly to the HEAD. To start doing this, open the Projects window and right-click the file you want to commit. In the context menu, choose Git ➤ Commit. In the Commit window, select the Select the Changes between Index and Working Tree toggle button. This displays the list of files that are not staged. Commit the file(s) as described in the "Committing Sources to a Repository" section that follows.

The status of the file in the HEAD displays in green to the left of the slash, as shown in Figure 10-3 earlier in this chapter.

The action works recursively if invoked on folders while respecting the NetBeans IDE flat folder content structure.

Editing Files

Once you have a Git-versioned project opened in the IDE, you can begin making changes to sources. As with any project opened in NetBeans IDE, you can open files in the Source Editor by double-clicking on their nodes, as they appear in the IDE's windows—for example, the Projects (Ctrl+1), Files (Ctrl+2), and Favorites (Ctrl+3) windows.

When working with source files in the IDE, there are various UI components at your disposal that aid in viewing and operating version control commands. These areas will now be explored—viewing changes in the Source Editor, viewing file status information, comparing file revisions, and reverting changes.

Viewing Changes in the Source Editor

When you open a versioned file in the IDE's Source Editor, you can view real-time changes occurring to your file as you modify it against the base version from the Git repository. As you work, the IDE uses color-coding in the Source Editor's margins to convey the following information:

- Blue: Indicates lines that have been changed since the earlier revision.

- Green: Indicates lines that have been added since the earlier revision.

- Red: Indicates lines that have been removed since the earlier revision.

The Source Editor's left margin shows changes occurring on a line-by-line basis. When you modify a given line, changes are immediately shown in the left margin, as shown in Figure 10-5.

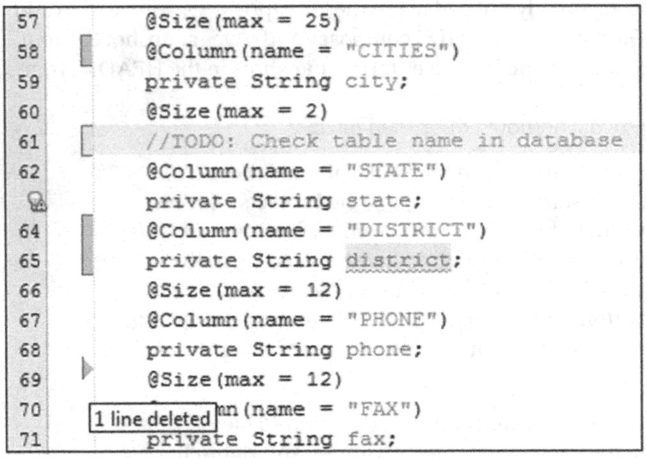

Figure 10-5. *Left margin shows changes*

You can click on a color grouping in the margin to make versioning commands available. For example, in Figure 10-6, you see the versioning buttons available to you when clicking a blue icon, which indicates that lines have been changed from your local copy.

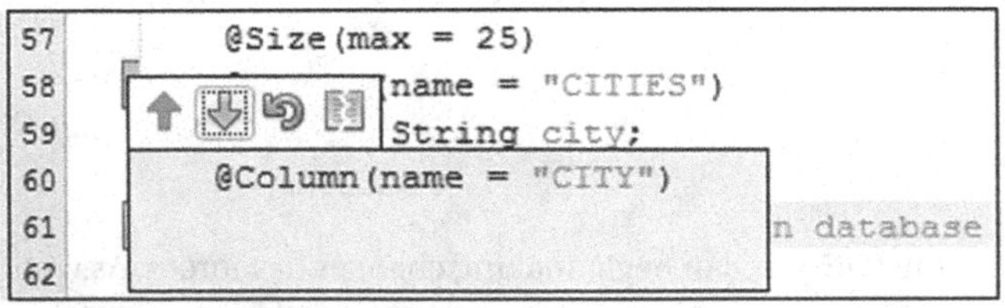

Figure 10-6. *Versioning commands for a color grouping*

The Source Editor's right margin provides you with an overview that displays changes made to your file as a whole, from top to bottom, as shown in Figure 10-7. Color-coding is generated immediately when you make changes to a file.

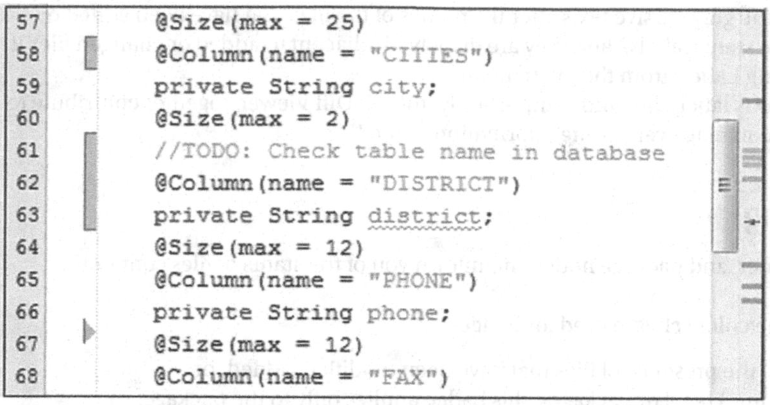

```
57        @Size(max = 25)
58        @Column(name = "CITIES")
59        private String city;
60        @Size(max = 2)
61        //TODO: Check table name in database
62        @Column(name = "DISTRICT")
63        private String district;
64        @Size(max = 12)
65        @Column(name = "PHONE")
66        private String phone;
67        @Size(max = 12)
68        @Column(name = "FAX")
```

Figure 10-7. *Right margin shows overview*

You can click on a specific point in the margin to bring your inline cursor immediately to that location in the file. To view the number of lines affected, hover your mouse over the colored icons in the right margin.

Viewing File Status Information

When you are working in the Projects (Ctrl+1), Files (Ctrl+2), Favorites (Ctrl+3), or Versioning views, the IDE provides several visual features that aid in viewing status information about your files. In Figure 10-8, notice how the badge (that is, the Blue icon badge on the expanded package) and the color of the filename coincide to provide you with a simple but effective way to keep track of versioning information on your files.

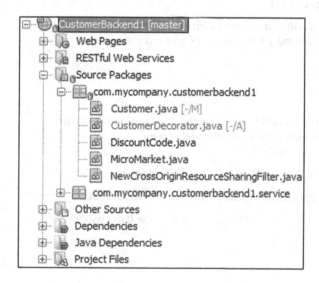

Figure 10-8. *Viewing file status information*

Again in Figure 10-8, notice the gray cursive texts after the names of the files that have been added or changed. These are known as "file status labels," and they are displayed adjacent to added or changed files if you select View ➤ Show Versioning Labels from the main menu.

Badges, color-coding, file status labels, and most importantly, the Git Diff Viewer, together contribute to your ability to effectively view and manage versioning information in the IDE.

Badges and Color-Coding

Badges are applied to project, folder, and package nodes and inform you of the status of files contained within that node.

The following list displays the color scheme used for badges.

- *Blue Badge:* Indicates the presence of files that have been modified, added, or deleted in your Working Tree. For packages, this badge applies only to the package itself and not to its subpackages. For projects or folders, the badge indicates changes within that item, or any of the contained subfolders.

- *Red Badge:* Marks projects, folders, or packages that contain conflicting files. For packages, this badge applies only to the package itself and not to its subpackages. For projects or folders, the badge indicates conflicts within that item or any of the contained subfolders. Color-coding is applied to filenames in order to indicate their current status against the repository.

- *Black:* Indicates that the file has no changes.

- *Blue:* Indicates that the file has been locally modified.

- *Green:* Indicates that the file has been locally added.

- *Red:* Indicates that the file is in a merge conflict.

- *Gray:* Indicates that the file is ignored by Git and will not be included in versioning commands (for example, Update and Commit). Files cannot be ignored if they are versioned.

File Status Labels

The IDE can display two status values for a file by means of "file status labels". File status labels can be toggled on and off by choosing View ➤ Show Versioning Labels from the main menu.

These are the file status labels that the IDE makes available:

- A status describing differences between the file's Working Tree and Index state.

- A status describing differences between the file's Index state and current HEAD commit.

File status labels provide a textual indication of the status of versioned files in the IDE's windows:

- A: Added

- U: Updated but unmerged

- M: Modified

- D: Deleted

- I: Ignored

- R: Renamed

The IDE displays status (new, modified, ignored, and so on) and folder information in gray text to the right of files, as shown in Figure 10-9.

com.mycompany.customerbackend1
Customer.java [-/M]
CustomerDecorator.java [-/A]
DiscountCodeaa.java [R/M]
NewCrossOriginResourceSharingFilter.java

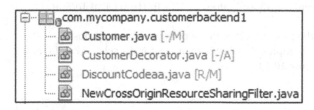

Figure 10-9. *File status labels*

File(s) in merge conflict feature the unmerged status that is generally annotated by red until the files are not resolved by your explicit action. The status label for unmerged file(s) depends on the scenario (for example, A/A is unmerged, both added).

Git Versioning View

The Git Versioning view provides you with a real-time list of all of the changes made to files in a selected folder of your local Working Tree. It opens by default in the bottom panel of the IDE, listing added, deleted, or modified files.

To open the Versioning view, select a versioned file or folder (such as from the Projects, Files, or Favorites window) and either choose Git ➤ Show Changes from the right-click menu or Team ➤ Show Changes from the main menu. The window shown in Figure 10-10 appears at the bottom of the IDE.

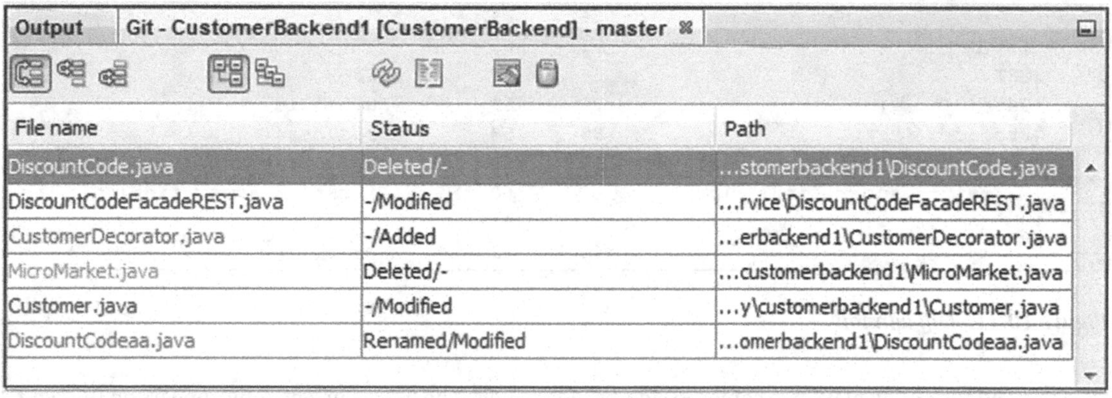

Output
Git - CustomerBackend1 [CustomerBackend] - master
File name
Status
Path
DiscountCode.java
Deleted/-
...stomerbackend1\DiscountCode.java
DiscountCodeFacadeREST.java
-/Modified
...rvice\DiscountCodeFacadeREST.java
CustomerDecorator.java
-/Added
...erbackend1\CustomerDecorator.java
MicroMarket.java
Deleted/-
...customerbackend1\MicroMarket.java
Customer.java
-/Modified
...y\customerbackend1\Customer.java
DiscountCodeaa.java
Renamed/Modified
...omerbackend1\DiscountCodeaa.java

Figure 10-10. *Git Versioning view*

By default, the Versioning view displays a list of all modified files within the selected package or folder in your Working Tree. Using the buttons in the toolbar, you can choose to display the list of files that have differences either between Index and HEAD, the Working Tree and Index, or the Working Tree and HEAD. You can also click the column headings above the listed files to sort the files by name, status, or location.

The Versioning view toolbar also includes buttons that enable you to invoke the most common Git tasks on all files displayed in the list. You can access other Git commands in the Versioning view by selecting a table row that corresponds to a modified file and choosing a command from the right-click menu.

Comparing File Revisions

Comparing file versions is a common task when working with versioned projects. The IDE enables you to compare revisions by using the Diff command. Several comparing modes—Diff To HEAD, Diff To Tracked, and Diff To—are available in the IDE.

Select a versioned file or folder (such as from the Projects, Files, or Favorites window). Choose Team ➤ Diff ➤ Diff to HEAD from the main menu. A graphical Diff Viewer opens for the selected file(s) and revisions in the IDE's main window, as shown in Figure 10-11.

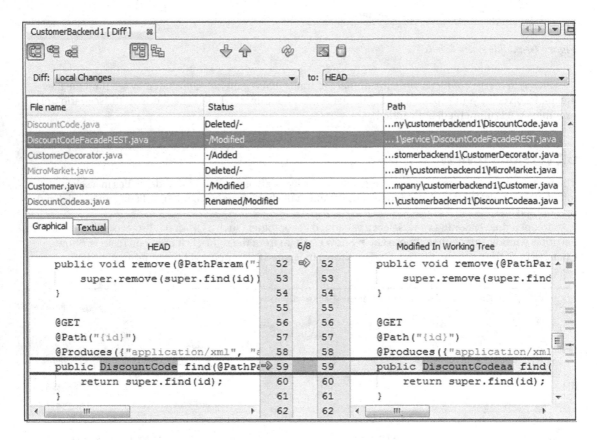

Figure 10-11. *Diff window*

The Diff Viewer displays two copies in side-by-side panels. The more current copy appears on the right side, so if you are comparing a repository revision against your Working Tree, the Working Tree displays in the right panel. The Diff Viewer uses the same color-coding used elsewhere to display version control changes. In Figure 10-11, green blocks indicate content that has been added to the more current revision. Red blocks indicate that content from the earlier revision has been removed from the later. Blue indicates that changes have occurred in the highlighted line(s). Other revisions can be selected from the Diff and from dropdown lists below the Diff Viewer toolbar.

The Diff Viewer toolbar also includes buttons that enable you to invoke the most common Git tasks on all files displayed in the list.

If you are performing a diff on your local copy in the Working Tree, the IDE enables you to make changes directly from within the Diff Viewer. To do so, you can place your cursor in the right pane of the Diff Viewer and modify your file accordingly or you can use the inline icons that display adjacent to each highlighted change. When you scroll on the right side, the left-side editor will scroll so that you can see the changes that have been made in comparison.

Reverting Changes

To throw away local changes made to selected files in your Working Tree and replace them with the ones in the Index or HEAD, select a versioned file or folder (such as from the Projects, Files, or Favorites window). Choose Team ➤ Revert Modifications from the main menu. The Revert Modifications window opens, as shown in Figure 10-12.

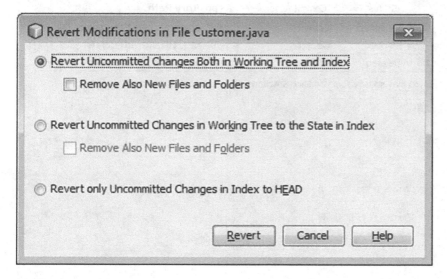

Figure 10-12. Reverting changes

Specify additional options (such as Revert Only Uncommitted Changes in Index to HEAD). Click Revert. The IDE replaces the selected files with those you specified.

Committing Sources to a Repository

To commit files to the Git repository, from the Projects window, right-click the file(s) you want to commit. In the context menu, choose Git ➤ Commit. The Commit window opens, as shown in Figure 10-13.

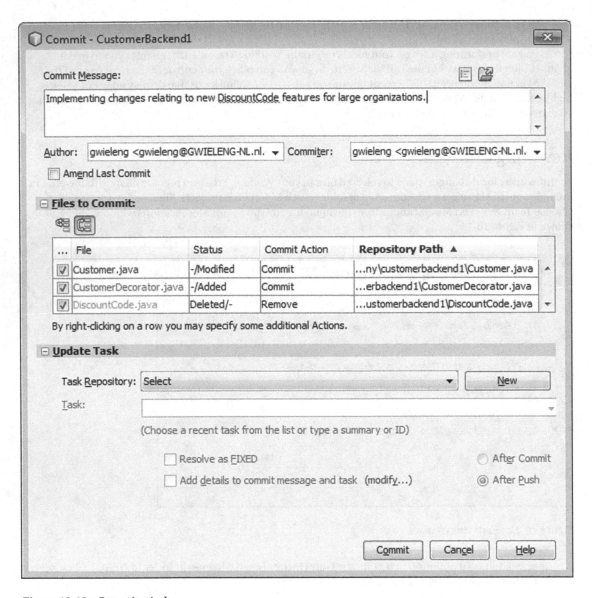

***Figure 10-13.** Commit window*

The Commit window contains the following fields:

- *Commit Message:* Text area intended for describing the change being committed.

- *Author and Committer:* Dropdown lists that let you differentiate between those who made the change and those who physically committed the file.

- *Files to Commit:* Lists all files modified, all files that have been deleted in the Working Tree (locally), all new files (files that do not yet exist in the Git repository), and all files that you have renamed.

Two toggle buttons that switch the mode in which the actual commit is to be performed are available here. Changes Between HEAD and Index displays a list of files that are staged. Changes Between HEAD and Working Tree displays a list of files that are either already staged or modified/created and not staged yet.

To specify here whether to exclude individual files from the commit, either deselect the checkbox in the first column called Commit or right-click a file row in the Commit Action column and choose Exclude from commit from the popup menu. To display the Diff Viewer here, right-click a file row in the Commit Action column and choose Diff from the popup menu.

- *Update Issue:* Section intended for tracking issues related to the change being committed. You need to install the JIRA or Subversion plugin to start tracking issues in the IDE.

Type a commit message into the Commit Message text area. Alternatively, you can do the following:

- Click the Recent Messages icon located in the upper-right corner to view and select from a list of messages that you have previously used.

- Click the Load Template icon located in the upper-right corner to select a message template.

After specifying actions for individual files, click Commit.

The IDE executes the commit and stores your snapshots to the repository. The IDE's status bar, located in the bottom-right side of the interface, displays as the commit action takes place. On a successful commit, versioning badges disappear in the Projects, Files, and Favorites windows, and the color-coding of the committed files returns to black.

Working with Branches

The IDE's Git support enables you to maintain different versions of an entire code base, by using branches.

When working with branches in the IDE, you can create, check out, merge, and delete branches. In the sections that follow, each of these Git terms will be examined and you will learn how to perform these actions in the IDE.

Creating

To create a local branch, if you want to work on a separate version of your file system for stabilization or experimentation purposes without disturbing the main trunk, in the Projects or Files window, choose a project or folder from the repository in which you want to create the branch.

In the main menu, choose Team ➤ Branch/Tag ➤ Create Branch. As an alternative approach, right-click the versioned project or folder and choose Git ➤ Branch/Tag ➤ Create Branch in the popup menu. The Create Branch window opens, as shown in Figure 10-14.

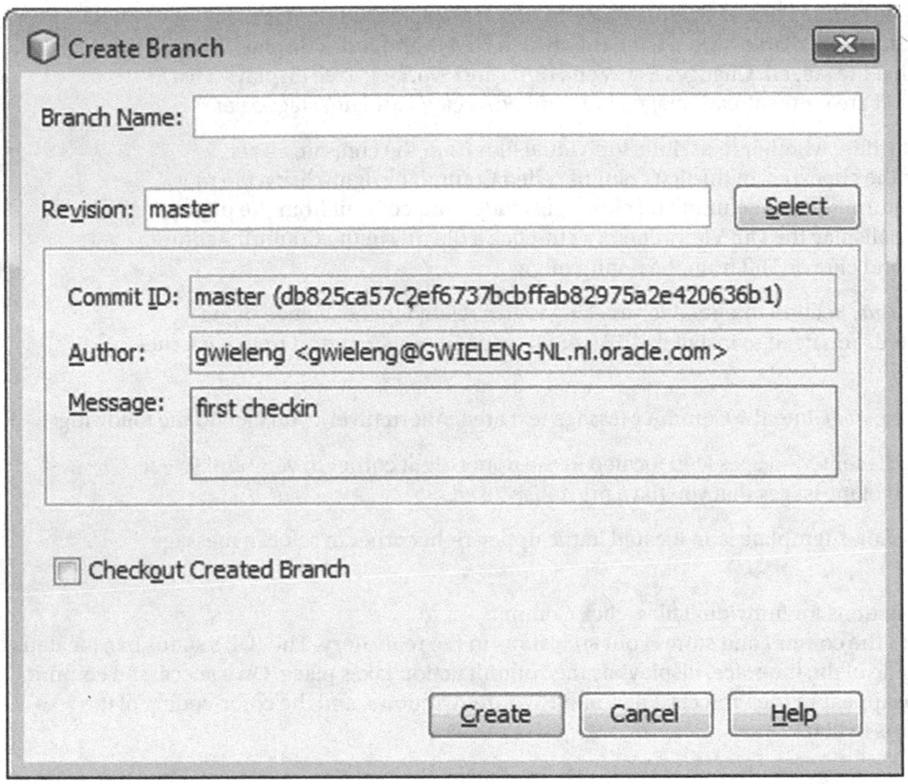

Figure 10-14. *Create Branch window*

In the Branch Name field, enter the name of the branch being created. Type a specific revision of the selected item by entering a commit ID, existing branch, or tag name in the Revision field or click Select to view the list of revisions maintained in the repository. Optionally, in the Select Revision window, expand Branches and choose the branch required, specify the commit ID in the adjacent list, and click Select. Review the Commit ID, Author, and Message fields specific to the revision being branched from and click Create.

The branch is added to the Branches/Local folder of the Git repository, which can be seen in the Git Repository Browser, as shown in Figure 10-15.

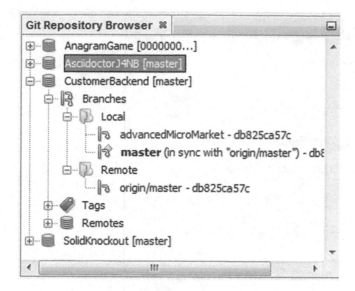

Figure 10-15. *Git Repository Browser*

You can open the Git Repository Browser by right-clicking a Git-versioned project and choosing Git ➤ Repository ➤ Browser.

Checking Out

If you need to edit files on a branch that already exists, you can check out the branch to copy the files to your Working Tree. To check out a revision, choose Team ➤ Checkout ➤ Checkout Revision from the main menu. The Checkout Selected Revision window opens, as shown in Figure 10-16.

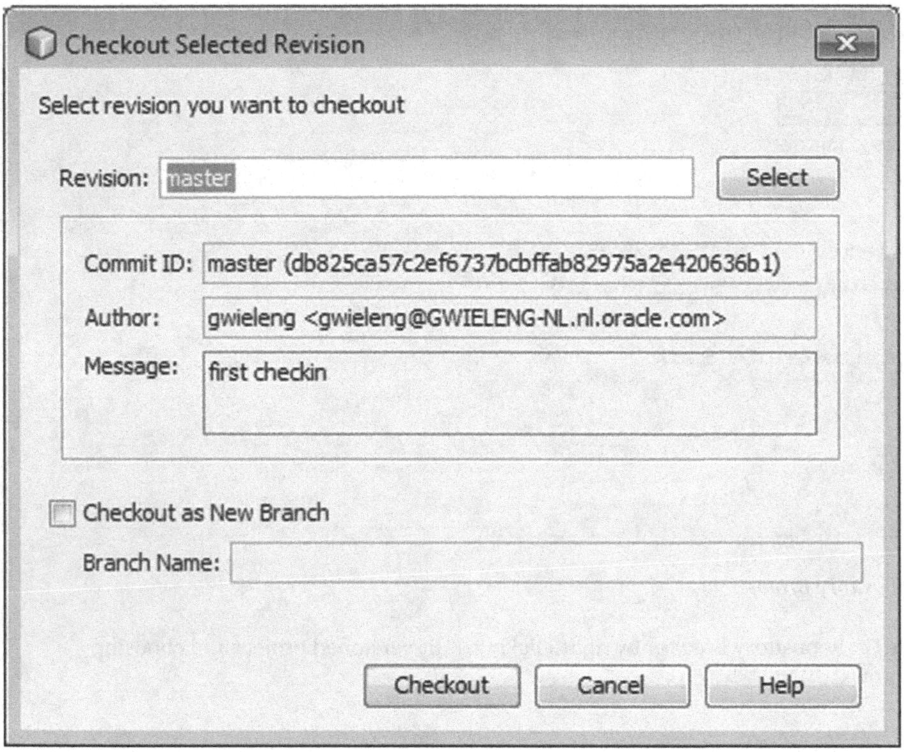

Figure 10-16. Checkout Selected Revision window

Specify the revision required by entering a commit ID, existing branch, or tag name in the Revision field or click Select to view the list of revisions maintained in the repository. Skip if you did not click Select in the previous step. In the Select Revision window, expand Branches and choose the branch required, specify the commit ID in the adjacent list if required, and then click Select. If the specified revision refers to a valid commit that is not marked with a branch name, your HEAD becomes detached and you are no longer on any branch. Review the Commit ID, Author, and Message fields specific to the revision being checked out. To create a new branch from the checked out revision, choose the Checkout as New Branch option and enter the name in the Branch Name field. Click Checkout to check out the revision.

Files in the Working Tree and in the Index are updated to match the version in the specified revision.

Merging

To port modifications from a repository revision to the Working Tree, choose Team ➤ Branch/Tag ➤ Merge Revision from the main menu. The Merge Revision window opens, as shown in Figure 10-17.

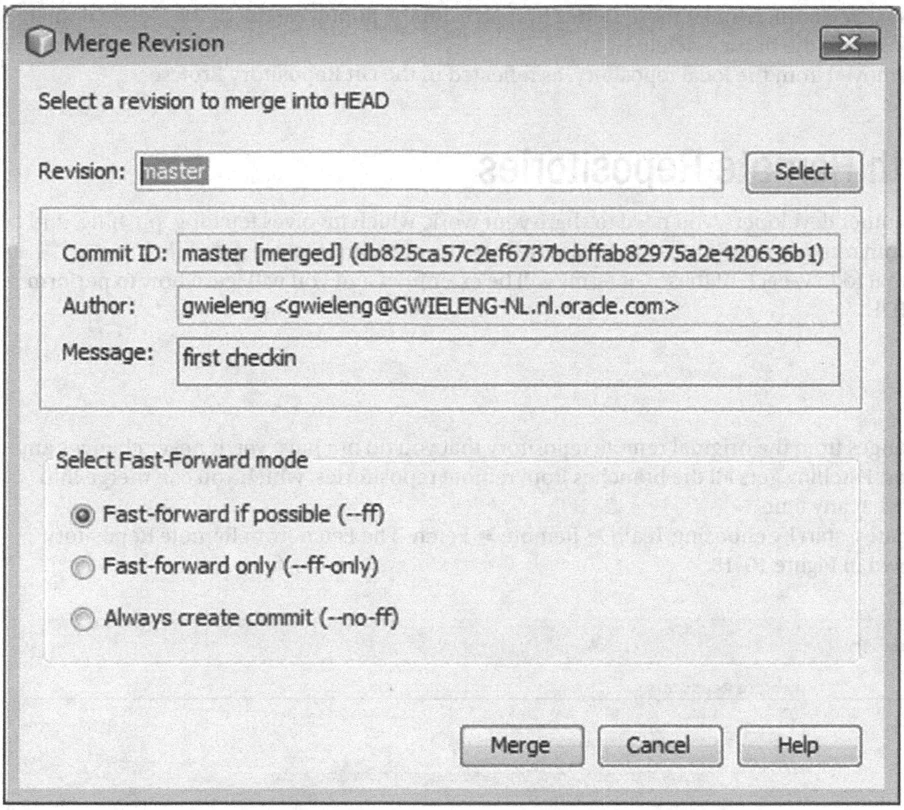

Figure 10-17. *Merge Revision window*

Specify the revision required by entering a commit ID, existing branch, or tag name in the Revision field or click Select to view the list of revisions maintained in the repository.

Skip this step if you did not click Select in the previous step. In the Select Revision window, expand Branches and choose the branch required, specify the commit ID in the adjacent list if required, and then click Select. Click Merge. A three-way merge between the current branch, your Working Tree contents, and the specified branch is completed. If a merge conflict occurs, the conflicting file is marked with a red badge to indicate this. After merging, you must still commit the changes in order for them to be added to the HEAD.

If the Master branch has diverged since the feature branch was created, merging the feature branch into Master will create a merge commit. This is a typical merge. If Master has not diverged, instead of creating a new commit, Git will just point the Master to the latest commit of the feature branch. This is a "fast forward". Passing --no-ff creates a new commit to represent the merge, even if Git would normally fast forward. A related explanation that can be helpful is found at the following URL: 365git.tumblr.com/post/504140728/fast-forward-merge.

Deleting

To delete an unnecessary local branch, choose Team ➤ Repository Browser from the main menu. In the Git Repository Browser, choose the branch to be deleted. The branch must be inactive, that is, not currently checked out into the Working Tree.

Right-click the selected branch and choose Delete Branch from the popup menu. In the Delete Branch window, click OK to confirm the branch deletion.

The branch is removed from the local repository, as reflected in the Git Repository Browser.

Working with Remote Repositories

When you work with other developers, you need to share your work, which involves fetching, pushing, and pulling data to and from remote repositories hosted on the Internet or on an internal network.

In the sections that follow, each of these Git terms will be examined and you will learn how to perform these actions in the IDE.

Fetching

Fetching gets the changes from the original remote repository that you do not have yet. It never changes any of your local branches. Fetching gets all the branches from remote repositories, which you can merge into your branch or inspect at any time.

To fetch the updates, start by choosing Team ➤ Remote ➤ Fetch. The Fetch from Remote Repository wizard opens, as shown in Figure 10-18.

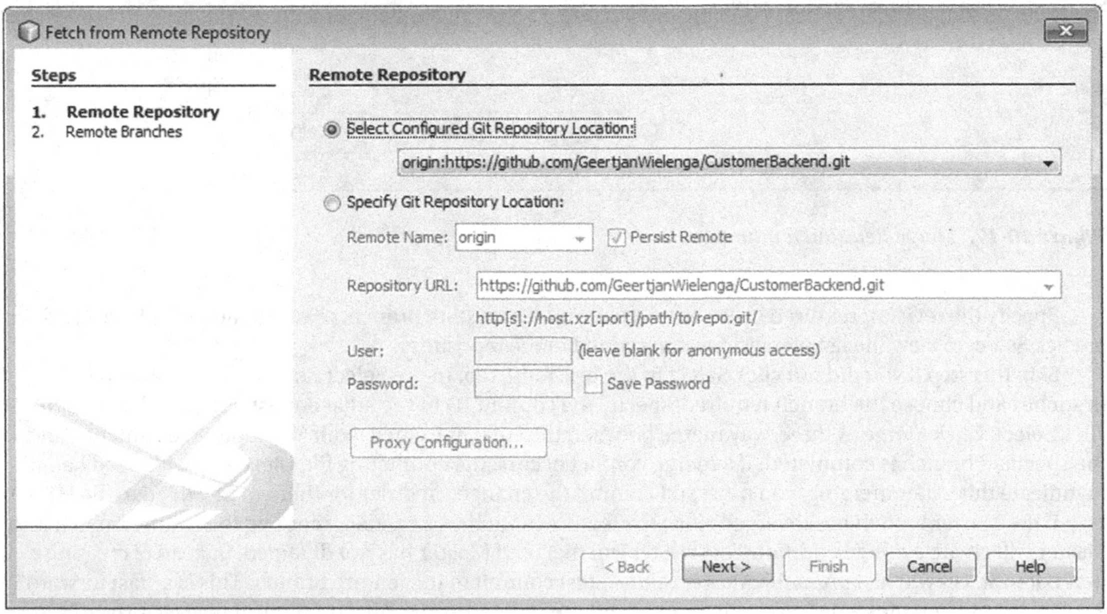

Figure 10-18. *Fetch from Remote Repository wizard*

In the Remote Repository step of the wizard, choose either the Select Configured Git Repository Location option (to use the path to the repository you configured earlier) or the Specify Git Repository Location option (to define the path to a remote repository that has not been accessed yet, its name, login, password, and proxy configuration if required). Click Next. In the Remote Branches step of the wizard, choose the branches to fetch changes from and click Finish.

A local copy of a remote branch is created. The selected branches are updated in the Branches ➤ Remote directory in the Git Repository Browser. Next, the fetched updates can be merged into a local branch.

Pulling

When pulling updates from a remote Git repository, the changes are fetched from it and merged into the current HEAD of your local repository. To perform pulling, choose Team ➤ Remote ➤ Pull. The Pull from Remote Repository wizard opens, as shown in Figure 10-19.

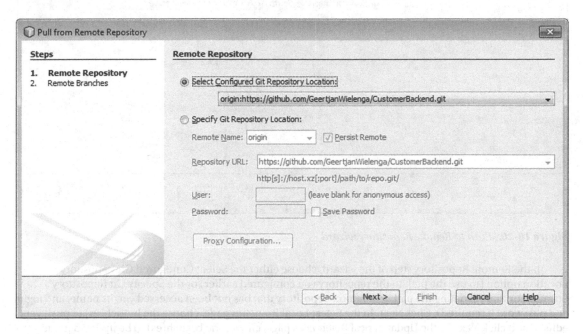

Figure 10-19. *Pull from Remote Repository wizard*

In the Remote Repository step of the wizard, choose either the Select Configured Git Repository Location option (to use the path to the repository you configured earlier) or the Specify Git Repository Location option (to define the path to a remote repository that has not been accessed yet, its name, and login and password if required). Click Next. In the Remote Branches page of the wizard, choose the branches from which changes will be pulled and click Finish.

Your local repository is synchronized with the origin repository.

Pushing

When you are going to push your commits into a repository and some other changes may have been pushed in the meantime, you need to pull and merge those changes first.

To contribute changes from your local Git repository into a public Git repository, choose Team ➤ Remote ➤ Push. The Push to Remote Repository wizard opens, as shown in Figure 10-20.

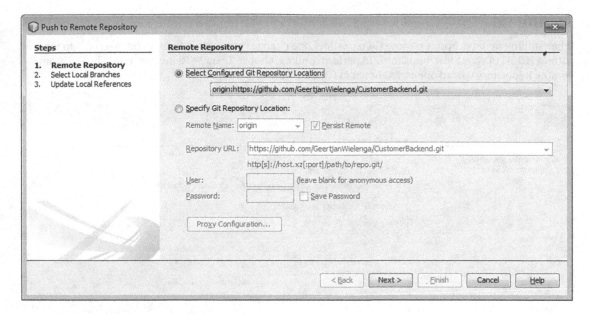

Figure 10-20. *Push to Remote Repository wizard*

In the Remote Repository step of the wizard, choose either the Select Configured Git Repository Location option (to use the path to the repository you configured earlier) or the Specify Git Repository Location option (to define the path to a remote repository that has not been accessed yet, its name, and login and password if required). Click Next. In the Select Local Branches page, choose the branch(es) to push your edits to and click Next. In the Update Local References page, choose the branch(es) to be updated in the Remotes directory of your local repository. Click Finish.

The specified remote repository branch is updated with the latest state of your local branch.

Index

■ T

■ U

Use Supertype Where
        Possible feature, 160

■ V

Vaadin, 94

■ W, X, Y, Z

Watches window, 202
        call stack window, 203
        changing values, 203
        fixed watch, 202
        `string` method, 203
        tooltip value, 202

Get the eBook for only $5!

Why limit yourself?

Now you can take the weightless companion with you wherever you go and access your content on your PC, phone, tablet, or reader.

Since you've purchased this print book, we're happy to offer you the eBook in all 3 formats for just $5.

Convenient and fully searchable, the PDF version enables you to easily find and copy code—or perform examples by quickly toggling between instructions and applications. The MOBI format is ideal for your Kindle, while the ePUB can be utilized on a variety of mobile devices.

To learn more, go to www.apress.com/companion or contact support@apress.com.

Printed in the United States
By Bookmasters